GHOSTS
OF GOLD
MOUNTAIN

BOOKS BY GORDON H. CHANG

Friends and Enemies: The United States, China, and the Soviet Union, 1948–1972

Morning Glory, Evening Shadow: Yamato Ichihashi and His Internment Writings

Asian Americans and Politics: Perspectives, Experiences, Prospects (co-editor)

Before Internment: Essays by Yuji Ichioka (co-editor)

Chinese American Voices: From the Gold Rush to the Present (co-editor)

Dhan Gopal Mukerji, Caste and Outcast (co-editor)

Asian American Art: A History, 1850–1970 (co-editor)

Fateful Ties: The History of America's Preoccupation with China

GHOSTS OF GOLD MOUNTAIN

The Epic Story of the Chinese Who Built the Transcontinental Railroad

GORDON H. CHANG

Houghton Mifflin Harcourt
Boston   New York
2019

For information about permission to reproduce selections from this book, write to trade.permissions@hmhco.com or to Permissions, Houghton Mifflin Harcourt Publishing Company, 3 Park Avenue, 19th Floor, New York, New York 10016.

hmhco.com

Library of Congress Cataloging-in-Publication Data
Names: Chang, Gordon H., author.
Title: Ghosts of Gold Mountain : the epic story of the Chinese who built the transcontinental railroad / Gordon H. Chang.
Description: Boston : Houghton Mifflin Harcourt, [2019] | Includes bibliographical references and index.
Identifiers: LCCN 2018042558 (print) | LCCN 2018051358 (ebook) | ISBN 9781328618610 (ebook) | ISBN 9781328618573 (hardcover)
Subjects: LCSH: Central Pacific Railroad Company—Employees—History. | Railroad construction workers—West (U.S.)—History—19th century. | Foreign workers, Chinese—West (U.S.)—History—19th century. | China—Emigration and immigration—History—19th century. | Chinese—West (U.S.)—History—19th century. | West (U.S.)—History—19th century.
Classification: LCC HD8039.R3152 (ebook) | LCC HD8039.R3152 C524 2019 (print) | DDC 331.6/251097809034—dc23
LC record available at https://lccn.loc.gov/2018042558
Book design by Emily Snyder
Printed in the United States of America
DOC 10 9 8 7 6 5 4 3 2
4500769694

Maps by Mapping Specialists, Ltd.; Excerpt on page 98 from *Homebase: A Novel* by Shawn Wong. Copyright © 1979 by Shawn Wong. Permission granted by Lowenstein Associates, Inc. All rights reserved.; Excerpt on page 121 from "Water that Springs from a Rock" by Alan Lau. Copyright © 1991 by Alan Chong Lau. Reprinted with permission. All rights reserved.; Excerpt on page 138 from *China Men* by Maxine Hong Kingston. Copyright © 1977, 1978, 1979, 1980 by Maxine Hong Kingston. Used by permission of Alfred. A. Knopf, an imprint of the Knopf Doubleday Publishing Group, a division of Penguin Random House LLC. All rights reserved.

For the forgotten

CONTENTS

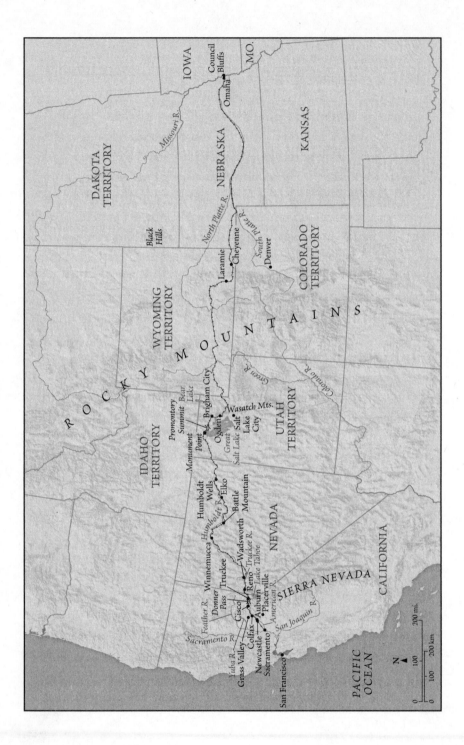

IOWA
Council Bluffs
Omaha
MO.

DAKOTA
TERRITORY

Missouri R.

KANSAS

Black
Hills

North Platte R.

NEBRASKA

Cheyenne
South Platte R.
Denver

Laramie

COLORADO
TERRITORY

R O C K Y   M O U N T A I N S

WYOMING
TERRITORY

Green R.

Colorado R.

Summit Bear
Promontory   Lake
Point Brigham City
Monument Ogden
Point Great Wasatch Mts.
Salt Salt Lake
Lake City

UTAH
TERRITORY

IDAHO
TERRITORY

Humboldt
Wells Elko
Battle
Humboldt R. Mountain

Winnemucca

NEVADA

Wadsworth
Truckee R.
Feather R. Truckee Reno Lake Tahoe
Donner Reno
Pass Truckee
Cisco Auburn American R.
Colfax Placerville
Yuba R. SIERRA NEVADA
Grass Valley San Joaquin R.
Newcastle Sacramento
Sacramento R. Sacramento

CALIFORNIA

San Francisco

PACIFIC
OCEAN

N

200 mi.

200 km
100
100
0

INTRODUCTION

Hung Wah stepped up into the private train car of James Strobridge, the field construction boss of the Central Pacific Railroad Company (CPRR). The wagon's well-appointed interior must have seemed a dark, cool oasis for the seasoned Chinese worker, offering a bit of welcome relief from both the blistering afternoon heat in the Utah desert and the bleak, monotonous scenery.

Hung Wah and Strobridge had come to know each other well over the previous five years during the construction of the Pacific Railway, or the Transcontinental Railroad, as it was popularly known. Two competing railroad companies had led the project: the CPRR, which began its work in Sacramento, California, and built eastward, and the Union Pacific (UP), which started in Omaha, Nebraska, and built westward. Their completed work, linked to already established rail lines in the East, forged a continuous road of iron across the entire country, making possible travel unprecedented in scale and speed. Now the two men were coming together at Promontory Summit, Utah, where a grand celebration had just concluded to mark the formal end of work. The date—May 10, 1869—has been immortalized by one of the

most famous photographs of nineteenth-century America: two massive steam engines, representing the CPRR and UP, meet head-to-head
in "East and West Shaking Hands" (below). The photographer, Andrew J. Russell, wanted to highlight the train's bonding of vast geographic space. Others at the time saw the rail connection as transfor-
mative not just for the nation but for civilization itself. Only
Christopher Columbus's discovery of the New World, an energetic
observer declared, surpassed the completion of the rail line in historic
importance.

    After the camera shots and public events, Strobridge gathered jour-
nalists, military officers, and other notables to mark the occasion in a
quieter way over drinks and food in his personal railroad car. In what
must have seemed a magnanimous gesture at the time, he invited Hung
Wah, who brought several other Chinese with him to share the special
moment, representing the thousands of Chinese who had toiled for
the CPRR and made possible what many had once claimed was an insurmountable construction challenge.
    Upwards of twenty thousand Chinese, 90 percent of the CPRR con-
struction labor force, had built almost the entire western half of the

Pacific Railway. The UP relied largely on Irish and other European immigrants and both black and white Civil War veterans for its labor
force. While the CPRR's leg of the railway ran to a little over half the
length of the Union Pacific's portion—690 miles compared to 1,086—
building the western section posed a considerably greater challenge.
The majority of the Union Pacific's line extended over relatively open,
even countryside, beginning in Omaha, where the country's existing
rail network ended. The CPRR, by contrast, faced a shorter but much
more arduous journey. Beginning in Sacramento, roughly at sea level,
it ascended almost immediately into the foothills of the Sierra Nevada
mountain range, climbing higher and higher until it reached elevations
of over seven thousand feet. To reach those heights, the workers of the
CPRR had to blast and dig their way through expanses of solid granite and brave some of the most dangerous working conditions imaginable. Chinese workers did what was widely considered at the time to
be impossible. They endured scorching summer heat in the high altitudes, dirt and choking dust, smoke, and fumes from the constant use
of explosives. They survived isolation, desiccating winds and thin air,
winter blizzards and freezing temperatures, as well as the ever-present
dangers of accidental explosions, falling trees, snowslides, avalanches,
cave-ins, illness, broken limbs, and plain exhaustion—all to realize the
federal government's great ambition of uniting the American continent with a central artery. These workers, in no short order, helped so-
lidify the westward future of the United States.

As a reflection of this herculean feat, the engravings on the legendary and ceremonial "Golden Spike" that symbolically united the rails
of the Central Pacific and Union Pacific railroads hailed the Transcontinental for bridging the Atlantic and Pacific oceans—reducing to
one week what had been a perilous three-to-six-month journey—and
healing the wounded nation. The Civil War had ended four years earlier, practically to the day, leaving a trail of destruction and a fractured
Union in its wake. "May God continue the unity of our Country," read
the engraving on one side of the Golden Spike, "as this Railroad unites
the two great Oceans of the world." The Chinese had played a heroic
and indispensable role in this achievement—and Strobridge, who had
played a leading role of his own in the project, now honored them for
their enormous contribution.

Strobridge had come far—not just in distance from Sacramento, where the CPRR's work began, but in his attitudes as well. Five years earlier he had strenuously opposed the proposal to hire Chinese workers. He argued with his boss, Charles Crocker, one of the so-called "Big Four," along with Leland Stanford, Collis Huntington, and Mark Hopkins, who served as directors of the CPRR, that the Chinese were not fit physically or temperamentally for the demanding work. Strobridge eventually relented, and Chinese, a few at first and then by the thousands, joined the construction effort. Proving themselves not just entirely capable but vital, in time they caused Strobridge to correct his error and drop his prejudice.

Hung Wah, for his part, had begun working for the CPRR in January 1864 after traveling to America from thousands of miles away in southern China. At Promontory he was in his mid-thirties, slightly older than most of the other Chinese, who were in their teens and twenties during construction, prime working ages for physical labor. He had received some education before coming to the United States and had a head for business, not to mention ambition: before Chinese were hired on to the CPRR, he was a prominent figure in Auburn, a town in the heart of the California gold country in the Sierra Nevada foothills. Agents of the CPRR turned to him to recruit workers, and he eventually became the leading Chinese "headman" over hundreds, and possibly thousands, of his compatriots working for the railroad. He handled their pay, living arrangements, and relations with the company. He had also survived years of personal difficulty and dangerous work, all the way through to the end.

Strobridge's invitation to Hung Wah at Promontory suggests they had developed a mutually respectful relationship — but it had not been easily forged. Strobridge was a demanding and intimidating supervisor who had earned a reputation for being especially tough on Chinese. He was as ferocious in appearance as in temperament: an errant explosion early in the construction effort had taken out one of his eyes, and an ominous black eye patch now covered an ugly scar. The Chinese railroad workers, in their lingo, called him "one-eyed bossy man."

Now Hung Wah and several other Chinese workers — possibly Ging Cui, Wong Fook, and Lee Shao, who had been part of the crew that had laid the last ties and length of track earlier in the day — found themselves not only inside Strobridge's personal car but also, probably for the first time in their lives, in close proximity to important white men. Perhaps Strobridge hoped that including the Chinese in his private event would make up for their absence in the public activities. Chinese had not been invited to attend the official proceedings, pose for Russell's historic photograph, or join the elite reception in the train car of Leland Stanford, the CPRR president.

The Chinese were weathered workmen. They were slight of build, sinewy after laboring for years clearing the land, cutting through dense stands of forest, putting down the roadbed, shoveling snow, blasting tunnels through granite, and laying track over the Sierra Nevada mountains in winter and across the vast deserts and plateaus of Nevada and Utah in the summer. They were dark brown in complexion, their skin leathered from living and working in recent months under the relentless desert sun. Their clothes, if they had not been able to change after work, would have been tattered, patched, and threadbare. We can see their shabby attire in other photos taken earlier that day. Their cotton tunics and baggy pants were blousy and designed for demanding physical labor in oven-like heat. Heavy American-made leather boots protected their feet. They wore soft, wide-brimmed cotton hats, not the woven-palm headgear from China they used elsewhere in other work. They dressed uniformly, like soldiers in an army.

Strobridge introduced Hung Wah and his co-workers to his other guests and brought Hung Wah to the head of the dining table. Standing, Strobridge warmly praised the contributions of the Chinese and expressed his appreciation for the essential role they had played in the project. The assembled all then also stood and gave three rousing cheers to the workers — no doubt the first time that these Chinese laborers had been toasted by a crowd of white people. This moment was the symbolic high point in acknowledging and honoring their contribution to completing the rail line.

The news article about the gathering nicely captured its significance for the Chinese, who were so often publicly disrespected, when it offered simply in a heading: "Chinese Laborers at Table." On no other occasion had the Chinese railroad workers personally received as sincere and spirited an appreciation of their long, dangerous toil.

The journalist who recorded the event does not mention whether Hung Wah responded to Strobridge's compliments or uttered any remarks at all. We do not know if he spoke. The news report rendered him mute, emblematic of the way Chinese in America were commonly presented then: Chinese railroad workers were acknowledged as ubiquitous and indispensable, but they were accorded no voice, literally or figuratively. We cannot hear what they said, thought, or felt. They were "silent spikes" or "nameless builders," evocative terms recently coined by scholars seeking to recover the experiences and identities of those Chinese who built the Transcontinental.

As with the news reports of the day, written history in the years afterward gives no voice or identity to the many thousands of these workers. In all of the many pages of serious writing about the construction of the Transcontinental Railroad, authors might describe the enormous efforts of the Chinese. They name but a few, however, let alone tell us something about them as living beings. The identities of Chinese in nineteenth-century America were elusive, and trying to recover them poses daunting challenges. The absence of documentation, mainstream unfamiliarity with Chinese life in America, and deprecation of their presence in the history of the country have rendered these workers all but invisible.

While the dearth of extant documentation from the Chinese workers can explain their shadowy presence in written history to a certain degree, prejudice through the years has relegated them to the margins of American life and memory in a more elemental way. Chinese were not deemed sufficiently important or interesting to include in sweeping narratives about the rise of the nation. In fact, in some instances Chinese are written out of the story altogether. At the 1969 centennial commemoration of the events at Promontory Summit, for example, Secretary of the Interior John Volpe extolled the Transcontinental as a monumental construction achievement of epic importance to the country. Only the vigor of "Americans" made it possible, he boasted. "Who else but Americans could drill tunnels in mountains 30 feet deep in snow?" Nowhere did he mention the Chinese, prohibited from becoming citizens by federal law and assuredly not embraced by his myopic vision of America. Nationalist celebration made no room for the alien Chinese, no matter how pivotal their role in the history of the nation itself.

Ghosts of Gold Mountain is the first book to attempt to fully address the inadequacy, amnesia, and insults that, for a century and a half, have relegated Chinese workers to the margins of history. It seeks to present a full account of the thousands who worked on the Transcontinental and their story as *lived experience*. The Chinese are presented not as voiceless objects of interest or as docile human tools, but as vital, living, and feeling human beings who made history. They were laborers, foremen, contractors, masons, cooks, medical practitioners, carpenters, interpreters, and teamsters. Thousands more Chinese associated with them as friends and relatives, as part of the immense supply chain that provisioned them for years, and, away from the track in their off-time, as gamblers, opium smokers, prostitutes, and devout worshippers of the gods and spirits who watched over them in their perilous work. Collectively they were the "Railroad Chinese," a wonderfully evocative term coined by "Lily," an immigrant from China whose great-grandfather worked on the Transcontinental, that captures their unique ethnic and class identity.

For five years, from 1864 to 1869, Chinese constituted by far the largest single workforce in American industry to that date, not surpassed in numbers until the Industrial Revolution in the late nineteenth century. Their massed presence along the construction route astonished journalists and travelers who witnessed them living and toiling under the most difficult of conditions. Writers described encampments of hundreds of tents, massed armies of workers, and thundering explosions of black powder and dynamite that recalled the cannon blasts of the Civil War. The Reverend John Todd, who delivered the benediction at the Promontory event, honored the central importance of the Railroad Chinese when he declared, "The road could never have been built without the Chinamen."

"The road," in turn, transformed America. The Transcontinental meant that travel across the country was dramatically reduced in time, expense, danger, and discomfort. Regional agricultural bounty gained access to the entire national market and to the great ports of the eastern seaboard and San Francisco on the Pacific. Exploitation of the immense coal, iron ore, timber, and other natural resources of the Rocky Mountain region became possible. The United States became the only advanced capitalist country in the world that enjoyed year-round direct access to both the Atlantic and the Pacific. Regional rail projects boomed post-Promontory, creating an even more efficient transportation infrastructure. Politically, the iron rails bound the United States as never before, while socially, the railroad made the Far West accessible to populations from the East, and in turn the Midwest and East now lay easily within reach for those from California, including Chinese. All this came at great cost, however, especially to Native peoples. The railroad invasion furthered the violent suppression of their autonomy and ways of life.

Despite their critical role in American history, the Railroad Chinese remain silent spikes to this day. No text generated by any Chinese railroad worker on the Transcontinental line in Chinese or English has ever been found, whether in the United States, China, or elsewhere. This is not because the Railroad Chinese were illiterate: a remarkable number, like Hung Wah himself, did read and write in their own language, an ability that many observers at the time noted. Many, including Hung Wah, also spoke some English. They were far from being meek and quiet, moreover; they could be a garrulous and disputatious lot, and they remained faithful and connected to family and village in China. Tens of thousands of letters traveled back and forth across the Pacific in the mid- to late nineteenth century. The Pacific Mail Steamship Company, the main American carrier in the Pacific, reported that in the single year 1876 alone, its ships carried more than 250,000 letters between China, Japan, and the United States. Yet remarkably, not a single message from or to a Railroad Chinese in this vigorous traffic has been located despite the most strenuous research efforts. Today there is nothing extant in their own words about their experiences.

What happened to these many words written long ago? Arson, pillaging, and the willful destruction of Chinese belongings by hostile nineteenth-century mobs in America help explain the absence of an archive, as do losses during these immigrants' many forced moves, ruin from earthquakes and fires such as at San Francisco in 1906, and the cruel devastation wrought by the many wars, civil upheavals, and revolutions in their land of ancestry. The habitual belittlement of their lives, and thus their archive, also deprived us of much of their record. Few, except perhaps their descendants and the exceptionally curious, wanted to know about the lives of Chinese laborers in America during the decades that have elapsed between their time and ours.

This presents a formidable challenge to the historian today: How does one give voice to the voiceless? How does one recover a sense of lived experience if there is nothing from the central actors themselves?

As a Chinese American, I had wanted to know about the Chinese builders of the Transcontinental ever since I was a youngster, but it was not until recently that I had the opportunity to engage in a sustained effort to recover their history. An international research project at Stanford that I helped establish and then co-direct took up these challenges and for more than six years conducted the most thorough study to date of the experience of Chinese road workers in North America. Scholars in North America and Asia and from disciplines ranging from history and American studies to archaeology, anthropology, and cultural studies scoured archives, family collections and memorabilia, government records, business papers, and archaeological reports, in English, Chinese, and other languages, to locate as much relevant material as possible. We also conducted oral histories with living descendants of railroad workers to learn about memory within families. This book draws significantly from the tremendous efforts of scores of scholars, students, and researchers around the world.

Though difficult, a recovery of a lost past is possible if imaginative efforts are made to understand the rich and expansive historical materials that do exist. Nineteenth-century writers wrote extensively about the Chinese, and their observations can be read in ways that move the Railroad Chinese from being objects for journalistic observation into the active center of the story. Years of dedicated research have also revealed substantial new documentation and sources in archives and libraries. Some of this rich material had simply been ignored as insignificant or bypassed as too challenging to use. Previous writers interested in the railroad had little or no familiarity with the history of Chinese American life and the wide array of sources from other dimensions of Chinese history in America that could be used to understand the railroad experience. There is Chinese-language material here and in China that was never consulted in any previous railroad book published in the United States. For example, poetry and folk songs express hopes, dreams, fears, and tragedy and offer insight into emotions and feelings. Railroad Chinese closely associated with other Chinese in California who wrote about their own lives, and this material provides further texture and context. Stories about the trials and tribulations of railroad workers circulated widely among the Chinese and, through repeated telling within families and community, have come down through the years to us today.

There is extensive business documentation, including payroll records and private correspondence and notes among the railroad magnates. From these we learn names, job categories, pay rates, labor organization, and the relationship of Railroad Chinese with the CPRR. We learn about working conditions and developments as the line pushed forward. We have photographs of the railroad's construction and can see actual images of the workers. Furthermore, in recent years, professional archaeologists have gathered an enormous amount of material culture left behind by the workers, which provides fascinating insight into their quotidian lives and the larger networks of their existence that connected them to their home villages and Chinese settlements throughout America.

Being attentive to the physical world of the Railroad Chinese — geographic location, terrain, weather conditions, and the natural and built environment — helps to capture a plausible sense of what the Railroad Chinese saw, felt, and experienced. While building the Central Pacific Railroad, they toiled outdoors, moving from the lush Central Valley of California, through the forests and canyons of Gold Country in the foothills of the Sierra Nevada, up into the high country of indomitable granite mountains, and then into the high deserts that seemed to stretch toward eternity in Nevada and Utah. Though long separated from them by the passage of time, we can recover a bit of what they encountered in the rural towns and wilds of California and what they felt out in the open during frigid winters and broiling summers, if we make the effort and use our empathetic imaginations.

The variety of historical materials that we do have, pieced together and used in creative ways, helps us reconstruct the story of the Railroad Chinese. Above all else, though, appreciating their elusive history begins with our placing ourselves in their position, at the very center of the telling, and trying to see the world from their points of view. Only by doing so can we begin to fully respect, and honor, their profound humanity.

This effort to recover their history begins with the origins of the Railroad Chinese in distant rural villages located in the Pearl River delta near Guangzhou (Canton) in southern China. They were "Cantonese" (a term commonly used to refer to an array of different regional and ethnic groups in southern China), who engaged in one of the great diasporas in human history. Numbering in the millions, they traveled across vast oceans to destinations in South America, the Caribbean, the Pacific, Southeast Asia, and North America, where, beginning in the early 1850s, one stream of this great migration became miners, farmers, fishermen, merchants, and railroad workers throughout California—or Gold Mountain, as they called it—and the entire American West.

The story then moves to the early experiences of Chinese in California, and to their lives and labor during the years they worked for the CPRR. This forms the core of the book. From the booming port city of San Francisco, where the vast majority of the Railroad Chinese disembarked, we will follow them across California's Central Valley to Sacramento, where the first tracks of the Central Pacific were laid, and then to Auburn, nestled in the foothills of the Sierra Nevada mountain range, where Chinese began to work for the railroad company en masse. Their numbers grew steadily as the line pushed farther east, deeper and higher into the Sierra. By the literal and figurative climax of the CPRR's journey over the Sierra, the completion of the Summit Tunnel near Lake Donner and Lake Tahoe, the Chinese formed roughly 90 percent of the company's workforce. It is no exaggeration to say that the effort could not have been completed without them. They labored—and died—among the peaks of the Sierra in some of the most extreme conditions imaginable. And when the work there was done, they continued eastward, into the tumbling hills of Nevada and the flat, baking expanse of Utah. By the time the CPRR united with the UP at Promontory Summit, hundreds—perhaps even thousands—of Chinese had died over the five years of the construction effort. Their industry, sacrifice, and contribution attracted great national attention, and for a moment it appeared that Chinese might be allowed to establish their place in the American family. Through the rest of the nineteenth century, thousands of Railroad Chinese dispersed throughout the United States and Canada, including for work on scores of other railroad construction projects. They began to settle in large cities and small towns throughout the United States. The moment of possibility for them, however, was short-lived. Chinese came to be seen as racial inferiors and competitors for work. Terrible violence and expulsion from America would be the bitter reward for their labor.

Thousands were driven out of the country and went elsewhere in the world for work and survival. Many returned to their homes in what became known as "railroad villages" because of their connection to the work of railroad construction. Those who stayed here helped establish the foundation for what we now call Chinese America. They built communities wherever the railroad could take them, opening the way for their compatriots who followed them across the country. Descendants of the Railroad Chinese are found everywhere here and around the world today.

Who were the Railroad Chinese? What did they do on the Transcontinental line? What were their ways of work and life? *Ghosts of Gold Mountain* speaks to these basic questions, as well as to more specific questions that have long intrigued those interested in the Railroad Chinese: How many toiled on the line? What kinds of work did they do? Did they actually suspend themselves in woven reed baskets down sheer cliffs to blast open the roadbed around mountains? What did it take to tunnel through the Sierra Nevada? What about the legendary strike of 1867, when three thousand Chinese put down their tools and confronted the railroad barons? Why did they strike, and what was the result of their collective action? How many Railroad Chinese died: several score, hundreds, thousands? How did America treat them after the rail line was completed? What is their place, and legacy, in the sweep of American history?

Central to this examination is the role of *chance* in the lives of the Railroad Chinese. Their lives were replete with choice, circumstance, accident, and luck, both good and bad. They may have believed in fate, as humans are wont to do, but their lives were filled with the unknown, including high risk to life and limb. They went out from their homes in south China seeking a livelihood, and even good fortune, but they also knew that life was precarious. Tragedy, injury, and violent death in the nineteenth-century Pacific and western United States were commonplace. Disease and mistreatment on the high seas in transit took many lives, as did villains in California who despised Chinese and targeted them for plunder and sport. Avalanches and snowslides swept countless Chinese down into Sierra canyons, and nitroglycerine accidental explosions could vaporize them. Political demagogues, after the work was done, campaigned for the exclusion and expulsion of Chinese from the nation, and scores of Chinese died in mob lynchings, arsons, and shootings. A high possibility of being killed by nature or at human hands was an assumed risk for the Railroad Chinese. Though they did not use the term, they constantly faced "a Chinaman's chance," a well-known phrase in the American racial lexicon that spoke to the precarity of Chinese life here.

Yet thousands upon thousands of the Railroad Chinese persevered. While most did not find their personal Gold Mountain, many did forge meaningful and productive lives in America. Some prospered and returned to China as heroes. One was the great-grandfather of Lily, who coined the term "Railroad Chinese," who brought a non-Chinese bride back with him from America. Many years later, Lily herself, of mixed racial heritage, emigrated to America, a place her family still called "home" after more than three generations of separation. Others prospered and stayed in the United States, where they helped form the beginnings of Chinese America. Recognition of their achievements is long overdue: their legacies should be honored and their spirits propitiated. The lost souls of those who died during the construction of the railroad, and the neglected lives and experiences of those who survived deserve nothing less. For while theirs is the story of ghosts past, in the present it is also an experience that resonates very much with the living. It is an epic story of dreams, courage, accomplishment, tragedy, and extraordinary determination.

1
GUANGDONG

In the second reign year of Haamfung, a trip to Gold Mountain was made.
With a pillow on my shoulder, I began my perilous journey.
Sailing a boat with bamboo poles across the seas,
Leaving behind wife and sisters in search of money,
No longer lingering with the woman in the bedroom,
No longer paying respect to parents at home.
— CANTONESE FOLK SONG,
MID- TO LATE NINETEENTH CENTURY

THE LANGUID BLUE SKIES AND THE GENTLE GREEN AND BROWN farm landscape reflect little of the human turmoil embedded in the place that the Railroad Chinese called home in southern China. In contrast with the natural beauty of the land are hundreds of multistory brick and stone structures called *diaolou* that rise far above the verdant treetops. Villagers constructed them as watchtowers and fortresses against the endemic banditry that plagued the region in the late nineteenth and early twentieth centuries. Today these structures are dramatic reminders of a long history of human suffering that defines this part of southern China.

By the tens of thousands beginning in the early nineteenth century, the people of this densely populated region, not much larger than seventy-five square miles, left for futures that would forever change families, ancestral village patterns of life, and the distant lands where they eventually settled. Far removed from the seat of imperial power in China's distant north and from the traditional centers of Chinese high culture and commerce, the "four counties," or the Siyi, an enclave along the southern coast of China, was their place of origin. An estimated one quarter of the population of just one of these counties, Taishan, or about 200,000 residents, left their homes in the nineteenth century for destinations overseas. Common farming folk though they may have been, the people of the Siyi, through their energy and enterprise, transformed places distant from their modest villages, homes, and farms. The *diaolou*, largely financed by funds sent back by successful Chinese overseas to protect their families that remained, are themselves evidence of the fidelity to home and the interconnectedness of the local and the distant.

The Siyi counties in the nineteenth century were Xinning (known later as Taishan), Kaiping, Enping, and Xinhui. They were among the most densely populated of the fifteen counties that made up the great province of Guangdong. With some 25 million in total population in the mid-nineteenth century and with a long coastline, Guangdong was the most strategically and politically important province in southern China. Almost all of those who came to the United States from China in the nineteenth century hailed from Guangdong.

Hills buffered the counties from the rest of the province, with the small settlement of Hong Kong to the east and the great city of Guangzhou to the north. Reclamation, with earth and rock along the many waterways and marshes that ran through the alluvial plain, enlarged the lands available for settlement and farming.

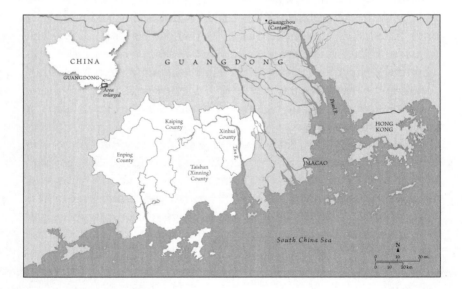

The soil of the Siyi is fertile, water from rainfall and myriad flowing waterways is plentiful, and the climate is inviting for the cultivation of rice, the staple of wet agriculture. A bright jade green color dominates the patchwork of tens of thousands of small family farms. Green was the color of growing rice, the waxy leaves of citrus and other fruit trees, the mulberry leaves fed to silkworms, and the palms whose durable fronds were used for weaving baskets, fans, furniture, and hats. Green was the color of the leafy vegetables and root crops that, along with foodstuffs from small freshwater ponds and the ocean, formed the distinctive local diet. Bamboo, the stuff of a thousand purposes, was everywhere.

The Siyi are part of the spreading delta formed by the plentiful waters of the Pearl River and adjunct waterways, known as the Dong, Xi, and Bei rivers, which flow from distant reaches in the west to the South China Sea. The Siyi lie roughly along the same latitude as southern Florida and, in feel and appearance, are akin to the lands in the vast spread of the Mississippi River delta. In fact, many Chinese settled in the Deep South after the completion of the Transcontinental Railroad because of its climatic and topical similarity to home. So too did they settle in the humid farm region of California's Sacramento River delta, where the waters begin to merge with San Francisco Bay. The people of the Siyi were sun and water people, both in their native lands and abroad.

The lands of the Siyi had been settled and intensely cultivated for a thousand years, and Americans encountering China in the early nineteenth century took note of the region's bounty. The Reverend William Speer, a well-known American missionary who resided for many years in the Pearl River delta, tried to describe it for folks back home. He fondly evoked its many villages "embowered in bamboo" and "a species of banyan and other trees," he wrote, that "meet the eye on every hand." Speer respected the sophisticated agricultural skills of the Siyi Chinese. "The level portion of the soil," he wrote, "is cultivated as only the Chinese know how to do in order to obtain the utmost possible returns from Nature. The view appears like a great garden bounded by ranges of hills." Extensive, undisturbed stretches of vegetation had long since disappeared, as they were cut away for human use over countless generations. Much of the wildlife in the farm areas had either been consumed or been driven away long ago.

The village was the nexus of life in the region. Modest coarse brick homes were clustered close together, with buildings sometimes sharing common walls. Families lived in intimate proximity to one another, with farmland lying away from the villages, unlike in America, where farmers usually lived far apart on their own land. Active social interaction, including the sharing of rumors or news about opportunities, was thus a feature of daily life and habit. The Railroad Chinese continued to enjoy this conviviality in America.

The next settlement might be an hour away by foot along dirt paths or by boat on small channels of water. A bit farther was the market town, a busy place of basic commerce, simple entertainments, and political and cultural life. "The narrow streets of the towns," Speer witnessed, "are densely crowded with men following every trade and means of procuring a subsistence which the necessities of human nature can suggest." The people Speer saw were traders, merchants, shopkeepers, artisans and craftsmen, peddlers, laborers, actors, healers, pawnshop dealers, moneylenders, cooks, butchers, weavers, artists, papermakers, makers of handicrafts and goods for local use and export, gamblers, and vagabonds. They were rich, poor, and middling, and varied in culture, education, and background. Such was the diverse social profile of those who left for America.

The Siyi people spoke different dialects of Chinese that were incomprehensible to other Chinese not from the same region. These widely varying ways of speaking came to be known generically as "Cantonese," which masks their considerable variability. The cultural, social, and ethnic mix of the region was rich and complex. Schooling was rudimentary for most but widespread. A few young men, including some who ventured to America, attained considerable learning, though most had only a very basic education.

Guangzhou city, whose roots go back two hundred years before the Common Era, lay within reach by small boat along the lattice of waterways that ran through the delta. Since AD 226, it served as the center of imperial authority in southern China and over the centuries became one of the commercial hubs of Chinese life. It helped anchor the so-called ancient maritime silk road, the vital and rich seagoing trade route that linked the Chinese empire with Southeast Asia, the lands of the Pacific, South Asia, the Islamic world, and even faraway Africa.

The Portuguese were the earliest Europeans who came by way of the ocean and initiated regular contact with Chinese along the Guangdong coast in the early sixteenth century. By mid-century they made Macao, a collection of small islands and a peninsula, the first permanent European settlement in East Asia. It was just about within sight from the coast of the Siyi.

A hundred other small islands lay along the crenulated Guangdong coast. The waters provided a rich bounty of sea life, which the Pearl River delta people harvested with nets cast from their boats. They processed their catch for the fresh markets but also preserved it with salt and sun. They would do so similarly when they came to California. Their rice-based diet also drew from a huge variety of dried, salted, and fermented vegetables, preserved fruits, herbs, fungi, dried flowers and buds, teas, nuts, legumes, and spices, all of which enlivened their meals, the center of family and social interaction. The southern Chinese remained strongly partial to their food for reasons of taste as well as social custom after they came to America.

The geography of the Guangdong coast made close central governmental control difficult and thereby promoted strong localism. Its proximity to the ocean and the possibilities it provided for distant travel also prompted an adventuresome spirit in its natives. The coastal region was a place from which one ventured out, but it also attracted smugglers, pirates, and foreigners who plundered, pillaged, and invaded, sometimes together symbiotically. The illicit opium trade promoted by the British beginning in the early nineteenth century first flourished in this very region. Opium brought from British colonial India flowed into the country along the porous shoreline. The accompanying banditry corrupted officials, debased society, and ruined the economy. Eventually millions, including many of those who migrated overseas, became addicted to the debilitating drug. The Anglo-Chinese War of 1839–1842, known as the First Opium War, began close by. The Siyi fishermen could easily hear the raging, thunderous cannon blasts and witness the sea battles between Chinese and British forces. In the Siyi's "good earth," human mobility, profound attachment to home, and social upheaval were all inextricably linked.

The Siyi people rarely felt what a North American might describe as cold weather, as the southern China coastal climate was semitropical. Intense sunshine was the daytime default condition for most of the year. Temperatures ranged from an average in the high 80s Fahrenheit in the summer to the 50-degree range in the winter. Ample humidity made the air thick and heavy through much of the year. Rainfall could be torrential. Even in the months of November and December, rain might continue for days on end. Snowfall might occur once in a century. The weather allowed continuous farming throughout the year, permitting farmers to enjoy two or three crops annually. As befitted the climate and their labor, Siyi people for most of the year wore light, loose-fitting garments made from cotton, straw sunhats, and the barest of footwear to traverse the wet or dusty fields. Children ran around barely clothed at all. The Siyi people may have worn padded jackets in the winter, but they could not have imagined donning the thick woolens, heavy leather boots, dungarees, and protective outerwear that California's mountains required for survival. Freezing temperatures and snow, and parched deserts such as those in Nevada and Utah, were known to them only from folktales and legends.

The Siyi have distinct seasons and storms that can be especially ferocious. Monsoon storms occur seasonally: in the winter and summer they hit the coastal area with tremendous force and torrential rains. These make sailing difficult, especially in the winter months. Most fearsome is the typhoon, a circulating tropical cyclone that whips wind around at fifty to one hundred miles an hour. Winds in Hong Kong have been recorded as reaching 150 miles an hour. Typhoons were an annual occurrence, usually during the summer, and regularly caused widespread death and destruction. They also determined travel patterns. Early spring, right after the Lunar New Year, was a good time to leave because of weather conditions. During the holiday, gathered family members could express best wishes for safe travel and for finding good fortune across the seas.

The people of the Siyi had deep attachments to their lands, but they knew they had not always lived there. It had been a frontier area in China's long historical terms, and family genealogies and village histories documented that their ancestors had migrated from elsewhere in China long ago. Many had arrived from northern or central China centuries earlier. The Siyi people closely recorded their family lineages, which for them meant the male lines, in order to conduct the rites to properly revere one's departed ancestors. By so doing, they also hoped to ensure that descendants would honor their own spirits for eternity. This central existential requirement shaped Siyi social life and culture and was faithfully continued in America. This focus on the family and ritual also meant that there was much shared knowledge about friends, families, and neighbors, including about those who emigrated.

There is no known full description by any railroad worker of mid-nineteenth-century village life in the Siyi, but a remarkable memoir of a Siyi man named Huie Kin, who came to America in the same era as the Railroad Chinese, tells us what his village life was like in the 1850s and 1860s, when he was a child. Much later, in 1932, when Huie Kin was almost eighty years old, he reflected on his life in China and America and published his "reminiscences" to help others understand the history of Chinese in America. During much of his life, he served as one of the most prominent Chinese Christian ministers in the country.

After coming to the United States, Huie, unlike most other Chinese immigrants, received a Western education and then settled in New York City, where he was the pastor of the First Chinese Presbyterian Church for almost forty years. He was never employed as a railroad worker, but he was well aware of the Railroad Chinese. He originated from the very same area as them and was raised in similar circumstances. His description of his childhood home, village, and local customs, presented in sensitive and poignant detail, is more than an individual story. It provides insight into a broadly shared experience. He arrived in America in 1868, just as the Transcontinental line was nearing completion.

Huie Kin was born in 1854 in Wing Ning, a small village in Taishan County. The Huie (also known as Xu) clan had come from northern China two hundred years earlier, in the seventeenth century. His village was "not far from the sea," as he described it, and was "tucked away among rice fields" and "hidden by mountain ranges." The clues he provides suggest that his village, like many in the hills of Taishan, was humble but not destitute. He claimed that its isolation provided a bit of protection from the rampant social turbulence in southern China during his childhood. Though his home was "only ninety miles from the provincial capital of Canton [Guangzhou], we were almost entirely isolated from the rest of the country." He knew nothing about the great events that were occurring not far away, including the devastating Taiping Rebellion of the 1850s that ravaged much of the prov-

ince and the Second Opium War of 1856–1860, during which the British
and French occupied Guangzhou for three years. Whether his ignorance of the turmoil was a result of the village's isolation or the inno-
cence of youth is impossible to say.

His family's brick home was typically modest. He, his two brothers,
and his father, along with the family cow, occupied one room that also
served as the kitchen. His mother had the other room, and because
the place was small, his two sisters slept in an ancestral temple at night
or in the village home for unmarried girls. It was a place where they
learned traditional female skills, arts, and ways from about six years of
age. It was also where they had their feet bound, a torturous practice
that many among the Han, the majority ethnicity in China, considered
necessary to make girls attractive for marriage. Huie's sisters joined
their parents and brothers during the daylight hours to work in the rice
fields. Shrines to three local deities (one that protected the family, one
for the welfare of the animals, and one for the kitchen, the place of
family sustenance) had their own dedicated spaces in the house. Protected rice chaff embers were always at hand for starting a fire in the
coarse brick stove. The family was middling in socioeconomic terms,
as were many that sent young men out to work overseas.

Huie's village, a hamlet really, was small—just fourteen households
in total, or about seventy people who lived in close physical proximity. They were all related. The houses were alike in appearance and
construction. Made from sun-dried bricks and covered with thatched
roofs, they were built in a U-shape and housed two or more related
families. This extended family, usually consisting of several generations, shared a common space, the central courtyard, where chickens
and pigs also resided. The homes were built on a north-south axis, with
the front opening to the south. A central hall physically connected the
living units. It served as a place for worship, special functions, and receiving guests.

The principles of *feng shui*, a belief system about the relationship
of human and natural forces and their proper ordering, governed not
only the placement of doorways, alleys, and home interiors but also
the deliberate arrangement of the entire village itself. At its north end,
considered its "back," a thick bamboo grove protected the village from
undesirable natural forces. Village common property lay at its "front,"
and included a playground, communal well, and fishpond. Every three

years, the right to raise, and then market, fish from the pond went up for public auction.

The villagers, bound closely together by lineage and tradition, believed in a complex cosmology of the given world and human existence, which they took with them wherever they went, including to America. They believed that human effort could positively affect what the uncertain future might bring. Before making any major decision, however, they would faithfully consult the heavens and spirits for guidance so they might act in accordance with powerful forces beyond their control. The Railroad Chinese tenaciously and openly practiced their traditional ways and rituals wherever they went, to the bewilderment of many Americans, who dismissed Siyi spiritual practices as superstition or paganism. Belief and ritual provided the Siyi people solace, if not actual help, in facing a precarious and insecure existence.

Spiritual practices occupied a prominent place within each family home but also for the entire village, which would maintain a village shrine (*shenkan*) and ancestral hall (*shentang*). The shrine was a small structure containing a platform for images of traditional gods and patron saints. Some villagers in the Siyi even claimed a new goddess, *Songjiu Funu*, who would care for the welfare of their many menfolk who went overseas. The village hall was a larger structure that held memorial tablets for many generations of clan ancestors and residents, as well as lists of village births and deaths. The hall also served as a small school for boys. Huie Kin attended a village school for a few years and learned basic reading, writing, and literature. Rudimentary literacy for males, even from small villages, was not unusual. For girls, education was rare, if not unheard of. Illiterate girls and women were said to be "blind," as Huie Kin sadly recalled, for they had to rely on males to read and write letters for them.

Life was structured around the rhythms of farming and the milestones of birth, marriage, death, and mourning. Everyone worked from an early age. Even the local wildlife seemed to prompt the work ethic: villagers construed the lyrical call of a local bird as saying, "Everybody work, everybody dig." Life did not allow for slackers. The missionary William Speer identified the industry the Chinese exhibited in California as inherent: "Ages of toil seem to have tamed the nature of the Chinese till now patience and diligence have become elements of both mind and body. They work because they love work, honor work and maintain happiness and self-respect by work. Work is a necessity of the muscular and mental, like food for the digestive, or air for the pulmonary system."

Huie Kin recalled that playtime for children was nevertheless still joyful, if sporadic, and community festivals were major happy events. The spring Dragon Boat Festival; a special girls' celebration in the summer; the Harvest Moon Festival in the fall; and, most important, New Year's (or Spring Festival) in the early spring according to the lunar calendar, structured the year. Everyday food was simple: basically rice, root crops, green vegetables, and some meat or fish a few times a month. Travel was by foot. Nothing was mechanically powered in any way. There was only human strength, fire, or elemental water or wind power.

Located a little farther away was a larger town where Huie Kin's father occasionally traveled to purchase salt, fish, and fruit, which he would in turn sell to neighboring farmers. Whether it was raising fish in the village pond for sale, buying and selling goods gathered from afar to neighbors, selling a surplus of the crop in the market town, or regularly using cash, many of the Siyi people were familiar with the basics of commerce. Experience with a rudimentary market economy, a varied mix of agriculture, handicraft, commerce, and fishing, prepared many of them for their ventures overseas.

Huie Kin might not have left behind the affection of his family and the familiarity of the village had forces far beyond Wing Ning not conspired to draw him away, for his world was not as isolated as he claimed at the beginning of his memoir—as Huie himself well knew. The European intrusion into China that intensified in the 1830s hit the southern region with special force, disrupting long-standing patterns of life, social relations, and the economy. As a young man in the late 1850s, Huie Kin also heard about ferocious ethnic fighting between "our people," the *bendi*, or the locals, as they called themselves, and the *kejia*, or Hakka, "guest" people, who spoke differently and loyally followed a dissimilar way of life. The *kejia* did not bind girls' feet, for example. The two had lived in close but hostile proximity to each other in Guangdong for hundreds of years, but in the mid-nineteenth century, their conflict erupted into wide-scale bloody war. Hundreds of thousands in the region died in the fighting. The region suffered terrible devastation.

The *bendi-kejia* conflict was linked to an even greater upheaval. From 1850 to 1864, the Taiping Rebellion, a millenarian peasant movement, challenged the ruling Qing dynasty founded by Manchus after they conquered China in 1644. The violent movement arose in the province next to Guangzhou and assumed control of most of China south of the Yangzi River for years. The civil war claimed upwards of 25 million lives. Another upheaval, the Red Turban Rebellion, named for the red headscarves worn by the fighters, also swept Guangdong during the 1850s.

The bloodletting associated with these conflicts was horrendous and infamous. Yung Wing, the most famous early Chinese to come to America, and 1854 Yale graduate, recalled seeing the gruesome execution grounds in Guangzhou where the provincial Qing viceroy put tens of thousands to death as punishment for their rebellion. The migrants from the Pearl River delta brought their fierce ethnic, regional, and political loyalties to the United States and continued their feuds in the hills of California in the 1850s and even during the construction of the railroad.

Huie Kin recalled that when he was young, he heard other, certainly more encouraging stories about the outside world from a young relative who had ventured overseas and returned to the village. He told "of strange cities, of people with red hair and blue eyes, and of solid gold nuggets in the mountains." A cousin who came back from California spoke about the riches at "Gold Mountain" (*jinshan*), so named because of the Gold Rush of 1849. (Australia, where Chinese went for gold later, became "New Gold Mountain.") These tales bewitched the young Huie Kin, who recalled that his mother had told him that once when he was in a feverish delirium, he babbled incessantly about nothing else but wanting to go to "Gold Mountain." He had contracted "gold fever." In the early days of out-migration from the villages, the lure of finding gold was a common incentive to leave home.

In this, Huie Kin was not alone. California in the mid-nineteenth century was a place of awe and wonder. "Gold Mountain," the extravagant but fitting name Chinese gave it, was sparsely populated, with fewer than 93,000 persons in 1850, when the state joined the Union, but it was clear to all that the land possessed a future of enormous possibilities. Its population grew quickly. Texas was larger in size, but what could compare with the magnificent harbor of San Francisco, the more than eight hundred miles of coast on the Pacific, the oceanic highway to Asia, the fertile soil of the Central Valley, the magnificent river systems, and astonishing sights such as Lake Tahoe, Yosemite, the redwood forests, and the towering Sierra Nevada mountain range? And then there was the lure of precious gold, discovered in the streams flowing out of the Sierra in 1848. No other place in the world then possessed such unspoiled wonders and attractions.

For Chinese, "Gold Mountain" meant the northern part of the state for much of the nineteenth century. The development of the southern region would come later, as the north was the location of seemingly inestimable opportunities and quick riches. It was also a very attractive place to reside. Its climate was temperate along the long coastal areas. Protected from the Pacific Ocean by a range of hills, the Central Valley, with some of the richest arable land in the world, could be hot and the air moist, much like the climate of Guangdong province, and attractive to anyone with farming in their blood. Unlike their home region in southern China, which had been densely populated and cultivated for more than a thousand years, California's extensive lands in the mid-nineteenth century, except around the settlements of Native peoples, were still largely untouched, their abundant resources untapped.

Two great rivers flow through the core of the state: the Sacramento, fed from the rivers coming out of California's northern mountain ranges, and the San Joaquin, with waters from the central and southern Sierra. Both rivers come together to form a broad delta that replenishes San Francisco Bay. The rivers were navigable for long stretches into California's interior and provided plentiful fresh water for life and irrigation. A short riverboat ride made the newly founded interior towns of Sacramento, Stockton, and Marysville easy destinations from the port of San Francisco. Other river systems, such as the American, Merced, Feather, and Yuba, offered further access into mining regions.

Chinese also settled along the Pacific coast, where they fished and harvested the ocean's bounty. Even San Francisco Bay itself provided natural riches for the picking. The Siyi people were well acquainted with fish, oysters, clams, abalone, crab, and sea vegetables. Their fishing villages—"China camps," as they were called—and farms supplied fresh and preserved food for the state's growing population and for markets back in China. Travelers to the young state reported seeing Chinese everywhere they went. From California, Chinese ventured out into Oregon, Nevada, and beyond. But it was luminous gold, coveted and esteemed in Chinese civilization from time immemorial, that first attracted them to America, and especially to California's mountain regions where the ore rested, waiting to be found. Over time, "Gold Mountain" became a metaphor for real and imagined places away from home where there were riches of all kinds to enjoy.

Though the Qing empire officially prohibited emigration from China, and—for fear of sedition—threatened with execution anyone who returned from abroad, many Qing subjects were undeterred by the edicts and left anyway. Over time, local officials gradually ignored the outflow. Migration to Southeast Asia, not very distant from Guangdong, had already long been a feature of the region's history. Making their way to and from the foreign-controlled ports of Macao and Hong Kong, Chinese travelers found ways to evade the authorities.

Eventually millions, the great majority being male, left, principally for Southeast Asia, but also for the Americas. "We youngsters were also caught in this fever for emigration," Huie Kin recalled. From the early 1850s, when they began to arrive in significant numbers, to 1868, the year when Huie Kin emigrated, an estimated 107,000 Chinese came to the United States. About 33,000 returned home, leaving about 70,000, the great majority from the Siyi. Few intended to stay on as permanent immigrants. Their original plan was to work, accumulate earnings, and return to live comfortably and die in their home villages. But the attractions of California, including work on the railroad, would amount to reason enough for many to stay abroad. Huie Kin and the Railroad Chinese were of a generation born and raised amidst war, rebellion, and the call of opportunity abroad.

For many Chinese who came to America, the journey was not an individual endeavor. Some traveled with close kin. For others, travel was a well-organized social process at every juncture, especially as migration became more routine and common. Future migrants would hear of the availability of work in America from fellow villagers or clansmen. They would follow the path taken earlier by other family members or fellow home villagers. Family, clan, and village connections formed the core of Chinese identity, and these connections continued long after emigrants left home. In America, blood ties and native place connections anchored Chinese work and commerce, and provided emotional support and sustenance.

Chinese labor recruiters and merchants arranged travel for many migrants, and associates of the recruiters or ethnic associations received the migrants in San Francisco. Some arrived on ships owned by Chinese in Hong Kong, but the great majority took passage on American or British vessels. The best-known lines, the Pacific Mail Steamship Company (PMSC) and, later, the Occidental and Oriental Steamship Company, formed directly by railroad companies, profited handsomely from the travel. From 1860 to 1874, more than 112,000 Chinese left from Hong Kong for the United States. Almost all of them arrived through the port of San Francisco.

The ship companies themselves encouraged emigration from China. In 1867 the PMSC began regular service between Asia and San Francisco and published its own newspaper, which promoted Pacific commerce and travel. In its first issue, dated January 1, 1867, the newspaper featured a long article in Chinese that told of glorious opportunities waiting for hardworking Chinese in the United States. Gold — and the country's nascent railroads — featured prominently.

A railroad company needed "the labor of thousands of workers," the article declared, to construct a transcontinental line from the town of Sacramento all the way to the distant Mississippi River. Ten thousand more men were needed to join the eleven thousand already employed, and there would be work for another three or four years. The construction of connecting rail lines into Arizona and Oregon had also begun. Moreover, there was work to be had in agriculture. The article also pointedly reminded readers that California was the "vast land where gold nuggets were discovered." The newspaper assured readers that monthly wages in America were $20 to $35, a grand sum for simple farmers. Steam-driven vessels would cut their travel time to half of what it would have been with sailing ships. Even better, Chinese businessmen would assist them in making specific arrangements. "The easy trip and large demand for workers," the newspaper explained, "makes San Francisco the best place in the world for the benefit of workers." It was an enticing message that reinforced what one heard through word of mouth. The promise of well-paying work on the railroad brought another Chinese teenager named Law Yow to America.

Gold Mountain, his friends and cousins had told him, was where one could "make lots of money, work on railroads."

The Chinese who were enticed by these announcements were mainly young men, who usually embarked on their long journey alongside others who shared their family and regional backgrounds. Two surviving passenger lists of ships from China that arrived in San Francisco in 1875 and 1876 provide insight into the collective identities of migrants from China in these years.

On February 15, 1875, the steamship *Alaska* docked in San Francisco with 801 passengers from China. Owned by the PMSC, the vessel had set out from Hong Kong, stopped at Yokohama, and then made its way across the Pacific. The captain and U.S. immigration officials compiled the list for the company on the basis of interviews with the passengers. All, or certainly most, were Cantonese, and the order of names is telling. Officials ordered these passenger lists not alphabetically but according to village of origin, or what was listed as "place of birth." Other identification information included age, occupation, sex, and last place of residence, which for all was simply given as "China."

The 801 passengers, all male, said they were from approximately 110 different villages, most being the home of five men or fewer. But the great majority of passengers, about 80 percent, traveled with a large number of others from the same village, and many shared the same surname. The largest group, for example, was from Sun Hing village, Seong Chun district, with fifty-three passengers. Of this number, thirty-two had the surnames Le or Lee, and ten were named Hong or Hung. The rendering of Chinese words into English was grossly inconsistent at the time, so it is possible that these two surnames were actually just one. All the passengers declared themselves to be "laborers," except for twenty-two youngsters who were listed as "student" and whose ages ranged from eight to twelve. These boys may have been on their way to join the Chinese government experiment known as the Chinese Educational Mission (1872–1881), which brought 120 young Chinese to New England for schooling. The oldest passenger was fifty, but the average age was early twenties, with many in their teens.

A second passenger list is from the *Gaelic,* originally from Liverpool, England. In August 1876 it landed in San Francisco with 192 passengers, mostly Chinese, though the ship could carry almost 700. The U.S. government official in Hong Kong responsible for determining emigrant status certified that all were "free and voluntary." Of the 192, one, a married woman, or possibly two are listed as adult females. (One child, Mock Kow, is described as being five years old "with its mother.") There is one female "student," and the rest are males, with the average age in the early twenties. Like the passengers on the *Alaska,* the Chinese are clustered by village name, the largest being Sun Neng village, Ha Chin district, and dominated by one or two surname groups. Chinese migration to the United States, these passenger lists confirm, was collective, closely connected to family, clan, and place of origin, overwhelmingly male, and young.

The migration experience of these passengers was probably similar to that of Huie Kin. Gold and the prospect of finding easy wealth inspired him, not work on the railroad, and individual ambition, not desperation, better explains his decision to leave the familiarity of home. As Huie would later claim, it was he and three male cousins, not their parents, who actually came up with the idea of leaving their village to go overseas and seek their fortunes. They devised ways to tell their fathers about the risky endeavor they were planning. While two of the boys were in their early twenties at the time, Huie Kin and the third of his cousins were only fourteen years of age.

None of their fathers objected. In fact, their families borrowed money to cover the $30 steerage fee for the young men's journey. Huie Kin's father put the family farm up as security for a loan. Huie remembered that his father actually said very little about the ambitious idea of leaving home, believing that his father "had quite a good business head" and understood the venture as an investment. Indeed, wrote Huie, his father had relatives who "went away poor as himself but came back with beautiful gold pieces in their pockets." The story could have been apocryphal, but it was repeated enough that it had the power of truth. It is also consistent with the conclusions of other historians that the out-migrants from the Siyi who came to the United States were not "the poorest of the poor" but were commonly mid-range in their socioeconomic position. It took resources to be able to travel. Loan contracts in the Siyi in those years often show that families like Huie's were able to put up some capital, usually land, as collateral for funds to support the efforts of young family members to travel abroad.

Huie Kin and his cousins assumed that their journey would be short-lived and they would soon return home better off. Huie, with his family indebted rather than himself personally, enjoyed more latitude in his choices overseas than did others who had to contract their future labor to pay for their passage. That form of travel became known as the "credit ticket" system, in which a contractor or employer advanced the cost of an individual's passage and was repaid, with interest, from the borrower's income in the United States. Though many European immigrants financed their passage to the United States in similar fashion, the practice itself became controversial for its alleged connections to systems of indentured servitude. The most vociferous and hostile forces against the Chinese in America often unfairly described them as servile and slave-like, exploited by Chinese merchants and contractors who used the hapless Chinese workers as coerced labor. This false characterization largely emanated from racial prejudice. As Huie Kin's memoir and other abundant evidence make clear, the male Chinese in America came as voluntary, free laborers.

The young Huie Kin and his cousins knew they had to be blessed with good luck to succeed in their venture, marked as it was by risks and uncertainties, but they could not know just how tragic and painful the costs would be.

Huie and his three cousins left their village before daybreak on a fine spring day in 1868, each with just a bedroll and a bamboo basket for their few personal belongings. The four travelers made their way to the sea, where they took a small boat to Hong Kong, about a day's journey from the Taishan coast. Sitting at the mouth of the Pearl River delta just downriver from Guangzhou, the port city had become a bustling trading center under British colonial rule, and its harbor had become the main point of departure for Chinese leaving their homeland for the United States. It was also surely the biggest agglomeration of buildings, ships, businesses, and people that a country boy like Huie had ever seen.

The trip to this staging ground had been brief and uneventful, unlike the next segment of Huie's journey. His little group had to spend a month in Hong Kong before they could book passage to the United States. They idled away their time along the busy piers in the harbor, observing, among other curiosities, Europeans. They had never seen such people before, with their "fiery hair and blue-grey eyes," as he put it. Though he did not mention them, Huie would also have encountered other fantastic sights, sounds, and people. Ship crews, passengers, and adventurers from Africa, the Pacific Islands, South Asia, and South America abounded. There would have been languages, music, dress, mechanical devices, foods, and displays of ways of living and wealth that were completely unfamiliar to the simple young villager. He would have seen guns, massive iron cannons, and disciplined military personnel keeping order. He could never have imagined the numbers of people, sailing vessels and warships, and the tall buildings and open public places in the central part of a rapidly growing Hong Kong.

When they finally boarded a ship to begin their journey, the vessel was every bit as striking as these new surroundings. Though paddlewheel steamships crossed the Pacific at this time, Huie Kin's was a tall sailing vessel with "three heavy masts and beautiful white sails." The entire crew was white, he recalled, though Asians, Pacific Islanders, and other non-Europeans frequently worked on board ships in the Pacific at the time. Many of Huie Kin's fellow passengers were other Chinese; others may have been Europeans or white Americans. Huie writes that he had no idea of the ship's route but only that the weather was warm and the ship made no stops along the way.

There were days when the doldrums, or windless days, left the sails limp, and the ship languished in the calm ocean waters. Headwinds occasionally pushed the ship backward, while storms dumped heavy rains on the wooden vessel, providing fresh water for drinking and washing. On one occasion, frightful rumors circulated among the passengers that the ship's officers had lost their way on the boundless high seas. Indeed, travel routes varied and had not yet been regularized because of inexperience with seasonal variations in winds and currents. Vessels typically relied on the clockwise circulation of currents in the northern Pacific: from Hong Kong, vessels went north past Taiwan, passed the east coast of Japan, and then turned eastward. They sailed north of the Hawaiian Islands. The return trip from San Francisco started out down along the California and Mexico coast to capture the equatorial current south of Hawaii that flowed westward.

Sailing conditions conspired to test the confidence of the young Huie Kin and the others. But nothing could prepare them for what happened next.

Suddenly, mid-trip, the eldest of the cousins and their selected leader died in an agony of fever and convulsions. Though Huie provides few details of the circumstances of his cousin's death, he does record his devastation. He remembers staring for hours into the inky blackness of the ocean, which received his cousin's shroud-wrapped body. His remains would never be returned to the village, which meant that his ghost, his spirit, would be lost forever in the bottomless sea. Later, the ghosts of Chinese who died in America and whose remains were not returned to their homes would likewise be stranded in a foreign land. It was a terrifying vision. "What was to become of the party now that our leader was gone?" Huie Kin wondered. "There was an uneasy feeling that his death could not but cast an evil shadow upon our venture."

The death of his cousin hangs over the rest of Huie Kin's account of his experience during his months in transit, and he provides few details about the mundane aspects of ocean travel. One wonders about the food that was available, the social dynamics among the cramped and anxious passengers, or their treatment by the white crew likely already possessed of a sense of racial superiority.

One journalist's report in 1870 about the voyage of Chinese to America tells that they were largely confined to quarters belowdecks, where they divided themselves into different social groups. They selected one from among them to cook and obtain rations from the crew. After the meal was finished, a Chinese passenger, it was observed, "reclines upon his couch, stretched on bamboo poles between decks, where he smokes his long-stemmed pipe, and goes to sleep to the sound of a Chinese guitar." They played cards and other games. Quarrels and fights occasionally broke out, but peace generally reigned, and they put on their best clothes to practice their rites. The Chinese "never fail to have altars, where they can offer their prayers." Reports of other voyages tell of considerably more stressful conditions, including agonizing seasickness, serious illness, terribly overcrowded quarters, and fighting. We can surmise that, much as with the lives these Chinese led before setting out for America, conditions on the passages varied widely.

Huie Kin's story speaks to several central issues that many scholars have considered over the years. For one, his village, though remote even in isolated Taishan county, was intertwined with the greater Pearl River delta, which had in the mid-nineteenth century one of the oldest and most developed market-oriented economies in China. Though of modest means, its people contributed to a larger agricultural economy and were not wholly ignorant of the transformation of East Asia. A culture of risk-taking and moneymaking encouraged individual economic ambition. Merchants bought and sold citrus, rice, seafood, silk, and handicrafts for profit. The nearby city of Foshan had produced metalwork and ceramics for domestic use and foreign trade for centuries. Huie Kin's description of life in his village, modest as it was, and his father's own supportive attitude, demonstrate his home's proximity to commercial culture and a broader motivation for him to try his luck. Indeed, scarcity alone does not explain out-migration in all cases. Rather, for Huie Kin and many others like him, opportunity beckoned, and they followed.

Paradoxically, the Siyi were relatively isolated within China but had more contact with the outside world than much of the rest of the country. The nineteenth-century intrusion of Europeans and Americans into China transformed the Pearl River delta area quickly and profoundly. The region was the first to experience the far-reaching combined impact of foreign soldiers, merchants, and missionaries. The Cantonese resented the arrogance of the British in particular and generally disliked all the unruly foreign sailors, merchants, and adventurers from abroad who disrupted Chinese life and order. Large, violent riots and protests were already a regular occurrence in Guangzhou as early as the 1840s. Foreigners considered the Cantonese, because of the constant friction with Westerners, to be the most anti-foreign of the Chinese. They also became the most familiar with the foreigner.

Huie Kin's account is markedly different from the experience of Chinese who migrated abroad on no initiative of their own under the "coolie" trade. Thousands of Chinese, he acknowledges, were taken as "slaves" to Cuba, "having been kidnapped and forcibly shipped there to work on the plantations." The coolie trade flourished in the region around Guangzhou from the 1830s to the 1860s, when moral outrage began to shut down the abusive system. One careful tabulation taken in 1859 determined that from 1847 to 1858, more than 28,000 Chinese left for Cuba on board seventy-one ships, most of European origin. More than four thousand of them died in transit, the death rate ranging from almost 15 percent on British ships to almost 40 percent on Peruvian. The death rate on American ships ran at 12 percent.

These tragic numbers reflect a broad pattern of forced labor in the history of the Chinese diaspora. Although chattel slavery was ended

by law in the British Empire in 1833, a system of indentured labor flourished throughout developing empires well into the nineteenth century
in the form of the coolie trade. Pirates and brigands provided hundreds of thousands of men from China and India for work on plantations and in mines around the globe. Many were prisoners taken
in ethnic wars; others were debtors or itinerants stolen off the land.
From the 1840s to the 1870s, traders took as many as 500,000 Chinese
to Peru, Cuba, and the Caribbean, most by way of Portuguese Macau.
The word *coolie* may have come from a Tamil term related to work;
perhaps it is no coincidence that in Chinese, a similar sounding word,
kuli, means bitter labor.

The Qing court attempted to suppress the brutal trade and imposed
the death penalty on those Chinese found guilty of trafficking in coolies. Scores in Guangdong were arrested by the authorities and executed, some on the spot where they were captured. A memorandum
from the governor-general of Guangdong to Emperor Tongzhi reported that between 1865 and 1868, authorities arrested almost sixty
traffickers for kidnapping, abduction, and other crimes including rape
and murder. Scores were executed in the years that followed.

Huie Kin's own journey, though touched by tragedy, appears fortunate
compared to the experiences of many others who left China, especially
under the murderous coolie trade.

In 1852 the Connecticut ship *Robert Browne* left Xiamen, in southern
Fujian province, supposedly for California, with more than four hundred Chinese on board. Nine days into the voyage the Chinese revolted,
killing the captain and several other officers and crew. They demanded
that the remaining crew return them to China, but after the ship ran
aground in the Ryukyu Islands, crew members regained control of the
vessel and, with the help of British naval forces, hunted down Chinese
who had escaped. Many were killed or captured. U.S. military authorities tried seventy of the Chinese and sentenced seventeen to death for
piracy. After a lengthy investigation by Chinese authorities, however,
the accused were transferred to local Chinese officials, who concluded,
on the basis of interviews with those involved, that the ship's captain
had deceived the laborers. Instead of going to California as he had told
them, he was taking them to Peru. The journey there and work in Pe-

ru's notorious guano mines were virtual death sentences. They also reported that the crew had cruelly abused them, throwing the ill while still alive into the sea and beating others. They had no choice but to revolt. The Chinese officials set them free.

Another American ship, the *Waverly,* was on its way to Peru in 1855 with 450 Chinese when it stopped in the Philippines after the death of its captain. Reportedly the crew, fearing an outbreak of dysentery on board and trouble from the restless Chinese, forced them belowdecks, killing a number in the melee. The crew locked down the hatches on the hold and, after a day had passed, ventured below and found that three hundred of the Chinese had suffered gruesome deaths from injuries and asphyxiation.

Other cases in the 1850s revealed that many American ships were carrying hundreds of Chinese to foreign destinations that were not clear to the passengers, often without their full consent. Investigations and interviews with those on board frequently revealed that the laborers had been deceived or forced aboard against their will. In the case of the *Messenger* in 1860, for example, the American captain maintained that the more than four hundred Chinese on board were in fact merely "cargo." He protested the efforts of Chinese officials to release them, saying that because he had properly paid his port dues in Guangzhou, he had acquired his "right" to them. He eventually succeeded in getting to Macao, where he fled to Cuba with his "cargo." American officials in Hong Kong and China were deeply troubled by this and other cruelties and dutifully reported the tragedies to Washington. In his report on the *Messenger,* U.S. minister to China John Ward informed the secretary of state that a thousand Chinese had died in incidents involving American ships in the last year alone. It was a "disgrace," he wrote, "upon our flag." Even though there was no firm evidence that Chinese entering the United States or Canada in the mid-nineteenth century were indentured or had been coerced into involuntary servitude, Congress in 1862 still passed legislation that outlawed American subjects and American ships from engaging in the coolie trade. The U.S. consulate in Hong Kong now had to verify that Chinese going to the United States had left of their own free will.

· · ·

After the tragedy of his cousin's death, the remainder of Huie Kin's voyage went uneventfully. He may even have experienced moments of beauty and joy, especially as his ship neared the California coast.

From the deck, if they were allowed topside, passengers might have seen great pods of dolphins racing alongside in the ship's wake, clouds of seabirds, mountainous gatherings of sea lions on rocks, migrating whales, and vast schools of fish and other enormous collections of sea life. Large-scale exploitation of the natural treasures of the Pacific had only just begun. If the ship arrived in California waters on a clear day, the vista would have been magnificent: the coastline was massive and dark, unending as far as one could see to the north and to the south, and the Golden Gate, the gap in between the sheer cliffs along the Pacific and the entryway into the harbor, was simultaneously foreboding and welcoming to travelers. The rocky crags of the channel would have towered over the man-made vessel, while swirling currents in the waters below toyed with the ship.

Once through the opening, the view opened out to one of the grandest natural harbors in the world. From on board an arriving ship, one could barely see the untouched marshes, flatlands, and gentle hills that surrounded the protected waters of the bay.

The Chinese must have felt great relief after the long, fraught voyage but also new anxiety. What would they encounter when they descended the planks to the motionless pier, so unlike the rolling vessel where they had lived for weeks, even months?

Huie Kin recalled that he could hardly contain himself when he arrived at the dock. The destination was "the land of our dreams," and the "feeling that welled up in us was indescribable." He wondered whether the joy of entering heaven could surpass the "ecstasy" he experienced on landing. But beyond the emotion that overwhelmed him, Huie could recall little about what happened after disembarking. "Everything was so strange and so exciting," he wrote, "that my memory of the landing is just a big blur." Countrymen speaking his local dialect gathered him and others from his district, cared for them for a few days, and then connected them with relatives who helped the arrivals find their way in the strange land. After two long months at sea, in September 1868 he had finally arrived in Gold Mountain.

2
GOLD MOUNTAIN

May our dear neighbors
Be brave in journeying,
Making a fortune depends on luck,
Don't be loath to depart now
When the chance comes,
Becoming rich from poverty is easy.
Returning home with much money
You will be smiling with happiness at the family reunion.
— NINETEENTH-CENTURY
SOUTHERN CHINESE FOLK SONG

WHEN HUIE KIN AND HIS TWO SURVIVING COUSINS DISEM-
barked in San Francisco in 1868, they joined a historic procession of
Chinese migrants to the United States that had begun decades earlier,
and that would stretch, through fits and starts, up until the present
day. Like the Chinese who worked on the Transcontinental, they found
themselves on the shores of a growing nation, one whose hunger for
labor would make a tenuous place for them, but whose racial prejudices would also keep them at its margins. Huie's entry into the country mirrors the experiences of thousands of other Chinese migrants
who would go to work on the Transcontinental, and sheds light on the
fraught place of Chinese in mid-nineteenth-century America.

Arriving in this unfamiliar country left a deep impression on many
Chinese migrants, who would vividly recall the experience years later.
In 1882, J. S. Look, a fifteen-year-old from Guangdong, arrived with his
uncle in San Francisco, and in the 1920s he reflected upon his experience. After he and the almost one thousand other Chinese passengers

disembarked from their ship, Look remembered getting to Chinatown and finding "it crowded with Chinese . . . There were so many of us that we had to sleep on the floors as there were not enough beds in Chinatown." Reversing the usual gaze, Look also observed "the Americans," as he put it. They "and their dress looked very funny to us, and we all laughed at the way the Americans dressed." But life was tough: "We were very poor at that time — many of the new arrivals had to go around and pick up cabbage leaves and vegetables and the culls of fruit at the various commission houses in order to obtain enough food upon which to live." The jobs available to Chinese were "limited to railroad work, laundry work, cooking and employment in canneries." Walking in the city was risky too, Look recalled, as "American boys would throw rocks at us."

Such violence was simply the street manifestation of a broader pattern of racialized, legally sanctioned discrimination against all Chinese, including Railroad Chinese, which was pervasive in the mid-nineteenth century. Over the preceding years, a few persons of Chinese ancestry had received citizenship because of local administrative error or by virtue of having been born in the United States, but immigrant Chinese were officially denied naturalized citizenship by federal law. The Nationality Act of 1790 granted naturalization privileges to "free, white persons" only. People of color were excluded. After the Civil War, the Civil Rights Act of 1866 and the Fourteenth Amendment to the Constitution, which was ratified in 1868, sought to ensure "birthright citizenship" to African Americans who had been born in America, but the 1790 act was not revised to address the naturalization of other non-whites.

As Look experienced when he arrived, scrutiny and mistreatment commonly greeted other Chinese newcomers upon their arrival in San Francisco. A veteran writer for the Boston-based literary journal the *Atlantic Monthly*, Albert S. Evans, vividly described one such moment in November 1869, about a year after Huie Kin stepped off his ship.

Reporting on the arrival of the *Great Republic* from Asia, Evans declared the scene "one of the most novel sights seen in America." A side-wheel steamship almost four hundred feet in length, it was one of the largest passenger ships on the oceans at the time. From 1867, when it began operating in the Pacific, to 1879, when a Pacific storm destroyed it, the single ship alone transported an estimated ten thousand Chinese to the United States. In 1869, its arrival in San Francisco stirred great excitement and commotion in the city. The size of the ship was itself a marvel, but what the vessel held provoked even greater curiosity: five thousand tons of cargo from Asia and almost 1,300 Chinese, many likely coming for railroad work, in addition to a couple of hundred Europeans and Americans.

Crowds of gawkers, attendants, workers, detectives, and a variety of authorities and officers gathered on the pier before the ship even came along dockside. Immigration processing in San Francisco occurred right on the wharf at this time. The captain of the city's police and his entire watch "armed with clubs and revolvers" stood by to keep order and inspect the arrivals. Up to a hundred Chinese merchants, "neatly-dressed and quiet, gentlemanly-behaved men," were on hand to collect their "consignees," as the Chinese under labor contract, were called. Almost all were Chinese males, according to the news report. The curious white spectators were not disappointed in what they were about to see.

After the ship pulled to the landing, Chinese men by the hundreds came up from steerage and crowded onto the main deck, "every foot of space being occupied by them," as Evans described the scene. They stood "in silent wonder" at the "new land" before them, and then, after all the other passengers had left, the "living stream of the blue-coated men of Asia" began to disembark (opposite). For two hours they came ashore steadily without interruption and packed the dock as they waited patiently for processing. Evans's detailed reportage provokes the imagination of the reader. The Chinese men, "all with the unusual and highly visible Manchu-imposed hair-style of shaved pate and queue hanging down to the waist, pour down the plank, with long bamboo poles across their shoulders, from which depend packages of bedding, matting, clothing, and things of which we know neither the names nor the uses." Evans continued: "They appear to be of an average age of twenty-five years,—very few being under fifteen and none apparently over forty years,—and though somewhat less in stature than Caucasians, healthy, active and able-bodied to a man. As they come down upon the wharf, they separate into messes or gangs of ten, twenty, or thirty each, being recognized through some to us incomprehensible free-masonry system of signs by the agents of the Companies as they come, are assigned places on the long broad-shedded wharf . . . [for processing by] the customs officers."

Evans surmised that all were of the "laboring class," none being students, businessmen, or merchants. "They are all dressed in coarse but clean and new blue cotton blouses and loose baggy breeches, blue cotton cloth stockings which reach to the knee, and slippers or shoes with heavy wooden soles." Their personal belongings were all in hand, and most carried "broad-brimmed hats of split bamboo, and huge palm-leaf fans."

Agents of the so-called Six Companies (*zhonghua gongsuo*), a consortium of Chinese mutual assistance associations based on county of origin, which non-Chinese misconstrued as commercial organizations, greeted the arrivals. Their orderliness impressed Evans: each group of workers, he observed, waited "in patience and perfectly soldier-like order," as customs agents and police searched for smuggled opium and other contraband. In contrast to the restrained Chinese, Evans describes the agents of authority in America as mean-spirited and brutal. He witnessed their "needless violence," and their free and frantic use of their clubs against the Chinese, whom Evans described as the "most orderly and methodical people." Without the unnecessary shouting and bludgeoning by the authorities, Evans said, the processing would have been completed in half the time. Eventually the Chinese were cleared and made their way along San Francisco's streets to the not distant Chinese quarter already known as Chinatown. Some went in horse-drawn wagons, but most walked or ran, with their shoulder poles, in "Indian file."

As much as the men fascinated Evans, he was captivated by the surprise appearance of several spectacularly attired young Chinese women, evidently the arranged brides for members of the Chinese merchant elite, who stood far apart from the male workers. One diminutive female especially mesmerized Evans: she emerged from a cabin with her attendant, he wrote, her "blue-black" hair elaborately coiffed, her facial makeup "'high art' in its perfection"; her tunic "of sky-blue satin, embroidered with flowers in bright-colored silk"; her trousers a darker blue satin and similarly embroidered; her "dainty little feet" were "encased in slippers of blue satin with gold-bullion embroidery and thick white felt soles and thin bottoms of polished wood." With dangling silver and precious stone jewelry from her hairpins to her anklets, she carried two fans to keep "her face hidden as far as possible from the public gaze." Evans, who apparently stood not far from the woman, could feel her anxiety. Female handlers quickly whisked her away to a wealthy Chinese husband waiting for his new wife. A bit later, more than a dozen other young Chinese women, probably indentured prostitutes, came down to the wharf to be taken by their "purchasers," as Evans called them, who placed them in the "charge of sallow old hags in black costume with bunches of keys in the girdles of their waists." These brothel madams, known as *laobao*, "will hold them in terrible bondage and collect the wages of their sin." The arriving women were dressed in simple "silk cotton tunics and trousers" and were "painted gaudily on cheeks and lips and wear on their heads the checked cotton handkerchiefs which are the badge of prostitution." As they were taken away to Chinatown and the Barbary Coast, San Francisco's red-light district, mobs of Chinese men nearly rioted along the streets. They shouted for female attention and lunged forward to try to touch or grab the women as they sat in the brothel wagons. What terror they must have experienced as they were led away into the strange engulfing city.

Evans wondered about the historical implications of what he had witnessed. In his estimation, the coming of the Chinese had incalculable consequences, not just for San Francisco or California but for the entire country. "The Chinese-labor question," he predicted, in a few years would "break down, revolutionize, and reorganize parties, completely change the industrial system of many of our States and Territories, and modify the destiny of our country for generations to come." He saw something historic that day in San Francisco. The "Occident and Orient stand face to face at last, and the meeting must signalize a notable era in the history of mankind."

The arrival of Chinese in San Francisco in significant numbers after the 1848 discovery of gold attracted widespread attention, as their appearance, social ways, language, and distance from home set them dramatically apart from the Euro-American population. Though much has been made of the Chinese as forming a colorful part of the Gold Rush, their actual numbers were modest. In 1850, when California joined the Union, only about five hundred of the almost 58,000 gold seekers in California were Chinese. Their numbers rose, however, after the relatively easy method of individual prospecting was replaced by mining operations that required hired hands. Among those ready to work were many Chinese. From 1852 through the early 1860s, approximately six to seven thousand Chinese arrived each year. Perhaps half of those who came to America stayed for just a few years before returning home; the other half made America their new permanent residence.

The initial reception they experienced was generally welcoming. In

May 1852, the state's leading newspaper, *Daily Alta California,* for example, described Chinese as a "worthy integer of our population" and optimistically predicted that "the China boys will yet vote at the same polls, study at the same schools and bow at the same altar as our own countrymen." In April 1854, a San Francisco newspaper reported on the recent arrival of nearly eight hundred Chinese from Hong Kong on board the *Lord Warriston.* More were expected to join the estimated twenty thousand already in the state. The newspaper then noted that the Chinese had already established a significant presence in the state: Chinese who had worked in mines and in San Francisco "were rising from extreme penury to comparative wealth." Though the newspaper described the character of these workers as clearly inferior in every way to the intelligence, morality, and abilities of the "Caucasian race," it observed nonetheless that the Chinese were becoming a vital element of the population. The "white men are naturally of the dominant race; they are all fitted to be masters," but who would serve them? There were no "black slaves" in the state, Indians were "fast dying out," and no white labor from the British dominions was to be had. Who would grow the food and staples and harvest them from the soil? "Roads have to be made, and railroads will soon follow," but "will the white man, in this country, follow such employments?" "Never," the paper declared, but Chinese would provide the muscle: they "are such a people."

In the mid-nineteenth century, despite the great attention devoted to the Chinese presence in the country, there was no firm agreement on how many had arrived. Confusion over the count emerged immediately at the start of an 1876 federal investigation into Chinese immigration. A federal commission tasked with determining the extent of the Chinese presence in the country and its implications for the economic, social, and moral well-being of the nation began its work posing a simple but basic question: How many Chinese were there actually in the United States? A parade of government officials, citizens, and Chinese came forward to offer wildly differing numbers.

Charles Wolcott Brooks, a prominent San Franciscan, believed that only 67,000 Chinese lived in the country, while the Reverend Otis Gibson, one of the best-known church leaders associated with Chinese, calculated 150,000 were on the West Coast alone. The Six Companies reported that 148,600 Chinese were then in the country according to its carefully maintained membership rolls. One member of the federal committee claimed that he would prove there were over 200,000 in the country. Other witnesses said they knew there were 60,000, 90,000, 110,000, or over 210,000 Chinese. In San Francisco alone, the estimate appeared to range from a low of 30,000 in the summer and fall to over 65,000 in the winter. The issue was never resolved, which fueled continuing anxiety among whites about the true extent of the Chinese presence.

Closely associated with the issue of numbers in the minds of forces hostile to the Chinese was the ongoing conviction, despite the 1862 act outlawing American participation in the coolie trade, that many Chinese were not voluntary workers but coerced indentured servants. "Free soil" California was not a place for such beings.

Independent journalists, however, closely investigated the circumstances of Chinese entry into the country and largely confirmed that Chinese had come freely. A detailed news report in 1869 specifically addressed the speculation that Chinese who worked on the Central Pacific Railroad were here involuntarily. A reporter for the *New York Evening Post,* then one of the most respected newspapers in the country and known for its favorable attitude toward the rights of minorities, wrote that "nearly the whole force which built the Central Pacific railroad were brought over as *free* laborers." They came under U.S. consul–approved contracts signed voluntarily and broke none of the U.S. laws prohibiting the coolie trade. An unidentified American businessman worked with Chinese merchants to recruit laborers, according to the newspaper, and many did enter into voluntary contracts. The basic terms were that the employers advanced the cost of passage and sent a deposit to a Chinese company in San Francisco to cover the return of remains in case of death. This was a form of insurance provided to the workers. In turn, the laborer agreed to work for a specified wage to pay off the advance; some executed a mortgage of real property as security for the loan. After working off the debt, the laborer was "free to make a new bargain or to go where he pleased." Individual Chinese had entered into contracts for their labor as early as the 1840s in California.

The news report described the Chinese who were coming to America as not from the "lowest class" of workers, like those sent to Cuba and Peru. Nearly all who came had "been educated to read and write," and because their many letters sent back to China provided "a vast amount of information" about America, those who followed them "know where they are going and what to expect when they arrive." The Chinese came to America to "improve their condition — to earn and accumulate money," and "if they decide to remain here, they will seek to have land and business of their own." The journalist's evidence was compelling and consistent with all other credible evidence at the time.

Nonetheless, the controversy persisted. At the center of it was the accusation that the Six Companies maintained a system that closely controlled and exploited Chinese workers. Its roots were in the 1850s, when Chinese leaders began to organize groups to attend to the needs of Chinese immigrants, provide assistance to newcomers, resolve disputes among themselves, and represent their interests to the wider society. The organizations were not commercial, though merchants dominated them, but mutual aid associations, known as *huiguan,* that represented the interests of migrants with same-place origins (*diyuan*), generally corresponding to counties in Guangdong. Merchant Cantonese often had formed these associations when they moved within China in aid of their businesses, but their form and function changed in America, a foreign and unfamiliar place. The Six Companies was a confederation of these separate *huiguan.* Most Chinese migrants and Americans who interacted with them and the Six Companies had a high regard for them and their purposes.

Still, Americans who were unfamiliar with the Chinese and their different ways could be uncomfortable and suspicious. For some, the *huiguan* and Six Companies were not just mysterious but possibly sinister. Sinophobes in America frequently accused the Six Companies of being "slaveholders," a most incendiary charge. The Six Companies, it was said, were a "government unto themselves," despotic, and anathema to American values.

The organization repeatedly defended itself against the accusations over the years. Knowledgeable white Americans who had extensive contact with the Chinese, including white Christian ministers who were long associated with them in China and America, defended the *huiguan* against these scurrilous accusations. Respected ministers such as the Reverend William Speer and the Reverend Otis Gibson, who had served in Fuzhou, China, for more than ten years before returning in 1865 to work among the Chinese in California, righteously condemned immoral and cruel practices such as the forced prostitution of young Chinese women, but also defended the Six Companies against slander.

"Why do the hundreds of intelligent Chinese Christians in America," wrote Gibson, citing evidence to support his point of view, "constantly assert that there is no such thing known among their people in this country as slavery, or bondage, except in the case of women." He posed his question rhetorically to emphasize his point. The Chinese who come here, Gibson declared, "in every case come voluntarily."

Leung Cook, a proprietor of the Tung-ching-lung store on Commercial Street in San Francisco's Chinatown, who hailed from Taishan, testified before a California state commission in 1876, providing a basic description of the Six Companies in his own words. He served as the president of the Ning Yeung association, the largest of the *huiguan* in the Six Companies. He reported that the organization was founded about 1853, after the Chinese first began to arrive, as they knew little of the English language and of American customs and needed help in "getting employment and in going from place to place." The sole purpose of the Six Companies, he said, was "to look after Chinamen here." He estimated that this association had a total of 75,000 members on its rolls, though the number was by then actually thirty to forty thousand because many had returned to China. He testified at length about the purpose of the *huiguan*. In his words, spoken through an interpreter:

> When my countrymen come to California, my company takes care of them, pays their boarding and lodging expenses. For this they collect, afterwards, from each man, five dollars. That is considered to pay back the amount due the company for its advances, for expense, and its trouble. When they pay it they get a paper or permit, and can then buy tickets [to return to China]. Where men are sick, poor and unfortunate, they remit the five dollars and give the permit anyhow. Where men are in debt to anybody, and the company finds it out, it will not give the permit. If the debtors are too poor to pay, they are allowed to go [back to China].

Leung Cook served as head of the association for just one year, as the presidency changed annually. Among his duties was to help his compatriots with their mail from home. The other important function provided by the association was to assist in returning the remains of the deceased to China. The Chinese, he informed the commission, "think a good deal of the remains of deceased persons, and when a person finishes his life, they take his remains back to China to show to some of his relations in order to have them remember and do honor to them," explaining, "It is a custom to do so." More than just habit, the practice provided essential existential comfort to those far from home, especially for the Railroad Chinese in their dangerous endeavor. Through the years, the associations dutifully repatriated the remains of thousands of Chinese who died in America for eternal rest in their home soil and with family.

The Six Companies helped Huie Kin, and thousands of other Chinese who arrived in the United States in the nineteenth century, make the transition to life in a new country, which they were themselves helping to shape with their presence, labor, and business acumen. In San Francisco, early on, Chinese established a complex community of businesses, residences, shops, association halls, theaters, gambling dens, brothels, and temples right in the center of the city. San Francisco's Chinatown, the "capital" of Chinese in America, still stands in the same original location. And while earthquakes and fires have reshaped the urban landscape of the port city, images of its early Chinese community survive, offering a precious link to the bygone world of the Railroad Chinese.

One of the most prominent photographers working in California at the time of the Transcontinental was Carleton Watkins, who established a studio on Montgomery Street in San Francisco in 1871, shortly after the railroad's completion. Located just a few blocks from Chinatown, Watkins' studio employed several Chinese to help produce his stereographs and other images, and the products of their labors often featured Chinese as well. More than thirty extant Watkins images have Chinese as the main or partial subject.

His photographs of Chinese in San Francisco show them in Chinatown stores, temples, restaurants, and smoking establishments. Two of his most arresting images are from the 1870s. "Chinese Women, San Francisco" (opposite) shows two fantastically silk-gowned women in a bright sunlit room full of Chinese tropical hardwood furniture, traditional string instruments, and art calligraphy. The partially visible elegant inscriptions declare that the owner of the artwork is a cultivated person. The setting is unlike anything most Euro-Americans at the time could ever have imagined existing on American soil. The women, who may be mother and daughter, seem relatively at ease; they do not appear to have bound feet (which suggests they are either Hakka or Manchu neither of whom engaged in the practice), and are clearly well-to-do. They hold painted fans, wear jade bracelets and rings, and are elegantly coifed and groomed. An opium pipe sits on the table between them. A few moments later, to judge from the shifting shadows, Watkins took a second photo, "Chinese Actor, San Francisco" (below), showing a young man in a spectacular Chinese opera costume. It must have shimmered and glowed with brilliantly colored silks and embroidery in red, blue, and gold thread. He may very well have performed for Railroad Chinese in the Sierra or when they came to San Francisco for a visit. The altar behind him features a fine ceramic rendition of *budai*, the "laughing Buddha," the spirit of goodwill and happiness. The flowering narcissus and citrus fruit, possibly pomelo, indicate it is the time of the Spring Festival or Chinese New Year, in late January or early February.

As early as the 1850s, Chinese photographers in San Francisco earned praise for the fine quality of their work. In 1854 a San Francisco newspaper reported on the photography of Ka Chau, who operated a "Daguerrian Establishment" and took pictures of Chinese men and women, though it seems none of his work has survived. By the late 1860s, at least sixteen Chinese professional artists and photographers were practicing their arts in San Francisco. The best known among them is Lai Yong, who worked from at least 1867 through the late 1880s as a photographer and portrait painter.

Though his life is still largely a mystery, Lai Yong's existing photographs show that the clientele for his portraiture and photography ranged beyond the Chinese community and included some of the most important figures in San Francisco. A handful of his *cartes de visite* and cabinet cards, popular forms of presenting photography at the time, provide remarkable views of Chinese in the years when Chinese worked on railroads. Unlike the images produced by many non-Chinese photographers of that era, Lai Yong's work does not have the feel of being "ethnographic," that is, a look at what was deemed foreign and exotic for the study or enjoyment of others, not for those in the frame. A common mark of ethnographic photography is a visibly uncomfortable subject, who often avoids looking into the camera's all-seeing eye. In contrast, Lai Yong's images, apparently taken in his studio in the heart of Chinatown, are of fellow Chinese, who appear relaxed and even pleased with the attention they are receiving. They had the means and desire to have their pictures taken by a person from their own community.

One striking image Lai Yong captured is of a Chinese male sitting with Chinese furniture, next to a flowering narcissus on a Chinese table (opposite, top left). He looks directly into the camera; his facial expression and body language are confident, strong, and even a bit intimidating. He wears a dark silk tunic and rimmed black hat popular with city Chinese men at the time. Lai Yong uses the same furniture for a portrait of a woman (top right), elegantly attired and coiffed and also comfortable as she gazes straight into the camera. She is composed and worldly. In another image, a confident young man holds a flower and a book. Other material that appear to be Chinese publications sit on the table shelf. His manner, clothes, and headwear express cultivation and refinement. Lai Yong's Chinese are distinct individuals with humanity and personality.

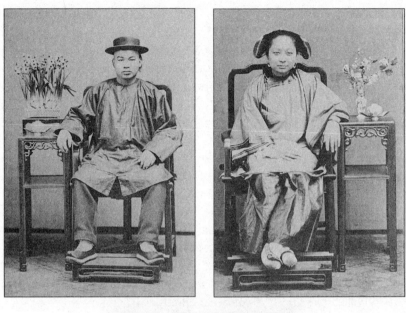

Photography was not the only medium that Lai Yong used for expression. As a polemicist, he became well known for his co-authorship of one of the most articulate statements decrying anti-Chinese sentiment in America. In 1873, while he was engaged in his photographic work, Lai Yong served as the lead author with four other Chinese to produce "The Chinese Question from a Chinese Standpoint." Directed to "the people of the United States" and translated and read before the San Francisco Board of Supervisors by the Reverend Otis Gibson, Lai Yong's eloquent statement angrily demanded fair treatment of Chinese in the country as mandated by international treaty and human decency. He defended his compatriots as "peaceable and industrious" folk who had "toiled patiently to build your railroads" and substantively contributed to the economy of the West. He and his fellow authors protested the "severe and discriminating" actions against "our people while living in this country" and argued that if the mistreatment of Chinese did not end, the treaties between China and the United States should be abrogated. All Americans should then remove themselves from China and the Chinese from America. *Stay at home and mind their own business,*" he emphasized, using an old admonition, "*and let all other people do the same.*" A few years later, Lai Yong, perhaps heeding his own declaration, himself disappeared from the San Francisco scene and returned to China.

The photography and writings of Chinese residents of San Francisco such as Lai Yong offer a colorful glimpse into the flourishing community that migrants like Huie Kin and J. S. Look—as well as countless Railroad Chinese—would have found when they first stepped onto California soil. So too does the dispatch from *Atlantic Monthly* writer Albert S. Evans, whose report on cargo of the steamship *Great Republic* upon its arrival in the city in 1869 provides vivid detail into that most important dimension of Chinese migrant life: diet. The items off-loaded from *The Great Republic* included coffee from Java, firecrackers, rhubarb, silk, and tea as well as other food items commonly enjoyed by Cantonese. There were tons of rice, dried fish, cuttlefish, "sharks' fins," and "preserved fruits, salted melon-seeds, dried ducks, pickled duck's eggs, cabbage sprouts in brine, candied citron, dates, dwarf oranges, ginger, smoked oysters, and a hundred other Chinese edibles and table luxuries." Railroad workers far distant from San Francisco would eventually partake of some of this comfort food from home.

Another keen observer of the Chinese newcomers was a young attorney and writer named Daniel Cleveland, who had recently arrived in California. The drama of the growing presence of Chinese inspired him to complete several studies about their entry into the state and the implications for the country. He sent one of his reports to the U.S. minister to China, who found it so useful he then forwarded it to William Seward, the secretary of state. Cleveland's private report was careful, factual, and decidedly sympathetic to the Chinese. He condemned the endemic violence and the overt social and legal prejudice against them. He believed that the Chinese deserved justice and that they would greatly benefit the country. Cleveland then completed a comprehensive four-hundred-page study on Chinese in California, which he hoped to publish but never did. It is unclear why, but the handwritten manuscript contains many keen firsthand observations, including an extended description of the landing of Chinese in San Francisco sometime in late 1868 or early 1869.

The treatment Cleveland described was considerably more brutal and controversial than anything experienced by Huie Kin and Look or observed by Evans. Cleveland reported that before any Chinese migrants were permitted to leave their vessel, labor contractors and their agents came on board to sort through the mass of passengers. Those identified as arriving through the "credit ticket" system, he wrote, in which the expense of transit would be deducted with interest from future wages, "are taken possession of by their white owners, and are treated like slaves, watched and guarded, until they reach the end of their journey, and are delivered to the Railroad Company." One scene especially disturbed him:

> [I] once saw a mulatto man, a petty officer on one of these boats, who had perhaps been a slave himself, taking advantage of his little brief authority to lord it over the poor Chinese. He maltreated them with a rough tyranny and keen relish as though it afforded him intense satisfaction to find human beings helpless enough to submit to his domination. The Chinese as helpless as a flock of sheep, look the picture of misery and despair, as they are huddled together upon the deck of the tug-boat listless and aimless, impotent against the force which keeps them in confinement. A small squad of resolute white men, armed with heavy bludgeons,

which they are not slow to use, keep vigilant watch over the Chinese to prevent their escape.

As Cleveland's report continues, after being taken by small boats directly from San Francisco Bay and then upriver to Sacramento, the men were forced into railroad boxcars, whose doors were closed and then locked by white overseers to prevent escape. "If they were culprits who had committed some heinous crime," Cleveland noted, "they would not be more closely guarded and harshly treated." During the ride, he says, some managed to open the doors and jump out to escape, but died when they hit the ground. The rest presumably wound up working for the Central Pacific. It was a terrible beginning for their lives in America.

The experience of arriving in America varied for individual Chinese, including those bound for railroad work. From the descriptions and recollections that we have, some, like Huie Kin, were exhilarated, while others, like Look, could find humor in the challenge of entering a new country and seeing new people. Others encountered an unanticipated nightmare. All faced great uncertainty. Few, if any, were prepared for what they would experience next.

3

CENTRAL PACIFIC

We young Chinese saw many strange things; the most remarkable being the steam-engine. We were told that those iron rails running parallel for a long distance were the "fire-car road." I was wondering how a car could run on them, and driven by fire, too, as I understood it, when a locomotive whizzed by, screeching and ringing its bell. That was the first iron-horse we had ever seen, and it made a profound impression on us.

— YAN PHOU LEE, IN JAPAN ON HIS WAY TO
THE UNITED STATES, SEEING A STEAM ENGINE
FOR THE FIRST TIME, CA. 1871

WHEN HUIE KIN STEPPED ONTO THE PIER IN SAN FRANCISCO in the summer of 1868, ten thousand Railroad Chinese were already toiling to get the line of the Central Pacific Railroad through the formidable High Sierra, the peak elevations of the great mountain range that runs like an indomitable spine down eastern California. The company had brought them onto its workforce four years earlier, and now they made up 90 percent of the massive army required for the construction project. At one moment in time, it appeared that Chinese were historically destined to become the most important migrant workforce in the western United States in the nineteenth century. China's population was huge and hardworking, and travel across the Pacific took about the same amount of time as getting from the East Coast of America to California.

China was embedded in the very vision of the Transcontinental itself when it first appeared as an entrepreneurial ambition in the 1840s. The most prominent early promoter of the idea was Asa Whitney, a prosperous merchant and a relative of Eli Whitney of cotton gin fame. Asa

Whitney had traveled to China in 1842 and very quickly enriched himself in the lucrative export trade. After just two years, he was wealthy enough to retire from work and returned home convinced that America's future lay in developing its commercial and cultural ties with Asia, China in particular. He energetically campaigned for the construction of a rail line to facilitate that trade.

As Whitney and other early boosters of a transcontinental railroad envisioned it, the line would span the three-thousand-mile-wide continent, link the country's heartland with the Pacific, and interconnect the commerce of the two great oceans of the world at a time when rail lines ran no more than a few hundred miles at most. Whitney's argument for the transcontinental line invoked a vision of providential destiny. In 1849 he declared: "The change of the route for the commerce with Asia has, since before the time of Solomon even, changed the destinies of Empires and States. It has and does to this day control the world. Its march has always been westward, and can never go back to its old routes . . . Through us [the United States] must be the route to Asia, and the change to our continent will be the last, the final change." The nation would become, in Whitney's view, the literal physical link connecting the mythic West (white America and Europe) to the East (China and the rest of Asia). Tens of thousands of inspired supporters across the country campaigned for his project and pressed Congress to back the plan. Among those who shared the vision was a young Leland Stanford in upstate New York, who listened as Whitney sought to persuade Leland's father to join his crusade for the rail line.

Other continental expansionists hailed the possibilities of American control of the Pacific, as Manifest Destiny, the conviction that the United States was meant to expand westward, grew ever more common. Chief among them was the insistent Missouri senator Thomas Hart Benton. In the 1850s Benton endorsed efforts to construct rail lines across the country and envisioned massive Chinese immigration to supply the anticipated labor needs of the American West. The Chinese, he believed, were essential if the country was to attain full economic and historical greatness. In an improbable flight of fancy, Benton was so convinced Chinese would soon become such a vitally important element in America that widespread marriage between the "yellow," as he called them, and the "white" must occur. "They must talk together, and trade together and marry together," he declared. "Commerce is a great civilizer—social intercourse as great—and marriage greater."

Similarly, William Speer, the early American missionary in China who returned to work among Chinese in America, saw their arrival here as monumentally important and providentially ordained. Their coming to America, he declared with no sense of exaggeration, was "excelled in importance by no other event since the discovery of the New World." Speer was convinced that the Chinese would make enormous contributions to the country's development, including to railroad construction. In January 1855, *The Oriental,* which Speer founded as one of the first Chinese-language periodicals published in the United States, predicted that soon "the boundless plateaus of the Western half of this continent, now desolate and almost unpopulated by any but the savage and scarce improvable destroyers of the buffalo, will be scattered with busy lines of Chinese builders of iron roads, that shall link the two oceans, and add to the wealth and comforts of the dwellers upon either shore."

Later in 1855, one early Chinese resident in the Sacramento area, a man identified as Sam Mill and elsewhere as Lam Tai-san, constructed a fully functioning miniature steam engine that could run on a track. Its display deeply impressed the public. The local newspaper called Mill "an ingenious builder" and reported that his work had been completed in an "exceedingly creditable manner." The model locomotive was twenty inches long, with a boiler, furnace, cylinders and pistons, and two sets of driving wheels. More than a colorful story, the account expressed genuine respect for the "Chinaman," as Mill was called, and is evidence that Chinese newcomers possessed notable technical abilities. They were not unskilled laborers alone. The Reverend William Speer, with relish, offered praise: "This *Chinese* locomotive and railroad were the first on the Pacific Coast!"

Not just in prediction and modeling but in actual practice, Chinese were early railroad workers in the New World. They may have worked in railroad construction in Cuba in the late 1840s and in Panama in the early 1850s. In 1854 the New York–based Panama Railway Company brought a thousand men from southern China to Panama to construct a trans-isthmus line. When the project failed because of ghastly working conditions—50 percent of the Chinese died from accidents, disease, and suicide—the railroad company sent the survivors to Jamaica and may have sent some to California.

Chinese began to work on real railroads in California in the late 1850s. In 1858 the *Sacramento Daily Union* reported that the California Central Railroad Company had hired fifty Chinese to work on its line in the Sacramento area and found them "very good working hands." They toiled from "sunrise until sunset," and, noted the paper, "the experiment bids fair to demonstrate that Chinese laborers can be profitably employed in grading railroads in California." At about the same time, Chinese also worked on a line that ran from San Jose to San Francisco, which is now the oldest line in continuing operation west of the Mississippi River.

Chinese in California, then, were already much more familiar with railroads than their compatriots in China. Few knew anything about them. The first lines were not constructed in China until the late nineteenth century, but descriptions of the "fire wagon" filtered back from Chinese returning from work abroad. These workers actually learned about railroads before scholars or officials in China. One of the first of these elite Chinese to see a train and write about it was a Manchu official known as Zhigang, who traveled overseas. He formed part of the Burlingame delegation, the first Chinese diplomatic delegation to come to the United States, in 1868, and a few years afterward published portions of his diary. His description reveals his fascination with the iron machine as well as his simple understanding of modern technology.

On April 16, 1868, he recorded that in the United States he "rode a fire-wheeled vehicle for the first time." The train was light, he wrote, "steady, and faster than Liezi [a legendary Daoist adept at] riding the wind." His effort to describe the train followed:

> It is constructed like a wooden house twenty or thirty feet wide and three times as long, with rows of seats, two columns of eight, each of which holds three persons, making [room for] forty-eight people in all. On both sides are rows of windows with three layers of glass, cloth curtains, and wooden shutters for protection against wind, rain, light, and dark. Each carriage has four iron wheels. In front is the fire-wheel engine wagon with a driver and

behind him two coal-wagon workers . . . The front wagon burns coal, heating water to produce steam, which goes through a tube to a compartment, causing a rod to expand and contract, which moves the wheels, which makes the train go . . . The speed of the train is double that of a steamboat, for a railroad takes much less power compared to paddling water.

Zhigang's description of the track, rails, and iron wheels are similarly simple, and he also notes the requirements for constructing the actual line: it "must be built straight" and "level," and "a tunnel must be built whenever a mountain is encountered, and a bridge whenever water is encountered." Zhigang does not mention seeing any of the Railroad Chinese then hard at work completing the very tasks he described, but it is likely that he did while traveling from San Francisco to the East Coast.

Political figures had at first publicly complimented the arriving Chinese. In January 1852, Governor John McDougal praised them before the state's legislature as among "the most worthy classes of our newly adopted citizens, to whom the climate and the character of California were peculiarly suited." He cited their industry and the value of their labor and considered offering economic incentives to increase their immigration. Even without such incentives, Chinese soon accounted for almost 20 percent of the working population in California. Some had distinguished themselves in local enterprise and established good reputations as trustworthy and capable businessmen, and many white employers continued to respect Chinese workers over the years.

Yet these "newly adopted citizens" found themselves living and working alongside many other Californians who had no interest in getting along with the newcomers. White southerners with strong racial prejudices, as well as anti-slavery, anti-black "Free Soilers" from the North, made up much of the state's young population. A wildly popular Massachusetts send-off song to those departing for California in the Gold Rush went:

> O! the land we'll save, for the bold and brave —
> Have determined there never shall breathe a slave;
> Let foes recoil, for the sons of toil
> Shall make California GOD'S FREE SOIL.

Suffering racial prejudices that festered throughout the country, Chinese came to be seen as a distinctly anomalous presence, even among the polyglot population that streamed into the state to seek their fortunes. Hostile descriptions emphasized the differences in their bodies and facial features, dress, language, customs, food, and behavior. Agitators accused Chinese of selfishly exploiting the state's natural resources and, as an allegedly servile workforce, undercutting the livelihood of white workers and their families. Culturally and racially, Chinese were condemned as unsuitable to become Californians, despite what McDougal and others had claimed. The Chinese presence in California became the most incendiary political and social issue in the state for the better part of the nineteenth century.

Anti-Chinese music, which voiced this prejudice, became a staple in western American popular culture. One song written in the mid-1850s and handed down through the years went:

> John Chinaman, John,
> > But five short years ago,
> I welcomed you from Canton, John—
> > But wish I hadn't though;
> Oh, John, I've been deceived in you,
> > And in all your thieving clan,
> For our gold is all you're after, John,
> > To get it as you can.

Lyrics of songs might not just be about Chinese but were also directed at them. The threatening chant of an energetic expulsion song went:

> Get out, Yellow-skins, get out!
> Get out, Yellow-skins, get out!
> We'll do it again if you don't go,
> Get out, Yellow-skins, get out!

Elite political support for this sort of ugly sentiment came from McDougal's successor, John Bigler, who reversed his predecessor's position and called for restricting Chinese entry into the state. In the spring of 1852, just a few months after McDougal's praise of Chinese, Bigler declared that he favored an array of taxes levied exclusively on the Chinese, including a Foreign Miners' Tax and head tax, and other measures to harass them out of the state. Chinese heard themselves described as slave-like "coolies," inassimilable, and damaging to the state's social "tranquility" and prosperity. (Not coincidentally, when civil war broke out a decade later, Bigler, a Democrat, would declare his sympathy for the Confederacy.)

One of the most eloquent Chinese responses to Bigler came quickly from San Francisco resident Norman Asing, a businessman originally from the Pearl River delta who claimed U.S. citizenship and was a prominent community leader. Writing in eloquent English for the *Daily Alta,* Asing condemned the governor's remarks as contrary to the history, practice, and law of the United States. Immigration, Asing maintained, had helped make the country great and respected in the world. Moreover, the Chinese were not a "degraded race," as Bigler had charged. Chinese respected honest labor and worked in many decent occupations, "following every honorable business of life." America, Asing declared, ought not to be a country with a racial hierarchy, a land with, in his words, an "aristocracy of *skin.*"

A decade later, Chinese again heard from the state's top political figure that they were unwelcome. This time the ugliness came from California's first Republican governor, and the future president of the Central Pacific Railroad: Leland Stanford. In his gubernatorial address in 1862, Stanford called for dramatic measures to address the "Chinese question." Attracting settlers to help populate the large state was of preeminent importance, he declared, but they had to be the right sort of people. "The settlement among us of an inferior race is to be discouraged," he urged, claiming that "Asia, with her numberless millions, sends to our shores the dregs of her population." Unless strong measures were taken soon, the governor averred, the state's very future would be jeopardized. Stanford branded Chinese "a degraded and distinct people" who exercised "a deleterious influence upon the superior race" and repelled "desirable immigration." He announced his eagerness to seek government action. Warm applause from the gathered throng in the state assembly chamber greeted these infamous anti-Chinese remarks, which today are still his best-known comments on the Chinese.

His expressed sentiments were apparently politically motivated and pandered to popular prejudices; in his own home and personal life

Stanford actually maintained close and even affectionate relationships with Chinese. Even as he publicly denounced Chinese, Leland and his wife, Jane, quietly maintained warm ties with them. In the summer of 1861, the couple purchased a ramshackle mansion in downtown Sacramento and staffed it with several Chinese workers, including a cook named Moy Jin Kee, who introduced his younger brother Moy Jin Mun to the couple. Jin Mun, who had recently arrived from China, also began working for the Stanfords. According to several accounts, Jane Stanford, childless at the time, became especially fond of the teenager and proposed to adopt him into the family. Jin Kee opposed the idea because Jin Mun's parents were still living in China, and because of the racial divide. Though never adopted into the family, Jin Mun remained close to the Stanfords. When he left their employ in the mid-1860s, Jane gave him a gold ring with his name engraved on it for remembrance. Jin Mun cherished the keepsake, according to the biographical information provided by his son, and proudly wore it for the next seventy years until his death in 1936. According to family history, Jin Mun worked as a foreman for Chinese workers on the Central Pacific Railroad in the 1870s.

Jin Kee, for his part, played a critical role in the life of the Stanford family. In 1862, the same year as Leland's inaugural address in which he expressed support for efforts to rid the state of Chinese, Jane Stanford developed a serious pulmonary infection that threatened her life. Western medical practices failed to improve her condition, but Jin Kee introduced her to Yee Fung Cheung, a Chinese traditional doctor who had arrived in California in 1850 and lived in the Chinese quarter of Sacramento. Yee used herbal remedies to treat Jane and restored her to full health. Yee himself later treated Chinese and white workers on the Central Pacific Railroad and became one of the most prominent and legendary Chinese medical practitioners in California.

In business, too, Stanford was not as ill-disposed against Chinese as his widely circulated public political position suggested. In just a few years it would be Stanford himself, as the president of the CPRR, who would be responsible for attracting more Chinese to America than any other single individual. What is more, throughout his life Stanford directly employed hundreds of Chinese on his many private and commercial properties around California, including at his stock farm in Palo Alto—the future site of the university that carries the Stanford name today. Ultimately, the political vitriol that Stanford directed toward Chinese migrants may simply have been the result of political calculation—a sadly familiar tactic, even at that stage in American political history. At the end of his life, Stanford rued his earlier prejudice against Chinese and expressed sincere respect for their industry and character. They had, of course, helped him become one of the richest men in the world.

The sectional conflict over slavery blocked progress in realizing Asa Whitney's dream of a rail line that spanned the continent. A transcontinental line would accrue enormous benefits to those along its route. Not only would there be huge federal subsidies and land grants to support its construction, but also states along the line would gain decisive economic, social, political, and strategic advantages. The railroad would be able to move people, equipment, and supplies longer distances and more quickly than ever before. The division between North and South, however, complicated all national politics. A divided Congress could not agree on any of the five proposed routes ranging from north to south. But the secession of southern states that precipitated the Civil War in the spring of 1861 finally allowed Washington to authorize the railroad's construction along a northern route that the South had opposed.

In July 1862, President Abraham Lincoln, who had been a lawyer for a railroad company early in his career, signed the Pacific Railway Act, selecting the CPRR and the UP to complete the first transcontinental railroad. The act pledged financial support in the form of land grants, bonds, and loans to the project. The two companies came into immediate competition with each other, as their present and future income and profits derived substantially from government support and anticipated income from passenger and freight traffic. Control of the line, including critical decisions on the specific route, depended on the amount of track a company laid. The federal government hoped that this competition would make construction more efficient and hasten the date of its completion, but it also encouraged financial malfeasance, slipshod work, political intrigue, bribery, and industrial sabotage. Eventually, the two railroad companies obtained millions of acres of public land in subsidies, and tens of millions of dollars in government support that supplemented private financing. The government's enormous expenditure of public funds in ways that were never fully clarified resulted in the great Crédit Mobilier scandal in the 1870s, which came to symbolize Gilded Age business-government corruption.

The UP line started near Omaha, the termination of the existing lines from the east. Construction did not begin in earnest until after the end of the Civil War, which released thousands of men for work. The UP hired army veterans, freed blacks, Irish and other European immigrants, and Mormons. The terrain they faced stretched over the slopes of the plains states, along river channels, and through Rocky Mountain passes. Supplies to build the line, including iron, tools, train engines and cars, and food, traveled relatively easily along established rail lines.

The almost 1,800 miles of track that the two companies would lay seemed an outsized ambition. It was the second-largest construction project in the world, after the Suez Canal, which was being constructed in Egypt at the same time. The *Sacramento Daily Union* provided figures to dramatize the immensity of the challenge just for the Central Pacific line. The newspaper calculated that laying track from Colfax, fifty-five miles north of Sacramento, where the line actually began, to the Great Salt Lake region in Utah, where the CPRR and UP might meet, would "require fifty thousand tons of iron, chairs and spikes, and one million one hundred thousand ties." A single train that could transport all the necessary iron would be twenty-eight miles in length, pulled by 416 locomotives. If one added the ties to this train and the additional locomotives, it would be fifty-two miles long.

That the CPRR would make it to Utah was not a given at all, and many were skeptical that it would even make it out of California. The construction challenges were staggering, including dramatic changes in elevation along the planned route in the Sierra: from just about sea level at the start in Sacramento, the line would rise more than seven thousand feet at Donner Summit after just one hundred miles. Extreme weather conditions in the higher elevations prevented work for as much as half the year, and laying roadbed through granite mountains required tunneling through the hardest rock. Almost all major construction supplies, including iron rails, spikes, connections, explosives, engines, and cars, had to be carried by ocean ships from the East all the way down past the tip of South America and up to California.

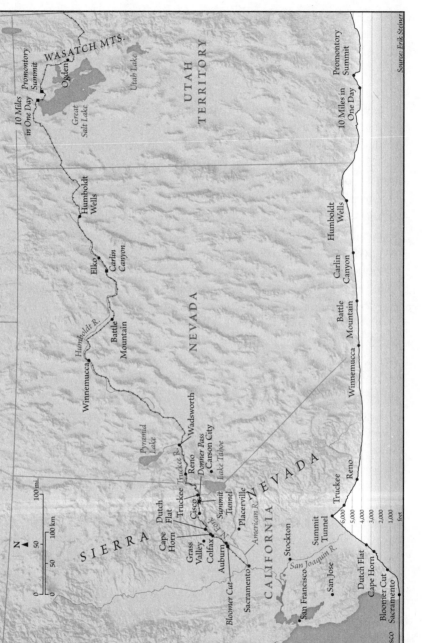

Source: Erik Steiner

Aside from the landscape and scope of the project, the difficulties of financing, scale, distance, politics, and the concurrent raging Civil War appeared insurmountable to many at the time. And above all, the fundamental and basic amount of human energy required to construct the line—that is, the elemental muscle, blood, sweat, and labor needed to make a way for a steam train to travel across the country— remained the most critical variable in the entire enterprise. Without the workers, there would be only debt and aspiration.

The CPRR would require massive numbers of workers, thousands upon thousands. They would be among the first industrial proletariat in America: paid with wages for their skills in metalwork, carpentry, explosives, earthmoving, timber clearing, water control, and drayage. All work, including forging the roadbed, tunneling, and laying the line would be manual. There were no steam shovels or mechanical earth-movers on this massive construction site, no power drills or tunneling machines, no motor vehicles to transport workers and materials other than on the completed sections of the rail line, no hydraulic pile drivers or diesel lifts. Work would take place out in the open, in all seasons and under all conditions except the most extreme. Living, for the workers, would also be out in the open for most of the year, except when they were furloughed because of the weather. The Pacific Railway would quite literally be "hand-made."

Governor Leland Stanford, who soon became the president of the CPRR, broke ground in January 1863 in a grand ceremony along the Sacramento River. Assuming office in 1861, Stanford had lobbied vigorously for federal government support for the construction of a transcontinental rail line. At the same time, he and the other Big Four established the CPRR in June 1861, anticipating the federal government's decision to back the project. A year later, President Lincoln signed legislation authorizing construction and providing limited financial support for the CPRR and UP, but work had not started because of difficulties in obtaining enough initial funding for the enterprise. Stanford and the other leaders of the CPRR were thought to be "a little off," even "insane" in thinking they could complete their portion of the task. Many thought that the company might reach the nearby foothills at the base of the Sierra, but it would never get through the formidable Sierra Nevada mountain range itself. Geography was one matter, and the lack of sufficient capital was another; but more challenging still was the shortage of labor.

Today, a memorial mural at the Sacramento site where Stanford turned the first spade to begin work depicts a few Chinese in the crowd, acknowledging their eventual role in the construction effort. In reality, the CPRR leadership, because of their racial prejudice, which they openly expressed, initially wanted only whites in their workforce. Just a few hundred white men responded to the CPRR recruitment efforts, however, and they soon proved unreliable; when word of a new strike of gold spread, they walked off the job. "It was impossible to get white labor," according to Lewis M. Clement, one of the principal engineers on the CPRR. The Union Pacific after the end of the Civil War tapped a robust labor market. The Central Pacific, by comparison, had almost none to draw from.

In part because of this lack of sufficient reliable white workers, the initial construction on the CPRR proceeded very slowly. In the first year and a half of effort, from January 1863 to June 1864, the CPRR line extended only as far as the small town of Newcastle, just thirty-one miles from Sacramento, and below a thousand feet in elevation. The High Sierra was not even in sight. The CPRR leadership had to consider radical measures. They thought about using Confederate prisoners even as the Civil War still raged. Later they wondered whether thousands of freedmen from the South could be brought west, or Mexicans brought north, to meet their immense need for workers.

The CPRR's labor predicament was no secret, even to Chinese. Sacramento's Chinese quarter sat just blocks from the site of groundbreaking and the CPRR's base of operations. The daily press closely followed the project and its problems, and those Chinese who kept up with current events must have wondered about the implications of the labor shortage and the possible opportunities for themselves. They likely discussed such things in their restaurants, associations, and gathering places. The ethnic news network throughout the state was well developed. Chinese household servants, of whom there were plenty in the residences of the railroad directors, would have been privy to frustrated private conversations about the company's problems. One of these inner sanctum workers was a man known as Ah Ling, a trusted and intelligent manservant of Charles Crocker. There is conjecture, even among Crocker's own descendants today, that it was Ah Ling who suggested employing Chinese on the railroad sometime in late 1863 or early 1864.

When Charles Crocker, or his brother E. B., raised the idea of using Chinese to other CPRR leaders, its audacity outraged and divided them. James Strobridge, the field construction supervisor beneath Crocker, pushed back. "I will not boss Chinese," Strobridge declared. Crocker was insistent, supposedly saying, "Did they not build the Chinese wall, the biggest piece of masonry in the world?" He then directed Strobridge to go to the town of Auburn to find Chinese workers.

Auburn, nestled in the western foothills of the Sierra Nevada thirty-five miles northeast of Sacramento, was on the CPRR route, but the completed portion of the line had not yet reached it. Strobridge knew the area well, having lived, married, and done business there for years before he went into railroad construction work. He may not have wanted to hire Chinese to work the CPRR line, but if he had to do it, he would have known that he could find them there.

The destinies of Strobridge, the CPRR, and Chinese in America converged and forever changed in Auburn, for it was there that Strobridge met a Chinese labor contractor who could provide him with workers. He was known as Hung Wah.

This was almost certainly not his actual name, even though it also appeared in the census record, which rendered it with Wah as the surname. The Chinese characters for Hung Wah, as we know from the court documents and his signature on later CPRR payroll records, are not words used for the name of a person. They were likely a designation for his business. "Hung Wah" translates roughly from Chinese as "working together harmoniously," nicely capturing the ideal of the organic social relationship Chinese employers would want to have with those they paid. Mistaking the title of a business for the name of the Chinese proprietor was common.

According to a brief news report in April 1931, when he passed away, Hung Wah was born in 1835 and, taking his chances, came to the United States in 1850. One of the first from the Siyi to arrive in Gold Mountain, he made his way, perhaps with relatives, to Auburn, in the heart of California's gold country. Census records, though often inaccurate, offer a possible glimpse into his background: the 1860 census identifies Hung Wah as being twenty-nine years old at the time and his occupation as "miner." He is described as "Mongolian" and is listed as having been born in 1831, not 1835, as given later. He lived with three other Chinese men: Sing Wah, twenty-four years of age; Sung Wah, age thirty-three; and Ki Sung, thirty years of age. Their appellations, likely an inaccurate rendering of their true Chinese names, and their ages suggest they were closely related—brothers or perhaps cousins. They lived next door to other Chinese. What these records fail to capture, however, is that Hung Wah was ambitious and entrepreneurial; he would make his fortune not in mining but in providing workers to those who needed them.

In the two years after the 1860 census, Hung Wah, no longer a worker himself and with some command of English, became a major supplier of Chinese labor to projects in Auburn, an early center of mining activity in the Mother Lode, as the gold country was called. Chinese had been a prominent part of the town's population since its founding soon after gold was discovered in nearby Coloma in 1848. In the 1850s, as many as 3,500 Chinese lived in neighboring Dutch Flat, making up more than half of the town's population and 30 percent of Auburn's population, or three thousand of the town's ten thousand residents. The American River and other gold-bearing waterways that abounded in the area attracted thousands from around the world. Roads connecting it to other mining towns made Auburn a transportation hub, and it became the county seat for Placer County. The Chinese may have found promise in the name "Placer," as it invoked the dream of gold: a "placer" is a rich deposit of minerals, including gold. Fertile farmland also lay close by. The town, at an elevation of 1,200 feet, saw little winter snow. It was a good place to live for both practical and symbolic reasons, and Chinese remained until they were driven out by the upsurge in the anti-Chinese violence of the late 1870s.

Chinese had arrived to prospect the rivers and streams in the area and also hired themselves out to work for whites and other Chinese on small and large mining operations. They frequently worked in teams on claims abandoned by white miners and, as in a cooperative, shared the proceeds. The work often involved skills that would later qualify and prepare them for railroad construction.

They even settled in neighboring areas with fearsome names like

Rattlesnake Bar, Murderer's Bar, and Poverty Bar, "bar" referring to a gravel formation in a river. Nearly all these towns in the Mother Lode had a Chinese quarter with stores, restaurants, boardinghouses, gambling and meeting halls, brothels, temples, and even theaters for touring opera troupes from China. In the 1850s, Chinese accounted for 30 percent of Placer County's population.

Chinese also patronized white-owned businesses, rented property from whites, and entered into commercial relations with them. The local newspaper encouraged whites to enjoy the shows at the Chinese theater, despite the language and cultural barrier. Stories in the press also circulated about the luck of some Chinese in making their fortunes. One fellow reportedly found a sixteen-pound lump of gold worth $3,300 near Auburn. The story no doubt stoked envy. The fellow immediately left for home, where he would receive a hero's welcome and inspire others by his good fortune to try their own chances in California. In the winter, when outdoor work could not be done, Chinese from surrounding areas swelled the town's Chinese population. Chinese also became local farmers and grew fruit and vegetables, such as beans and tomatoes, for the miners and others. In the 1850s and 1860s, Chinese established themselves as an integral, though largely separated and tenuous, part of Auburn life.

The region also experienced ugly anti-Chinese violence from its earliest days. In 1853, in neighboring Nevada County, "Ling Sing (a Chinaman)," as the record constantly refers to the miner, was shot fifteen to eighteen times in the back by a white man. Court documents tell of his brutal death at the hands of George W. Hall and two accomplices who wanted Ling Sing's belongings. A district court first convicted Hall of murder on the testimony of several Chinese eyewitnesses, but Hall appealed and took the case to the California Supreme Court. The court did not deny the facts of the crime but threw out the verdict, citing a state statute that forbade the testimony of non-white people in cases involving whites. Hall walked away a free man, and *People v. Hall* stayed on the books for twenty years before it was overturned. Where Ling Sing is buried is not known.

Violence against Chinese soared. With dramatically curtailed legal protection, Chinese became easy targets for robbery and abuse. Daniel Cleveland, the early acute observer of Chinese life in California, condemned the discrimination. "In no other civilized country," he informed top officials in Washington, D.C., "would the Chinese be debarred from the right of testifying against those who had wronged them in person or property." He believed that hundreds of Chinese had been brutally murdered in the state, with the perpetrators known and unpunished.

In this volatile environment, Hung Wah still managed to establish himself as a person of importance and standing. In 1862, a year or more before Strobridge approached him in Auburn, he became embroiled in a conflict among several white businessmen who wanted to undertake a large gold mining operation in one of their claims along the American River. The specifics of the dispute are obscure, but the summary of the civil proceedings provides fascinating information about Hung Wah. Court documents show that Hung Wah contracted with one of the involved parties to provide and supervise up to 150 Chinese workers to build and operate long flumes to wash huge quantities of gravel to extract gold. In return, Hung Wah was to receive a stunning 60 percent of the gold dust collected from the operation. Presumably he paid the workers from his share, which the principals must have expected to be significant, given the scale of the operation. Also, Hung Wah was to receive an additional small percentage held by the principals to cover provisions before the ore could be collected, amounting to thousands of dollars in cash. Differences over expenses incurred in supplying the Chinese workers appear to have been at the center of the conflict among the business partners. In the court proceedings, Hung Wah's comments are summarized in English, with no mention of the use of an interpreter. Although he signed his business agreement "Hung Wah Company," in clearly written Chinese characters, evidence suggests that he had a decent command of English, including written English. He had legal representation and appears to have represented in turn many other Chinese who had observed the signing of the contract and were eager to join his crew.

The court documents indicate that Hung Wah enjoyed the respect of the involved parties as well as of the court itself. Perhaps most surprising is repeated mention that Hung Wah operated a store and lived with a "family," though the reference may have been to male relatives, not to a wife or children, as there is no evidence that he was married. Chinese males married both Chinese and non-Chinese females in America, though not in great numbers, and would formally record the union. In these years, usually only financially successful Chinese in California could afford to have families, sometimes even financing the travel of an arranged bride from China.

In August 1863, a few months after Leland Stanford broke ground for the CPRR operation, Hung Wah advertised his labor contracting services in the Auburn newspaper. He declared in English, "I will furnish any number of Chinese laborers to work on Rail Roads, Wagon Roads, or Mining Claims," doing so "at the lowest cash rates." Hung Wah claimed that he had "experience in the business" and access to "facilities" to obtain "any required number of men." Notably, he deliberately listed "rail roads" first among the construction projects. His claims were bold, but he backed them up by providing the name of William McDaniel, a prominent local businessman Hung Wah had worked with, as his reputable reference.

It may have been McDaniel, who was widely known for having close dealings with Chinese, who introduced Hung Wah to construction supervisor Strobridge. Or perhaps Strobridge, who had his own personal ties to Auburn, had simply read Hung Wah's advertisements in the local paper. It was likely during Strobridge's visit to Auburn when Hung Wah and Strobridge met. Regardless of how the two men found their way to each other, one thing is certain: their meeting quickly led to a mutually beneficial business relationship that had historic consequences.

The January 1864 payroll record of the CPRR is the first firm evidence of Chinese joining the construction effort. Years later, Charles Crocker recalled that the company began to hire first "50 Chinamen" and then "50 more" and "50 more," and put them to work just north of Auburn on what was known as the Dutch Flat–Donner Lake Wagon Road, which the CPRR would use for access. On the payroll record, Hung Wah signed his name in Chinese as receiving almost $675 for "Chinese laborers" and "per diem," which may have been expenses for supplies and food for about twenty-five workers. Hung Wah and a man named Ah Toy, who is listed as a supervisor, are the only Chinese names on the roll. The next month they appear again as receiving similar amounts. The names of the individual workers on the line are lost forever. But the legacy they were about to forge remains with us to this day.

. . .

At first, the CPRR put the handful of Chinese laborers to work on light grading, but they worked so well, the company quickly hired more and more until they became the main construction force. By early spring 1865, two to three thousand Chinese worked the line, largely recruited from among the Chinese already living in the state. Many more would join them soon.

These workers greatly outnumbered the eight hundred white employees who were supervisors over the Chinese, teamsters, craftsmen, and laborers, too. The Chinese impressed their bosses back in Sacramento, who initially paid them on average $26 a month in wages, about a dollar a day, with one day off from work each week. They paid for their own room and board and lived together in temporary outdoor camps that moved along with the line. The company, in its need to attract workers, believed its pay was better than what the workers received in mine labor. It was, however, less than what the CPRR paid white workers, who received perhaps 30 percent more in wages. This race-based differential was common practice at the time. White workers, even laborers, were paid significantly more than Chinese, who still found the work attractive. The wages they received were much higher than what they could make in China. Gold Mountain had become not only a place where good fortune might be found in the ground, if one was lucky, but also a place where attractive wage-paying work could be had almost without limit, at least until white labor targeted Chinese as competitors.

The leadership of the CPRR knew they needed an army of muscle to complete the construction task before them, but at this early stage of the project, they could not anticipate how difficult the work would become and how many workers they would require. The general route up from the Central Valley was not a mystery, but the upper reaches of the Sierra were not well known. The engineers learned about the topography and geology as they went along. There was no firm, detailed blueprint. Surveying and determining the actual route had to be done as the construction army advanced. And few had seen, let alone lived through, the winter snow season in the high country. None could know that the winters in the next two years would in fact be among the worst in history. None had any inkling of the extraordinary measures the Railroad Chinese would have to take to build, and survive, through the extreme conditions that lay just ahead. No one in

the world had ever tackled, or even seriously imagined, what was required to tunnel through mountains of defiant granite and construct a
roadbed through frozen ground, ice, and forty-foot snowdrifts. Nothing prepared them for the challenge of building and then protecting a
vulnerable ribbon of rail through the mountains. Would the Railroad
Chinese have continued to work for the CPRR if they had known that
killer snow and landslides would sweep many of them away, taking
their young lives?

All this was to come.

The country traversed by the CPRR in its first year and a half of
work was the most hospitable it would face, but progress had been
pitiful. The CPRR line had advanced less than fifty miles, and the High
Sierra, the company's greatest challenge, was still off in the distance
—a towering wall that blocked the western line of the railroad from
the vast expanses of Nevada and Utah, where the two halves of the
Transcontinental were to connect. The terminus where the CPRR and
UP would meet was undetermined and dependent on work yet to be
completed. Their business resources, finances, influence and power,
and future profit depended entirely on the miles of track they could
claim. Nothing was certain except the relentless press of competition
between the ambitious leadership of the two railroad companies to
have their workers lay as much track as possible, as quickly as possible.
Whether the CPRR's Railroad Chinese would succeed in conquering
the Sierra Nevada was yet to be seen.

4
FOOTHILLS

[In late January] a black bird, called by us wu-hou, because its cry was like that, came about this time, and also the cuckoo. The black bird would call "Wu hou, wu hou," and the cuckoo would reply, "Ko kung ko ch'o, ko kung ko ch'o," which the farmers thought sounded like "Everybody work, everybody dig."

— HUIE KIN, *Reminiscences*

THE ROUTE OF THE CENTRAL PACIFIC RAIL LINE THROUGH California traveled across some of the most varied and dramatic landscape anywhere in the world. The CPRR's starting point along the Sacramento River lay a bit above sea level in elevation. The air in summer there is stifling, thick with moisture from the surrounding waterways. Just one hundred miles northeast lies the start of the granite mountains of the Sierra Nevada range, among the most rugged in North America. The pass over Donner Summit, named for the ill-fated party trapped by winter snows in 1846, lies at over seven thousand feet in altitude. Surrounding peaks are even higher, at more than nine thousand feet. The air is thin and challenges the lungs. The rail line had to overcome this intimidating barrier to reach the eastern side of California and beyond to the expansive high plains and deserts of Nevada and Utah.

In summer, gentle grasslands blanket the area around Sacramento, but eastward the landscape quickly changes to oak-and-shrub-covered hills that yellow in the dry heat. Farther on at the lower elevations of the Sierra, cooler temperatures encourage vast, dense stands of pine, fir, and other conifers. Overhead, the High Sierra soars above the tree line. The scenery becomes rugged, with barren rock and shrubland.

High mountain meadows and thousands of snowmelt pools and lakes form stunning vistas. Tahoe, the Washoe Indian name for the largest alpine lake in North America, lies there.

The Central Valley can have heavy rain but rarely sees snow. Snowdrifts at the higher elevations rise twenty to forty feet or more in winter and cover the ground well into summer, which can also see ferocious wind and thunderstorms. Snowstorms as late as July are common in the Sierra. Through the changing seasons along the route of the railroad in California alone, the Railroad Chinese faced frigid temperatures and towering snowdrifts; vast fields of deep mud and slush that made walking, let alone the use of horse-drawn carts, almost impossible; and blazing sun, especially at the higher altitudes.

Spectacularly beautiful scenery and plentiful wildlife accompanied the intimidating terrain and climate. Great populations of bears including grizzlies at the time, wild sheep, deer, and fish lived in abundance in the hills, mountains, and waterways. Small mammals, birds of great variety, rattlesnakes and other reptiles, brilliantly colored butterflies, wasps, and bees entertained, nourished, and tormented those who lived in the wilds. The Railroad Chinese had never encountered flora and fauna as rich and as varied back in their homeland.

The railroad, as no other manmade machine did to the same extent, challenged and disrupted this natural environment. The steam engine, with its noise, fumes, and insatiable appetite for fuel, vanquished the stillness of mountains and forests. Track sliced through and permanently scarred the land. The railroad invaded, and ended, the isolation of wilderness.

Though a railroad conjures images of continuous linear movement and of the predictability of terminals and schedules, constructing the iron road was a very different reality. Building the Pacific railway was discontinuous, disconnected, erratic, and unpredictable. The construction schedule was punctuated with delays, work in fits and starts, frenetic activity interposed with halting progress, gruesome deaths and constant danger, and disruptive human behavior from top to bottom. Problems with securing funding, the vagaries of weather, the indomitable and imposing topography, the unpredictability of the supply chain from iron to food, changes in engineering, routes, and work plans, calculating and disputatious leadership, and the challenges of

quality and quantity of labor were the only constants. There was nothing simple, smooth, or predictable about this construction effort, the
most massive to that point in American history.

When they were put to work for the CPRR in early 1864, the Railroad Chinese set about laying a line that had been only generally
mapped earlier by surveyors and engineers. They favored making the
route as straight and level as possible and with a steady rise up the elevations that locomotives could handle. Nature had to be shaped, cut,
filled, packed, and bridged. The line had to twist and wind gradually
around unavoidable topographical obstacles. The Railroad Chinese,
using only picks and shovels, wheelbarrows, carts, and horses, cleared
the dense brush and forests, graded, cut through steep rises and hills
that blocked the straightaway, filled deep ravines, laid down the ballast, set the ties, and spiked the iron rails. They used blasting powder
to crack stone and packed earth. With hands and muscle, they moved
thousands of tons of earth, gravel, and rock. Weather conditions allowed them to work at the lower elevations almost throughout the
entire year. Ahead, though, lay the perilous work of getting the line
around soaring cliffs, across plunging ravines, and through the intimidating granite of the Sierra Nevada. The immensity of the challenge
that landscape and weather would present far exceeded anything that
the workers, and the directors of the company, could conjure in their
wildest imaginations.

No account of the experience of working on the line for the CPRR
by a Chinese is known to survive. We can only imagine what the
lived experience may have been like, but the diary of a young Union
Army veteran who arrived in San Francisco by ship from New York in
December 1864 provides a rare sense of the challenges of living and
working on the line, even for one who occupied the relatively privi-
leged position of a member of the railroad's professional engineering staff. Stephen Allen Curry, who was deeply devout and a sensitive
observer, hoped he would find rewards that would make his perilous journey to California worthwhile. After landing, he quickly made
his way to Sacramento, where he met Leland Stanford and engineers
Samuel Montague and Lewis Clement, who hired him to join their

staff. In February 1865, about a year after Hung Wah and his compatriots had started work on the CPRR, Curry was sent out to help plot the line through the mountains. As dramatic and beautiful as California's scenery and wildlife were, they could not compensate for the terrible living conditions he would have to endure. The description of the difficulties Curry recorded in his journal only begins to suggest what the construction workers' diaries might have told us if they had survived.

On his way to the high country in early March, Curry stayed for a few days near Illinoistown, soon renamed Colfax, on the route of the line. It lay at 2,400 feet in altitude fifty miles from Sacramento. Curry walked or rode on horseback much of the way, as the completed rail line was still far from reaching the town. "Weather showery. Some snow on the ground, roads terribly muddy . . . Wet feet for two or three days has given me some cold." After a week's stay at Shake Shanty, the name of the rough cabin in which he lived with fellow engineers for several weeks, he writes that he is already "lonely and sad." As one who had endured the Civil War, Curry had experienced hardship before, but nothing had prepared him for his work surveying the railroad route. "What a home for white men," he wrote.

In late March 1865, he added a long entry to his diary about an especially difficult workday a few miles east of Illinoistown. "Yesterday morning we began putting reference points near 'Cape Horn,'" he wrote. "It was a difficult job, and almost perilous. The bluff stands at an angle of 70°, and where the line runs it is more than 1200 feet above the bed of the north fork of the American River, which runs and roars at its base." Chinese would soon be working at this dangerous location, which became the focus of one of the most controversial episodes in the construction history of the railroad.

On April 3, an early spring day in much of the rest of California, Curry encountered snow and frigid weather in the mountains. "Very cold last night, ice on water an inch thick this morning," he recorded, and on April 7 he wrote: "The ground was white with snow this morning and the snow was falling rapidly. Pretty hard for a new camper in a muslin tent very carelessly and badly pitched. There is a prospect of a deep fall of snow. At night, the snow changed to rain during the day —a cold dismal, drenching November rain . . . The tent leaked badly and blankets became wet—everything wet and dirty. Standing by the fire to warm one's feet incurs the necessity of a wet back." His resolve and hope shaken, Curry confides, "I submit and commit myself to God and hope for better weather or better shelter," but the next day is actually worse, and he fears he will get "badly sick." Then he writes: "April 10th. Sun rose clear and bright. Snow 6 inches deep. A storm of hail, snow and rain thunder loud and reverberating grandly among the hills. Were driven to camp. News of the surrender of Lee and his army. Praise God from whom all blessings flow."

Over the next several weeks, Curry passed through the booming town of Dutch Flat, learned about Lincoln's assassination, and encountered Chinese, and though the weather slowly improved, he continued to suffer. He struggled with bouts of diarrhea, blistered and raw feet, and demanding work assignments. He complained about having to work through snow, being able to sleep just a few hours a night on the unforgiving ground, and fending off mosquitoes, numerous rattlesnakes, and repeated illnesses. The pious young man passed by sites with frightful names like Robber's Ravine, Hell's Kitchen, Dead Eye Gulch, Deserted Ranch, and Devil's Peak, as well as a place called, embarrassingly to him, Horse Cock Cañon, so named, in his modest words, for a "perpendicular shaft of conglomerate rock."

By mid-May 1865, he had had enough. "Curry sick," he writes of himself in the third person. "Have decided to quit this R.R. by the first of June," he notes, adding, "I pray that providence will follow me and sustain me as in the past, for I feel very weak." The physical challenges of living and working in the Sierra had become too much for him. He finally ended his surveying work near the summit of the mountain range in view of Donner Lake, at six thousand feet, and the surrounding snow-capped peaks. Several months later, Railroad Chinese would arrive in the area to start the arduous work of tunneling. Returning to San Francisco to depart for home, Curry prayed "for future protection from accident and danger during the voyage."

Though he had occupied a skilled position for the Central Pacific, five months was enough for Stephen Allen Curry. His diary includes no speculation or musing about what life would be like for the construction workers who would follow him; the struggle of his own day-to-day existence occupied him completely. He could not have imagined what winter would be like in the summit area. But surely, in a quiet, prayerful moment, he must have thought to himself: Thank God I am not a construction worker. Look kindly on those who will be.

By mid-1865, around the time when Stephen Allen Curry finished his survey of the railroad's route into the highest reaches of the Sierra, several thousand Chinese were toiling for the CPRR far below and to the west, pushing the railway's line across the Central Valley and toward the forbidding mountains. Many of these men had been miners in the Sierra foothills gold country, not far from the CPRR route. A growing number came directly from China, where labor agents recruited them to travel to California to work.

Practically overnight, Chinese had come to form the backbone of the railroad construction army that shaped, filled, and covered the earth and laid the bed and track, all by hand. Their early labors concentrated on stretches of line that lay well below the upper reaches of the Sierra, yet these efforts nevertheless stagger the imagination for the energy and ingenuity required to push forward.

A photograph taken over a decade after the completion of one these projects gives some sense of the scale and ambition of the CPRR even at this early phase of its construction. The iconic "Filling in Secret Town Trestle" (opposite) is the best-known photograph that includes Railroad Chinese workers within the frame. Photographer Carlton Watkins, who took the pictures of Chinese in San Francisco we saw earlier and was later famous for his grand images of Yosemite and other California landscapes, took this photo around 1876, when Chinese were completing in-fill work around the great trestle near Colfax that had been erected a decade earlier to span a deep ravine. Chinese are not likely, however, to have been the main workforce in its original construction, but we can see that the workers in the photograph are Chinese because of their characteristic hats. They labor alongside handcarts transporting a staggering amount of soil and rock. With a magnifier we can see that in addition to several Chinese standing in the lower left of the photo, who were likely posed, there are perhaps hundreds on the far right and in the background who are breaking down hillsides, filling carts, and pulling them to where the fill was needed. They appear to have completed an astonishing amount of work and would do even more. Eventually they completed the entire in-fill, making the wood trestle unnecessary, and it was removed.

It was hardly the only such project—or the first. In May 1865, the Chinese workers began their assault on what was called "the big fill." Located near Auburn, it may have been the first big project tackled by many of the Railroad Chinese. Three hundred and fifty men, with thirty carts and thirty-five wagons, filled a gully a thousand feet long and fifty-three feet deep in the middle. Once the project was finished, they laid track atop its length. At nearby Wildcat Canyon, hundreds of other Chinese used wheelbarrows and hundreds of horses and carts to transport immense quantities of dirt scraped from "many acres" a "long distance away," according to a reporter, to fill the great chasm. Massive excavations were also common throughout this section of track. Two cuts just past Clipper Gap measured four hundred feet long and fifty feet deep each. At Wildcat Summit, the cut through the earth ran 941 feet deep and required the removal of an estimated thirty thousand cubic yards of earth and rock. At Star House Gap, the cut ran eight hundred feet long and thirty-seven feet deep; at George's Gap, the cut was 1,150 feet long and thirty-six feet deep. Huge embankments often also had to be constructed to protect these passes to keep them open. One at Wildcat Summit extended one thousand feet and stood forty-five feet high. Bridges five hundred feet long spanned steep ravines. Carpenters were mainly Euro-Americans, though Chinese also helped build the structures.

While the names and identities of nearly all of the thousands of Railroad Chinese have been lost to history, the payroll sheets of construction companies affiliated with the CPRR, though scattered and incomplete, contain tantalizing information about the identities and duties of some of the Railroad Chinese who were working for the company around this time. These payroll sheets are the closest thing we have to personnel records; from them we can find several hundred Chinese names, almost all of them labor contractors or "headmen," and bits of information about some other individuals; we have no records listing the names of the thousands of workers in the construction ranks.

Records we do have show that Chinese worked mainly as laborers, but also as waiters, cooks, blacksmiths, and helpers of various sorts. Frustratingly, and with just a few exceptions, Chinese names are rendered in ways that make identifying actual individuals with any accuracy impossible. Few full proper names are given, and most of those are listed in an informal way that was customary for Chinese males in their home areas. For example, on "Payroll Sheet #128, April 1865," under "China Labor," we see this column of names, all Chinese (except for "Sisson's," which was the name of the largest labor contracting company):

Ah Fong's Men
Billy Yang's Men
Ah Gou's Men
Che Noa
Foo Sing
Hung Wah
Sisson's Time
Wang Wan
Ah Wy
Ah Kung
Ah Coons

Cum Sing
Hung Wah

Below each of the principal entries on this list appear Euro-American names—presumably identifying supervisors or foremen attached to the contractor. Large amounts of money follow each main entry, the sums ranging from a low of just over $100 for one contractor to almost $4,000 for Hung Wah, whose name appears in two entries. Several other Chinese received over $3,000, though Hung Wah is the only one who signs his name, in Chinese, for receipt of the funds. "Paid" is simply scribbled for all the others.

All the entries on this payroll sheet appear to be for labor contractors. Indeed, up to *five hundred* Chinese labor contractors provided perhaps half of the five to six thousand Chinese laborers who worked for the CPRR in these first years of construction. According to extant payroll records, most appear to have been responsible for a team of twenty-five or fewer workers and may have worked alongside them.

Some contractors provided several teams, while still others were responsible for hundreds of men. Among the most prominent contractors were men identified simply as Ah Fong, Ah Yow, Ah Coon, Cum Sing, and Ah Wing, but the vague rendering of their names and absence of any other identifying information make it impossible for us to know much about them, including their formal names. "Ah" was a common diminutive that Chinese used among themselves. The Chinese may not have tried to help the company understand their individual identities, or perhaps the company itself was just not especially interested in learning.

The Chinese contractor who furnished the most workers by far was Hung Wah. Although the documentation is incomplete, construction company records show that he provided just twenty workers in early 1864 and a few more in the following months. But a year later, in April 1865, the payroll number ballooned to almost 140 men. In May, the number was 250.

An early group photograph of Chinese workers in California may show one of the first Railroad Chinese, Lim Lip Hong (previous page, front row, second from the left), and others. One of them may even have been Hung Wah. Perhaps he is sitting in the center of the group.

Hung Wah's good fortune would continue in the coming years. The number of workers under his command appears to have increased further through the rest of 1865 and into 1866. By April 1866, Hung Wah would be responsible for more than five hundred workers, according to the payroll sheet from that month. During that spring and summer, Hung Wah would provide even more workers each month, peaking at more than *nine hundred* workers on the July 1866 payroll sheet, almost one quarter of the total construction workforce. In that month alone, Hung Wah would receive almost $28,000 to distribute. In today's dollars, that would be $784,000.

We know nothing about how Hung Wah handled the money that passed through his hands. No records survive of his accounting system, his management methods, the individual identities of the workers he paid, the relationships he maintained with them, or their view of him. By custom, however, the workers would have originated from the same area as Hung Wah and spoken the same local dialect. Hung Wah's established record of steady and significant increases in his labor force also indicates that workers had confidence in his integrity and believed he would do right by them. He had developed a solid reputation and had won their trust, a fundamental element in long-term Chinese work relationships. In contrast, other Chinese contractors, because of unscrupulous business dealings and mistreatment, became targets of workers' wrath. Chinese workers, after all, were not passive and could decide for whom they would work.

What is clear, in any case, is that many of the Railroad Chinese were businessmen comfortable with handling money, making transactions, supervising labor, and interacting with management. Those whose names appear on the aforementioned payroll sheet, for example, seem to have been responsible for teams of twenty-five to fifty workers in multiple camps, which are listed. The amount of pay issued in gold or silver computes to almost a thousand Chinese workers, assuming an average pay rate of $26 a month per worker for twenty-six days of work, from first light to sundown.

These Chinese workers deeply impressed the once skeptical leaders of the CPRR. Edwin B. Crocker, brother of Charles, retired justice of the California Supreme Court, and the CPRR's attorney, privately provided an insider's report on the progress of the railroad in an April 1865 letter to a close friend. Crocker wrote that Chinese then constituted a "large part" of the workforce, or approximately three thousand hands, he wrote, and "they prove nearly equal to white men, in the amount of labor they perform, and are far more reliable." Chinese were doing "all kinds of labor, blasting, driving horses, handling rock, as well as the pick and shovel." His friend would be "astonished," Crocker wrote, to see the amount of work the Chinese had completed: they were "moving the earth and rock rapidly." Moreover, they were disciplined. Crocker assured his correspondent that there was "no danger of strikes among them"—although before long, the Railroad Chinese would dispel this rosy assessment.

In a July 1865 report to stockholders, Leland Stanford himself indicated that Chinese had become "an important element of labor" for the company. A few months later, he issued an even more expansive assessment and declared they had simply become indispensable. Stanford did not characterize Chinese in the demeaning ways he had just a few years earlier when, as governor, he called for restricting them from the state. Instead, he praised their qualities and tremendous contribution to the construction effort.

In October 1865, Stanford submitted an official public report to President Andrew Johnson on the CPRR's work as required by Congress, which had authorized public money for the Transcontinental. Thousands of Chinese, he observed, were then working for the company. "They are quiet, peaceable, patient, industrious and economical," he wrote, and they are "ready and apt to learn all the different kinds of work required in railroad building." Stanford concluded that not only were the Chinese becoming as "efficient as white laborers," but also they were "more prudent and economical" and were "contented with less wages." In contrast, white workers were not even joining the CPRR, as they "preferred employment other than in railroad work."

Stanford also directly addressed the suspicion that Chinese were servile indentured laborers under the control of unscrupulous Chinese merchants. Such a view, Stanford adamantly maintained, was completely unfounded. Chinese leaders were "intelligent business men who promptly advise their subordinates where employment can be found on most favorable terms. No system similar to slavery, serfdom or peonage prevails among these laborers," whose wages "are always paid in coin each month." Stanford confidently predicted that as many as fifteen thousand Chinese would be working for the company in the next year, making it possible for the CPRR to complete its work in the time required by Congress.

Company leaders also described Chinese as engaged in a wide range of work, including the most dangerous. In his end-of-year report to the company, chief engineer Montague observed that Chinese "are becoming very expert in drilling, blasting and other departments of rock work." In his own report, Stanford reflected on the tremendous progress made in 1865, and declared that the CPRR had completed the most challenging and dangerous work ever faced by a railroad company. The achievement was epic. For instance, "heavy rock excavations" that should have taken eighteen months to complete had "been pushed through in from four to five months" because of the "great vigor" of the effort.

In September 1865, after the line reached Colfax, fifty miles from Sacramento and at 2,500 feet in elevation, the earth presented its greatest challenge yet to the construction crews. Just east of the town, the huge, steep mountain known as Cape Horn stood in the way of the line. Surveyor Curry had helped plot the route at this site. There was no way to avoid the mountain's intimidating presence, which is why it was named for the treacherous southern tip of South America, where the Atlantic and Pacific Oceans meet and around which all ships had to pass through dangerous waters. From Cape Horn mountain, one could also take in spectacular views of the surrounding countryside. The wild American River far below the route of the line. One of the most vigorously debated questions in the history of the Central Pacific's effort to get through the Sierra centers on what happened at this location.

Many railroad histories tell of Chinese lowering themselves from the top of the mountain in baskets woven from reeds and using hand tools to carve a ledge for the roadbed or hole and place explosives to blow away the stubborn rock. Hanging dangerously in the wind, with nothing but natural fibers keeping them from the void below, the Chinese, it was said, would sometimes not make it back up in time before the ferocious detonations, and they would be lost forever. This dramatic mental image was so compelling, it became emblematic of Chinese suffering and sacrifice on the Central Pacific. From Oscar Lewis, author of the influential history *The Big Four,* to writer Maxine Hong Kingston, in a famous passage in *China Men* in which her grandfather, suspended in a hanging basket, sexually engages the earth, many writers recounted the dramatic story. The baskets were also immortalized visually in paintings and illustrations.

As insistent as those who vividly relate such stories are, others vociferously challenge the veracity of these accounts. They are based on a myth, it is said, and nothing more, propagated and embellished by those who want "politically correct" history about minorities instead of the real truth. In 1927, goes the debunking argument, a public relations agent of the Southern Pacific Railroad invented the legend of the baskets to entertain travelers as they rounded Cape Horn promontory. According to this tale, Chinese were supposedly lowered in "bosun's chairs" to work on the cliff face. Subsequent writers embellished the account over the years, with wooden chairs becoming woven baskets. The account was allegedly recycled repeatedly without firm evidence until legend became assumed truth. Confirming the debunking argument was the apparent absence of any mention of the use of baskets at Cape Horn, or anywhere else, in private correspondence, archives, or journalism before 1927. There simply was no textual or visual evidence to substantiate the claim, it was said. Moreover, the actual surface features of Cape Horn made the use of baskets unlikely, if not impossible. The mountain's sides were not close to standing vertical but sloped in a way that would have made the use of hanging baskets impractical. There were no projecting ledges from which men could be lowered in baskets and dangle to work effectively. Another highly charged controversy associated with Cape Horn is the claim that more than three hundred Chinese fell to their deaths during the construction of the roadbed there. Firm evidence for this latter belief has yet to be found.

The issue of the baskets is another matter, however. Recently overlooked accounts from long before 1927 contain firm evidence that substantially supports the claim that Chinese did in fact use ropes and chairs as well as woven baskets in construction work in the Sierra. Whether these instances took place at Cape Horn or at other nearby locations is not clear, but the "baskets story" is now more compelling than ever. It is *not* mere legend, as some skeptics argue.

An 1869 tour book by a traveler who took the Transcontinental Railroad soon after it was completed described encountering Cape Horn and related what he was told: "When the road was in course of construction, the groups of Chinese laborers on the bluffs looked almost like swarms of ants, when viewed from the river . . . When the roadbed was constructed around this point, the men who broke the first standing ground were held by ropes until firm foot-holds could be excavated in the rocky sides of the precipitous bluffs."

Several accounts written in the 1870s provide similar descriptions of the Chinese laborers held up by ropes so they could create footings for work on the roadbed around an area that appears to be Cape Horn. One describes the Chinese being lowered five hundred feet down from the top of a cliff, with 1,200 feet of void below them. Frederick A. Bee, a prominent businessman who also was in the railroad business, testified in 1876: "I have built railroads. I have hung them [Chinese] over the sides of rocks where no white would trust himself, as the Pacific Railroad Company has done."

One of the first mentions of the actual use of baskets was in a volume published by "Nelsons' Pictorial Guide-Books," a respected travel series. *The Central Pacific Railroad: A Trip Across the North American Continent from Ogden to San Francisco,* published in 1870, provides a vivid description of the Cape Horn area. According to the guide, a traveler at Cape Horn sees "one of the wildest and most magnificent ravines in the Sierra Nevada. The [American] river is here confined between two perpendicular walls, each about 2000 feet in height, which are washed perpetually by the boiling waters, and leave not an inch of ground for the foot of the would-be explorer." The traveler goes on to say:

> The swiftness with which the train flies down this tremendous incline, and the suddenness with which it wheels round the curves, produce a sensation not to be reproduced in words. The line is carried along the edge of declivities stretching downwards for 2000 or 3000 feet, and in some parts on a narrow ledge excavated from the mountain side by men swung from the top in baskets. The speed under these conditions is well calculated to try even the steadiest nerves. And as we sweep past each rugged height and grisly precipice it is impossible not to be stirred in one's inmost soul by the grandeur of the moving spectacle.

The most stirring description of the construction at Cape Horn comes from a young woman, Isabella L. Bird, who traveled across the country in 1873 and wrote private letters to her sister about her experiences, which were later published. One letter includes this striking account of the high point of her trek through the Sierra:

> The light of the sinking sun from that time glorified the Sierras, and as the dew fell, aromatic odours made the still air sweet. On a single track, sometimes carried on a narrow ledge excavated from the mountain side by men lowered from the top in baskets, overhanging ravines from 2000 to 3000 feet deep, the monster train *snaked* its way upwards, stopping sometimes in front of a few frame houses, at others where nothing was to be seen but a log cabin with a few Chinamen hanging about it, but where trails on the sides of the ravines pointed to a gold country above and below. So sharp and frequent are the curves on some parts of the ascent, that on looking out of the window one could seldom see more than a part of the train at once. At Cape Horn, where the track curves round the ledge of a precipice 2,500 feet in depth, it is correct to be frightened, and a fashion of holding the breath

and shutting the eyes prevails, but my fears were reserved for the crossing of a trestle-bridge over a very deep chasm, which is itself approached by a sharp curve. This bridge appeared to be overlapped by the cars so as to produce the effect of looking down directly into a wild gulch, with a torrent raging along it at an immense depth below.

In this account of what she was apparently told, Bird seems to locate the use of baskets a bit east of Cape Horn and higher up from the American River than where Cape Horn is usually placed. The photograph of Cape Horn taken several years before her journey shows the dramatic precipice of the location (below).

But the most compelling and contemporary evidence of the use of baskets in the Sierra at large is a news account by an unidentified traveling correspondent for a Massachusetts newspaper, the *Pittsfield Eagle*, in 1868:

The most thrilling scene that came under my observation was in the Sierra Nevada on the Central Pacific. Here the road is built on the side of a precipice 2,400 feet above the base, and the slope is so steep that the Chinamen who did the work were let down in baskets, and in this position drilled holes and charged them in the side of the mountains. At one time there were 460 of these charges connected by a fuse, exploded at one time. Masses of rock weighing many tons, fell to the bottom with terrific fury. When the debris had ceased to fall, the echoes were still reporting among the distant hills. So stunning was the shock that I would never willingly witness the like again.

Half a dozen other newspapers in the East also published this account in its entirety, bolstering its credibility. No past or present challenge to this widely circulated report has been found, further supporting its veracity.

Lastly, the topography made the use of baskets impracticable, some have argued. A view of Cape Horn today shows that the slope is only about 45 degrees. The report of chief engineer Montague, the chief engineer of the CPRR, however, presented a very different picture of the physical conditions as he saw them in 1864. Cape Horn, he wrote, "is a precipitous rocky bluff, about twelve hundred feet in height above the American River." Furthermore, "the dip of the ledge," he observed, "is about seventy-five degrees, or nearly perpendicular." Construction of the roadbed, according to the engineer, would therefore "necessarily be mostly an excavation" to form a ledge cut into the rock face, since building retaining walls around the rock would be "unsafe" and "impractical." Several months later, Stephen Allen Curry, the young surveyor, described the slope of Cape Horn very much as did Montague. Curry estimated the incline at 70 degrees. The large difference in estimates of the incline of the slope at Cape Horn might be explained by human intervention: over the 150 years since the work was completed, railroad companies have remade the area several times, significantly altering its incline and shaping it into its present appearance.

Though there are still questions about exactly where and when the "baskets" were used, the use of them by Chinese laborers in constructing the rail line at a perilous location in the Sierra cannot be dismissed as myth. Several narratives from the time explicitly describe Chinese using what are identified as "baskets" in the Cape Horn area. There is also firm evidence of the use of baskets in railroad construction elsewhere after the Pacific Railroad was completed, most notably on a portion of the South Pacific Coast rail line through the rugged Santa Cruz Mountains that Chinese worked.

The mystery around the use of baskets by the Railroad Chinese is ultimately about the details of their use, not about the actual occurrence. They may not have "dangled" over ledges, for example, but may have used them to sled down unstable slopes that made firm footing impossible. It is a shame that there are no photographs to prove how and when they were deployed. Few photographs of the CPRR construction effort show laborers actually at work. Yet these images still attest to the extreme danger and hardship the Railroad Chinese faced as they drove deeper and deeper into the Sierra Nevada.

Around the same time that Chinese began joining the CPRR in large numbers, the company hired a capable photographer named Alfred Hart to document and publicize the company's work. The railroad was far removed from the daily reality of most Americans, and the company believed visualizing the work was of vital importance not just for the public's edification but for company business. Public officials, investors, future freight customers, and prospective passengers had to be able to see the wonders of the Far West and the accomplishments of the railroad company. It was helping transform the nation.

Hart, who had come to California from Connecticut shortly before the CPRR began its work, captured hundreds of images of the construction effort from 1864 to 1869. He was also a portrait artist, yet he did not photograph any individual Chinese, or any other identified worker, for that matter. Groups of forlorn Paiutes and Shoshones appear in some of his work, faces clearly presented but identified only by a tribal name in the photo title, and in a few stills he depicts Jane Stanford boating on Donner Lake or Leland Stanford at the events at Promontory Summit. But for the most part, in Hart's images other humans and work animals are largely ciphers, distant figures with indistinct facial features. The only function of their physical bodies in the frame is to help viewers appreciate the phenomenal magnitude of work and the daunting challenges of location and environment. Many photos contain no humans at all but just buildings, trestles, railcars, and other human-made products that display the dramatic imprint of the company on a landscape that defied the imagination of those who had not witnessed it in person.

Despite — or perhaps because of — the fact that his compositions prioritized the construction and scenery over CPRR laborers, Hart's work impressed company officials. E. B. Crocker, who became his good friend, reported to Huntington in New York that Hart's railroad images were "universally admired" in California. The company sent many of them to Huntington for his use in raising capital.

The photos could not have failed to impress easterners. Hart's pictures were among the first to capture the rugged, brutal, and majestic scenery of the California mountain region. In time, as work on the CPRR line progressed, he would share with a rapt nation images of some of the most distant and treasured vistas: the High Sierra, the summit and Donner Lake region, and the broad deserts and plains of Nevada and Utah.

Groups of Chinese are clearly visible in many of Hart's images and may appear in many others even if they cannot be clearly distinguished through the crowds, shadows, or distance. Though it was not Hart's evident intention, his images today provide stirring visual entry into the environment and conditions of life on the construction line.

Photography was still in its technological infancy. Hart used glass plate negatives, a stereograph box camera with a manual lens cap, and a spindly mount to hold his fragile equipment. These features effectively determined his decisions about subject matter, location, time of day for shooting, season, and even captions. He had to consider lighting, accessibility to locations for himself and his equipment, work schedules, and of course his own safety. He had to avoid or minimize taking photos where there was vigorous movement: humans toiling, machines operating, lumbering work animals, trees shaking in the wind, and of course falling rain, sleet, snow, and darkness. Running water in streams and rivers emerged as ribbons of white gossamer. His lenses allowed him, it appears, to take only limited medium-range or distant images. He captured much that is arresting, but he could photograph only a minuscule amount of what he witnessed.

Hart's work nevertheless stimulates the imagination to consider what it might have been like to work on the line. In "Blasting at Chalk Bluffs Above Alta — Cut 60 Feet Deep," taken sixty-five miles from

Sacramento, and "Bank and Cut at Sailor's Spur—80 Miles from Sacramento" (both below), dramatic scenery towers over the scores of workers who are transforming the earth. In one photo, they cut away a towering hillside to make way for the line; in the other, an incomplete raised roadbed rises from two directions to cross a deep ravine. Humans had to move a staggering amount of earth and stone to carve the line through dense, virtually untouched evergreen forests and imposing landscape. Too far removed from the camera, the individual workers are obscure, but their clothing and hats identify them as Chinese.

Scores of Chinese workers who appear in these photos use hand tools, carts, and work animals. As with almost all the photos containing Chinese, they appear to be working in isolated teams, and only a few white workers or supervisors are occasionally visible. Other photos show white workers together exclusively. The workforce in these photos was segregated.

Little sense of human energy comes from the images of the Chinese workers, who appear strangely still and distant because of the technology of photography at the time, but the massive amount of cleared ground, moved earth, and shaped roadbed evidences the stupendous effort expended when the camera was not present. Hart occasionally provided the basic dimensions of the cuts and embankments in some of the photo captions so that viewers could properly appreciate the enormous scale of the construction endeavor. His photos, however, reveal only a small portion of the actual work on the line. He could get to only a few of accessible work sites and had very little time to work. Hundreds of other important locations, with their innumerable workers, were never visually recorded.

In some instances, the absence of humans in an image serves to accentuate the monumentality of the construction challenge. In "Horse Ravine Wall, and Grizzly Hill Tunnel—77 Miles from Sacramento" (above), a massive retaining wall, tons of moved earth, a sharp cut into

the hill, and the ragged, forbidding mouth of a tunnel into the mountain dwarf a few Chinese workers, draft animals, and carts that are visible at a distance. Towering above them are jagged and unfriendly
trees, ominous sentinels witnessing the violation of their land. Nothing serves to inform a viewer that hundreds of Chinese, who worked
at this location before the image was captured, were responsible for the
stunning transformation. The retaining wall stands mute, but its distinctive construction form of fitted stone, with no mortar, is evidence
that it is the product of traditional masonry techniques brought from
China. Scores of similar walls hold up the roadbed and prop up hillsides all along the line. After this photograph was taken, workers laid a
solid roadbed, ties, and iron track on which a behemoth steam engine
and train could safely run. The most famous of these walls remains
standing today. A historical marker informs travelers now of "The
Great Chinese Wall" along Highway 40, just off of Donner Summit in
the Sierra Nevada.

Captions for some photos explicitly include references to Chinese. Photo number 1129, which is probably by Hart, is titled "Wood Train and Chinamen in Bloomer Cut" (opposite). The photo shows Chinese on board a freight train full of wood moving through one of the CPRR's imposing early construction challenges. An immense mound of rock embedded in natural cement near Auburn blocked the route and required a cut of one thousand feet in length and up to sixty-two feet deep. A crew of workers, European and Chinese, labored from February 1864 to May 1865 to complete the job, hailed at the time as the "eighth wonder of the world."

Bloomer Cut, which was completed around the time when Stephen Allen Curry resolved to quit the railroad business, may well have been the location where some Chinese first began work for the CPRR. About a score of them can be seen in Hart's image: roughly a dozen men, standing or seated among the blocks of wood that fill the train's hopper wagons. The Chinese man closest to the camera moved during Hart's exposure of his glass negative, creating a ghostly presence in the reproduced image. Like so many of his brethren standing farther back in the car in this image and others, he is rendered as an apparition—a spirit wandering higher and higher into the Sierra Nevada, toward where the mountains meet the sky.

5
THE HIGH SIERRA

Great-Grandfather built the railroad through the Sierra Nevada in difficult seasons. Night was a time of peace. On warm nights Great-Grandfather would move away from camp to sleep, away from the night workers. There was a river nearby the camp, and farther upstream, the falls. He always walked beside the moonlit river at night, the cascading water glowing white with the reflection made his footsteps visible.
— SHAWN WONG, *Homebase: A Novel*, 1979

IN THE SIERRA, THE SKY ON A CRYSTALLINE CLEAR NIGHT IS spectacular, bejeweled with innumerable points of brilliant stars, the vast heavenly expanse of the Milky Way, and a moon almost too bright for the eyes. As they began their eastward ascent into the highest reaches of the Sierra in 1865, the Railroad Chinese would have looked to the phases of the moon to guide and structure the rhythm of their existence. Though they worked head-down toward the earth during the day, the Railroad Chinese looked up to the heavens at night, and especially to the moon, to determine where they were in the cycle of the passing year.

Since time immemorial, Chinese used the waxing and waning of the moon to calculate their calendar time. As farmers, they watched the sky to know when to plant and when to harvest. They knew from the moon when to expect the four defining moments of the year: the summer and winter solstices and the spring and fall equinoxes. Each month began with a "new" moon, or no moon, and a big full moon marked the middle of the month, the fifteenth. Though not as precise as the Gregorian calendar, which is based on the earth's revolution around the sun, the lunar calendar was simple to understand and follow. One just had to watch the skies at night and keep track of the moon's phases.

For the Railroad Chinese, the New Year began with the second new moon following the winter solstice, the longest night of the year. This meant that the Chinese New Year usually occurred somewhere between late January and late February. Traditionally the occasion was celebrated with great delight; it was the time to reunite with family, revere ancestors, honor deities, ward off evil spirits, and beseech the gods to bestow good luck and fortune in the coming year. Chinese called these most important days the Spring Festival, *chunjie,* the celebration that marked the coming of spring and the promise of life's renewal. Some Railroad Chinese traveled all the way back to China to be with family, but most stayed in California and spent the time with friends.

Qingming, the important festival back home that honored one's ancestors, occurred after the spring equinox, but in America, where there were few burial tombs to clean, the occasion was less significant to Railroad Chinese. The time of the fall equinox in mid-September was another matter. This is when the mid-autumn festival, *zhongqiujie,* occurred. It was also known as the Moon Festival because of the huge harvest moon that illuminates the night sky. It would be an especially nostalgic, even sad time for the Railroad Chinese, as the full moon traditionally symbolized life's wholeness and the joy of family. But for the Railroad Chinese isolated in the mountains of California far from home and their loved ones, the shining full moon reminded them of their separation and existential incompleteness. Were their family members, seeing the same full moon back in the village, also wondering when there would be reunion?

During the construction months from spring to fall, the Railroad Chinese could watch the gradual changes in the sky each night. One of the most prominent formations they followed illustrated the bittersweet story of the Cowherd and the Weaver Girl. The legend, which had originated 2,500 years earlier, was about two young lovers who had displeased a powerful, spiteful goddess. She banished them to the heavens, transformed them into stars, and separated them for eternity. They became what in the West are called Altair and Vega, located on opposite sides of the vast Milky Way in the night sky. During the summer, the two stars move slowly in tandem toward the vault of the sky as part of the Summer Triangle. Then in mid-August, when the stars reach their highest point, it is said that a flock of magical magpies forms a bridge that allows the two lovers to visit each other, but for just one day. The star points then start to drift down, ending the annual cycle. The Railroad Chinese would know that summer was coming to an end. And as fall approached in 1865, the change of seasons foreboded a new and arduous phase in the Central Pacific's colossal construction project.

In August 1865, Leland Stanford hosted visiting speaker of the house and soon to be vice president of the United States Schuyler Colfax, other dignitaries, and prominent eastern journalists who had been invited to travel along the line as far as it had been completed into the Sierra and inspect the CPRR's work. Stanford proudly described it as an effort "of great magnitude and National importance." The official party was astounded to see thousands of Chinese working in the mountains. One eyewitness described seeing their multitude everywhere, "shoveling, wheeling, carting, drilling and blasting rocks and earth." There were then four thousand workers in total, an estimated 90 percent Chinese and 10 percent Irish. At campsites, the travelers saw hundreds of Chinese sitting on the ground having their meals. Gulping down rice with chopsticks from bowls, they ate their repast of familiar food made by Chinese cooks with great gusto. For these visitors from the American East, these novel scenes of the unfamiliar Chinese appear to have made an impression almost as memorable as the monumental construction project itself.

In terms of quality, the work on this prodigious project, declared one leading railroad engineer who inspected the line, would "compare most favorably in every respect with any railroad in the United States." Though it was likely not his intention, his assessment complimented the Railroad Chinese, for it was they who were largely responsible for the construction. Yet the product of their labor to this point was nothing compared to what they would accomplish next. In fall 1865, the company wanted to hire thousands more Chinese workers as the crucial assault on the High Sierra was about to begin. Getting past the summit in the next couple of years was essential if the company was to control the critical rail traffic between Nevada and California and survive financially. The CPRR sent workers to the higher elevations, where they were to carve and blast out the tunnels needed to get through the granite mountains.

After Cape Horn, the railroad route became more rugged and dangerous, with steep ravines, sharply dropping cliffs, canyons, and frigid, rushing rivers fed by the high country snowmelt. Earth and rock formations became irregular, with complex intermixed masses of ancient oceanic crust, limestone, gravel, and volcanic rock, including ever greater amounts of granite, as the elevation rose. The fields of granite become batholiths, immense spans of solid rock miles across in width. Glaciers over tens of thousands of years in the past had weathered and polished these surfaces, making them slick when any moisture touched them. Cold temperatures turned them into colossal ice cubes. Ancient glaciers had also sliced through the mountains, creating soaring, fantastical rock formations. Edges of granite split by explosions could be as sharp as knives.

The CPRR workers would have to use sledgehammers, five-foot-long steel drills, gunpowder (also known as black powder), and nitroglycerine, a liquid explosive, to attack the stubborn Sierra. As if the risk of injury in the rugged land was not bad enough, these rude tools made the job even more treacherous. Many of the Railroad Chinese, however, were probably familiar with black powder, which their ancestors had invented in the ninth century and was commonly used in fireworks, guns, and cannons back in their home region in China. An imperial gunpowder production facility began operation in that area in the early nineteenth century.

Dramatic weather changes also quickly made the already difficult construction challenge even tougher. Early torrential rains made the fall of 1865 one of the wettest on record. Carriage and cart travel over the clay soils of the foothills became impossible. Dense, clinging mud was the worst enemy of movement. Workers on foot and hundreds of pack animals had to laboriously transport supplies, even including hay for the horses, up into the snow country, where sleds could then be used. Deep mud immobilized one carriage in the middle of the Gold

Run settlement for six weeks before it was extricated. Water runoff collapsed cuts, which then had to be reworked.

Snowfall began in September, and starting in October storms followed one another almost continuously for the next five months. Towering banks of snow covered the completed track and the intended route. Even five to seven coupled heavy locomotives could not drive a snowplow through the packed thirty-foot drifts. Railroad Chinese were ordered to work around the clock, day and night, to clear the track and roadbed by hand, but the snows became too heavy and the men had to move east of the summit before they could return to work in the higher elevations.

Thinking about working and living out in the open in the Sierra to build the Central Pacific for months, even years in sum, challenges even the most lively of imaginations. It does not help that we have no written records of the workers' own experiences, nor that the company that employed them took so little interest in their day-to-day lives. By using different forms of evidence from the past in creative ways, however, we can recover portions of this human drama.

Archaeology provides one way forward. Researchers have studied thousands of objects, food remnants, fire pits, and other site landscape found at the former living encampments and work areas of Railroad Chinese. This material culture is what remains of daily life and tells us about their quotidian existence. Considered together with other bits of evidence gleaned from periodical literature, historical photography, business records, and contemporaneous personal observations about Chinese in America, it lets us begin to form some idea of what the lives of Railroad Chinese in the Sierra may have been like.

To be sure, the experience of individual Railroad Chinese varied tremendously; there was not one Railroad Chinese experience but many. Geography, season, weather, and work demands constantly changed. Few Chinese resided and worked in one established location for more than a few weeks or a season before moving on along the line or leaving work altogether. At the summit area, where work continued for years, some may have resided in one camp for months or years. But turnover also appears to have been high, and the railroad company never wanted to keep more workers on the payroll than necessary. The company constantly moved workers to different locations to meet construction scheduling and needs. During the depths of winter, the company released workers, who would move to a nearby town or perhaps all the way back to Auburn or San Francisco. Some resided in a base location and then traveled out to work, while others moved along with the advance of the line. Most lived outside under the open sky together with those with whom they worked during the day.

Yet at all of these living sites along the CPRR, and many other railroad lines throughout the West, Chinese left an abundance of material culture that exhibits remarkable consistency. The common origin, make, and style of found ceramics, utensils, and other remains of everyday life are evidence of a well-functioning network of commodity production in China and system of distribution in America. A sophisticated trans-Pacific, trans-America supply chain linked remote and widely separated Chinese labor camps with one another and with China. The work camps of the Railroad Chinese were simultaneously dispersed, distant, interconnected, and comparably provisioned. Archaeological evidence shows that objects found on Chinese railroad workers' campsites in California were often like those used in their home villages and produced in the Pearl River delta. Identical or similar items related to diet, medical care, and leisure activity can be found in California, Nevada, Utah, Montana, Idaho, Oregon, Washington State, Texas, and elsewhere in the West. Fully intact rice bowls, other eating ware, large food storage containers such as brown-glazed stoneware jars, wine jugs, and small vessels for foodstuffs, as well as pieces of these objects, have been gathered along multiple rail lines, their concentrations indicating the sites of Chinese labor camps long ago.

Consistency in found objects at different campsites points to comparability in ways of living, but studies of former campsites also reveal important differences. The living circumstances of different groups of Railroad Chinese could vary considerably. Duration of habitation is one variable, but arrangement was another. Some sites were well organized into distinct areas, such as for sleeping, eating, cooking, and socializing. Others appear to have been more haphazard. Some were rather small in size, accommodating perhaps a few dozen workers. Others were large. Chinese campsites in Utah ranged from a tenth of an acre to more than twenty-four acres in area. In the Sierra, Railroad Chinese usually resided in canvas tents, varying in size from some that held four persons to others that could hold as many as twelve. Some campsites are distinguished by deliberate shaping of the ground for sleeping and eating areas or by the arrangement of stones for foundations and fire pits for cooking, which can still be seen today.

Large rectangular depressions in the ground denote areas where eating and social life under tenting probably occurred. Smaller dugouts served to help shelter residents from the wind, cold, and snow. Wind, especially through passes such as at Donner, could be constant and desiccating. The unceasing flow of wind drained bodies and dried out skin. Rough foundations of gathered rock and rough tent platforms point to longer habitation. Residential segregation was the norm: Chinese and non-Chinese lived separately from each other, as indicated by the refuse collected by archaeologists. The material culture is usually clearly identified as being either predominantly from China or from the United States and Europe. Even if Chinese and whites lived on the same site, the Chinese typically lived in a section more exposed to the elements or to pests such as mosquitoes. The spatial arrangement of living reflected the general racial hierarchy and inequality enforced by the CPRR.

Observers of the construction effort sometimes provided eyewitness descriptions of these Chinese work camps. One reporter who hiked along the road under construction in 1867 described encountering Chinese so numerous they were "thick as bees." He stumbled past one of their encampments and disabused his readers of any notion that the Chinese camp was picturesque or romantic, with "snow-white canvas" tents sitting atop fragrant pine; rather, in his demeaning words, it was more like "a collection of dog-kennels," simply made of wood shakes and standing about four feet high, six feet wide and eight feet long." These were likely hastily built for the short term.

Author Daniel Cleveland wrote differently in 1869 about the campsites he saw: "[The Chinese] live in little villages of cloth tents, containing from 50 to 500 inhabitants. As the work progresses, they fold up and remove their tents and establish their villages at other points along the line of the road. What yesterday was a noisy Chinese town is today but a barren waste, with only rubbish and debris to mark that it was once a settlement." After work, once the sun had set, Cleveland witnessed a quiet scene of some charm. The tents at night, he wrote, "are illuminated with candles, and groups of Chinese can be seen gambling, smoking opium, visiting or engaging in household labor."

At Summit Camp, at more than seven thousand feet in elevation and at the crest of the route through the Sierra, Chinese lived for four years in what became a small town to complete the grueling work of boring tunnels through the granite mountains. Photographs and archaeological evidence show wooden buildings that housed them there. Photographs (below), however, could not fully record the grim conditions the workers faced, such as those they had to live through during the ferocious winter of 1867–68, when more than forty storms hit the summit. Snowdrifts rose to forty-four feet and more in height. Temperatures regularly fell to below zero Fahrenheit. Blizzard winds could hit a hundred miles an hour through the passes. The summit area is one of the snowiest places in the lower continental United States.

Snow buried not only the portals to the tunnel but entire living areas as well, requiring workers to dig tunnels through the snow to get to and from their living camps to the tunnel work in the rock. According to the chief tunnel engineer for the CPRR, John R. Gilliss, Chinese even had to live beneath the snow for months at a time. They constructed chimneys and air shafts up through the snow. Tunnels linked storerooms and blacksmith shops. Some snow tunnels were as much as two hundred feet in length and high enough to accommodate two-horse sleds that carried broken rock out of the tunnels to dump outside. Workers also hollowed out large caverns in the snow so they could build retaining walls to protect the track. They used hoists to lower wall stones down through shafts in the snow to men working beneath. Sudden snowslides carried many away to terrible deaths. Accounts of such brutal living and working conditions would be barely believable had the information not come from top company leaders themselves. Lewis Clement, the CPRR chief engineer, testified that management had decided tunnel work had to continue uninterrupted through the ferocious winter, in his words, "no matter what the cost." Clement spoke primarily in financial terms, but the company's attitude clearly had tragic human consequences. James Strobridge, the construction boss, indicated that the toll of human life during that season was staggering "In many instances our camps were carried away by snowslides," he recalled. "Men were buried and many of them were not found until the snow melted the next summer." In one instance, Chinese tried to escape an avalanche by taking refuge behind a protective rock. They were buried anyway under fifty feet of snow, and their bodies were not found until it melted in the spring. Revealed was the ghastly sight of dead Chinese standing, still holding their shovels in their stiff hands.

• • •

During late spring, summer, and fall, the peak work seasons in California's mountains, the workday lasted from sunup to sundown, averaging about ten to twelve hours a day, though shifts in the tunnels were shorter because of the difficulty of the work. At the end of a day's labor, the teams of Railroad Chinese, covered in sweat, dust, and grime, returned together to their living spaces, washed down their bodies, as was their custom after working, rested, ate an evening meal, and perhaps smoked some tobacco or opium before retiring. Moderate opium smoking was not incompatible with labor and opium was not then illegal. Its use was not hidden from the company. The workweek ran six days, with rest on Sunday, when workers recuperated and attended to washing their clothes, grooming, and other personal matters, including tending to their queue, a long braid of hair behind a partially shaved pate. China's Manchu rulers required men to adopt the hairstyle, and most kept it after traveling to the United States. The workers also enjoyed singing, storytelling, drinking rice wine and American whisky, and gaming, all popular leisure activities among the Chinese in California. If they were close to a town, lottery salesmen might even visit the camp to sell tickets. One could get lucky and win enough so that he and perhaps his friends could leave the line altogether.

Potent odors permeated Railroad Chinese campsites. Scores, if not hundreds, of workingmen lived in close proximity. Privies were nearby and crudely made. Meat and fish were butchered out in the open, food was cooked outdoors in woks, and water was boiled at smoky fire pits that burned constantly. An evening meal might feature salted fish, a favorite dish with a pungent aroma that attracted Siyi people as much as it repelled non-Chinese. The blue smoke from strong tobacco and opium hung over the site and mixed with the sweet aromas of alcohol. Chinese herbal remedies made with herbs, bark, seeds, roots, and dried insects and animals slowly steeped in open pots set among coals, releasing vapors ranging from musty to stomach-turning. Body sweat, unwashed work clothes, socks, boots, well-used bedding, and old canvas tenting produced additional smells that assaulted the nose. Crisp, clean mountain air was found elsewhere, away from the camp.

Food and diet were integral to the health practices of Chinese. Indeed, the lines between health maintenance, healing, and food consumption were thin, even nonexistent. According to traditional Chinese belief, tea, which the Railroad Chinese drank in copious amounts, was essential not just for hydration but for general well-being. Tea carriers brought fresh tea brewed from mountain waters in kegs to replenish large barrels and canisters for the workers along the route. Observers noted much lower instances of dysentery and other stomach ailments among Railroad Chinese because their drinking water was boiled. Soups were not just nourishing; they could also be tonics for ailments and body restoration. Chinese ladle soup spoons are among the most common items found at former campsites.

The Railroad Chinese tenaciously maintained their preference for the flavors and food culture they enjoyed in their home villages. They drew on a well-established network of grocers, importers, and local Chinese food producers to provide familiar foodstuffs, cookware, eating utensils, tableware, and other familiar necessities. Shipping manifests, business receipts and ledgers, and the observations of writers indicate that Chinese imported not just their staple of rice but a large array of foodstuffs from their home areas not found in America. These ingredients included preserved meats; dried fish, shrimp, and other shellfish; dried legumes; different forms of dried noodles; and preserved vegetables, including dried seaweed, teas, and other desiccated foods for reconstituting. Given the problems of supply across long distances and storage, relying on dried and preserved foods would make a great deal of sense. Other commonly imported foods included condiments such as soy sauce, wines, vinegars, salted beans, fermented sauces, spices and herbs, and other flavorings. An invoice for goods received by a Chinese merchant in San Francisco in 1854 listed "oranges, pomelos, dry oyster, shrimps, cuttlefish, mushrooms, dried bean curd, bamboo shoots, narrow leaved greens, yams, ginger, sugar, rice, sweetmeats, sausage, dry duck, eggs, dry fruit, salt ginger, salt eggs." Expensive or specialty items are found on other invoices and were used for celebrations and banquets. Treats included candied fruits and sweet spiced confections, the delicacy known as dried birds' nests, fish fins, tamarind, bean sauces, *bêche-de-mer* (sea cucumber), and liquors and wines of various sorts.

Speaker of the House Schuyler Colfax probably tasted these and

other specialties during the bountiful feast he enjoyed when he visited San Francisco's Chinatown in August 1865, after he had witnessed
Chinese constructing the CPRR in the Sierra. The Chinese Six Companies hosted him and dozens of other leading political and business
leaders at a "state banquet" that lasted six hours, held at the Hang
Heong Restaurant on Clay Street in Chinatown. The restaurant reportedly served 336 dishes through 130 courses presented in "three
acts." The repast equaled or even surpassed what could be had in
their home region. Chinese cooking ingredients, even the very rare,
were not wanting in California. Some unusual items, such as bear
paw, were probably even more available then in California than in
southern China.

Inventory in a Chinese store in Calaveras County, California, in 1865
included many of the items already mentioned as well as cooking oil,
Chinese cigars, medicinal herbs, firecrackers, writing paper, candles,
clothing, and Chinese bottles. Chinese cooks had access to traditional
iron and copper pans, knives, chopsticks, ladles, tongs, mills, ceramics of many kinds, and bamboo, wood, and lacquer ware. Everywhere
Railroad Chinese went for work, they consumed similar foodstuffs.
Markets in Chinatowns today still carry the same items.

Railroad Chinese likely consumed large quantities of fresh food produced by other Chinese in California and Nevada, as they had at home
in the Pearl River delta. As early as the 1850s, hundreds of Chinese established fishing villages around San Francisco Bay and along the coast
at Monterey and north to Humboldt Bay. The abundance of sea life
would have astonished any fisherman: salmon, sturgeon, smelts, sar-
dines, abalone, crabs, clams, oysters, and shrimp filled northern California sea waters and were there for the taking. Chinese also established fishing camps along the Sacramento River and in its delta for
freshwater fish and other foods. The bounty from their enterprise exceeded local demand, and they exported highly valued dried shrimp
and fish back to China.

In the mountain areas of California, still largely pristine, fish and
game, including trout, salmon, wild fowl, deer, and bear, lived in abundance. Chinese had guns for self-protection and hunting and were
known to be resourceful in procuring food and developing food sourc-
ing. To provide an ongoing source of fresh protein, a Chinese fish-

erman might have introduced catfish, for example, into a lake near Summit Camp where Chinese lived. Nonindigenous catfish, likely descendants of such early stock, are still found there and in other ponds along the route of the CPRR.

Southern Chinese have the reputation of eating anything that moves, including cold-blooded snakes and any warm-blooded animal with four legs, and animal life was plentiful in the mountains. To supplement their supplies, resourceful camp cooks could have used some of their daylight hours while the workers were on the line to hunt and forage, though all the noise and commotion from construction probably scared away much wildlife. In California and Nevada, Chinese and Native people were in contact; there is evidence of exchange of local foodstuffs for Chinese ceramic ware. Given the remote and difficult conditions in which they worked and lived, the Railroad Chinese certainly must have eaten poorly at times, but probably not consistently so. Animal bone remains recovered from Chinese railroad work camps do not exhibit the heavy processing associated with starvation diets. Food supplies could actually have been ample, as it would have been in the interests of the company to provision them well, especially since the Chinese were paying for their own food. Journalists at the time often wrote that the Railroad Chinese commonly ate a more varied and better diet than white fellow workers, and possibly even better than they had in China. For at least some Chinese railroad workers, it does appear that their diet in the United States was more nutritious than in China. One forensic study of the remains of a group of Chinese railroad workers, though not on the CPRR, indicates that they had been undernourished as children and ate better in America.

Other evidence exists that suggests that the Railroad Chinese did not just subsist but could eat well. A report in 1870 claimed that the rations for Chinese railroad workers per diem, per man, were two pounds of rice; one-third ounce of tea; one pound of beef, pork, or fish; one-third pound of vegetables; and a small quantity of lard or oil. These "rations" may have been the maximum amount a Chinese could purchase from the company store, not what the men actually consumed, which would have been considerably more than they would have eaten at home. A pound of meat per day in the Pearl River delta was unheard of. Poultry, an item for special occasions in China, was regularly available to the Railroad Chinese. Indeed, the availability of good food may have served as an incentive to join the construction effort. Their food may have far exceeded in quantity and quality what miners scattered throughout the mountain areas in small camps consumed.

California Chinese farmed and grew produce for their compatriots and for the general market wherever they went, including in Nevada. Hundreds of Chinese raised vegetables, hogs, and poultry in the 1850s and 1860s in the Sacramento area and in the mountains. In 1860, Chinese operated thirty-six truck farms in Placer County, more than half of the total number for the county. In 1870 there were sixty-three. A map locating Chinese truck farmers operating in 1870 shows that scores farmed all along the route of the line: the location of clusters of these Chinese farms reads like a train schedule: Sacramento, Newcastle, Auburn, Clipper Gap, Colfax, Dutch Flat, and nearby Grass Valley and Nevada City, and then Truckee, where Chinese cultivated small farms right next to the railroad line. They grew vegetables, including Chinese vegetables from seeds brought from China, for summer and fall consumption but also crops that could be consumed throughout the harsh winters. In Truckee they cultivated cabbage, turnips, carrots, parsnips, beets, and onions, all of which was cold-stored. Chinese also became familiar with American canned goods, evaporated milk, meat cuts, wheat flour, brandy, whisky, gin, ham, lard, mustard, salad dressing, and bouillon. Bottles of Lea & Perrins Worcester sauce abounded at Railroad Chinese camp sites.

Their meals invariably attracted the attention of non-Chinese who were unfamiliar with their food and style of eating. Journalists reported seeing the Railroad Chinese having their breakfast of congee with vegetables; they used chopsticks and carried their own mess kits. Sketches of them in their work camps show them cooking in woks and eating fresh-caught fish. Their heavier meals likely consisted of stews of root crops from local sources, soups, and stir fries enlivened with garlic, fresh and preserved vegetables, bits of cured meats, salted fish, or other seafood, and other Chinese ingredients from home. Old fire pits include rocks arranged to hold iron woks, and recovered butchered animal bones display traditional cutting techniques using Chinese cleavers. Some recipes might pass for Chinese food available in America today, but the daily repasts were probably quite different, given the rough conditions and availability of ingredients.

When he was a youngster, "Pappy" Clay spent much time among Chinese railroad workers, and later, when elderly, he fondly recalled having meals with them. He described one dish that he frequently enjoyed and described in interesting detail. He remembered that the Chinese cooks built their own ovens and cooking areas in the dirt banks alongside the tracks.

> Each cook would have the use of a very big iron kettle hanging over an open fire and into it they would dump a couple of measures of Chinese unhulled brown rice, Chinese noodles, bamboo sprouts and dried seaweed, different Chinese seasonings and American chickens cut up into small pieces including, heads, legs, and all plus more water than what would seem necessary and still the kettle would be only half full. When the cook stirred up the fire the concoction began to boil, then the rice would begin to swell until finally the kettle would be nearly full of steaming nearly dry brown rice with the cut up chickens all through it.

Each worker then ladled the meal into a "big blue bowl" and used chopsticks to down it all. They drank plenty of tea on the side.

On special occasions, however, the Railroad Chinese would have enjoyed celebratory repasts of meats and specially prepared treats. The workers would have expected these from their district associations or employers as part of their due. Chinese cooks at the summit area constructed fire pits that accommodated woks and ovens large enough to roast whole pigs, a Chinese celebratory favorite.

Provisioning the Railroad Chinese was itself a profitable business. Though no specific evidence as to the practices of labor contractors such as Hung Wah has been found, information from journalists and from the archives of other Chinese labor contractors suggests that the contractors made money not just by bringing workers to employers but also in supplying food, opium, liquor, and other commodities to them. In Auburn, Hung Wah had been a labor contractor as well as a merchandiser of goods. He sold food, and perhaps provided cooks who handled and prepared the food, to his contract workers, producing a steady cash flow. Other Chinese labor contractors operated similarly, preferring to make money mainly from provisioning rather than by taking larger percentages from wages. Unlike suppliers of European immigrant labor on the East Coast, who usually took a cut from wages or a flat rate for each worker supplied, the large California companies that recruited thousands of Chinese workers for the CPRR appear to have operated more like their Chinese contractor counterparts.

The Sisson, Wallace Company, for example, became the largest contracting company for the CPRR. It had been founded in Sacramento in 1857 as a general merchandising and Chinese import enterprise and in 1866 began to recruit workers in China for the CPRR. The company had offices in Hong Kong, San Francisco, Truckee, and other towns along the route. It asked for relatively little compensation for the actual contracting service but required that it control provisioning of food and supplies. Keeping the cost of supplying workers low encouraged the company to hire greater numbers. Profits could then be made from providing tools, clothes, liquor, opium, and food to the workers. The arrangement was lucrative, especially for the Crocker family, which benefited at each level of the operation. Charles Crocker, a director of the CPRR, also headed its main construction company, Crocker Construction. As a boss of one company, he therefore essentially paid himself as the head of the other. It in turn worked with Sisson, Wallace, a labor contracting and supply company. Workers purchased supplies from its stores. Clark W. Crocker, one of Charles's brothers, became a chief partner of Sisson, Wallace. Labor provision was adjunct to, and supportive of, provisioning. Merchandising goods to sell to newcomers looking for gold was the way the CPRR directors all first became successful in California, after all.

The business records of a man named Ah Louis, who in the 1870s became the most important Chinese labor contractor along the central coast of California, show a similar pattern of operation. Ah Louis had been born in the Siyi and arrived in San Francisco in 1861. He worked in Oregon for a few years, including possibly as a railroad worker, and then settled in San Luis Obispo. There he went into the business of labor contracting. He was responsible for recruiting hundreds of Chinese workers for the Pacific Coast Railroad, which extended into southern

California. He also sold groceries and supplies to the contracted work-ers. He may have even offered them what might be called a "full meal plan," in which he charged them for the food and its preparation, or a "partial plan," whereby he supplied raw foodstuffs.

The Railroad Chinese were frugal and resourceful in shaping im-plements for their daily use from discarded materials. Objects from la-bor camps found today include storage containers, funnels, strainers, and even bean sprout germinators made from reused metal. There are gaming pieces fashioned from recycled materials. They used their ingenuity to craft things they apparently had difficulty obtaining. Rail-road Chinese, however, were also surprisingly wasteful: the aston-ishing array and quantity of discarded artifacts indicate that living in scarcity was not their lot, at least a good part of the time. Commonly found at the sites of former railroad camps are many discarded per-sonal items, such as Chinese-made toothbrushes, which first orig-inated in fifteenth-century China, fashioned from boar's bristles threaded through holes in flat bone handles. Metal buttons and buck-les, straight-edged razors, clasps, and brads, as well as Chinese fasten-ers indicate that the Railroad Chinese wore a combination of West-ern and Chinese clothing and footwear, especially American leather and rubberized work boots. During the winter they wore thick coats, probably woolen, mittens, and heavy scarves, all items they would not have had in China.

A vast quantity of items related to health has been found at for-mer Chinese labor camp sites too. Small glass vials held pills, pow-ders, or oils, such as peppermint, common in Chinese health prac-tices. Larger bottles held tonics that were to help blood circulation, energy flow, and digestion. Special wines infused with natural ingre-dients were taken to remedy stomach pain, indigestion, weak appe-tite, depression, or irritability. Railroad Chinese complemented their traditional remedies with Western patent medicines made from herbs, minerals, water, alcohol, and opiates. They used plasters, poultices, and Chinese and Western drinking alcohol for therapeu-tic uses, such as for skin, muscle, and internal injuries and massage. Scrapers of various sorts were used to move internal body energy and relieve ailments. Qing dynasty coins abound and were used as gaming pieces and talismans but also in folk remedies. Practitioners knowledgeable in Chinese medicine frequented the camps and knew how to use such implements and materials. Opium paraphernalia, such as pipes and storage tins, is also evident at the camps. Miners and Railroad Chinese paid cash for the highest-quality opium. Chinese wording on the label of an opium tin from approximately 1859 found at a campsite guarantees that the product was top quality and not "fake goods" from smugglers. The maker requested of the customer, "Please recognize our trademark."

Railroad Chinese even ate from ceramics that originated in their home region. Chinese ceramic potsherds found along the route of the Transcontinental can be traced to specific kilns seven thousand miles away in the Pearl River region. The ceramics exhibited familiar bright glazes in a variety of colors and traditional designs, including blue on white and luminous blue-green. Almost all items carried decorative motifs of lovely flowers, elegant bamboo, and even auspicious words and symbols. One of the most commonly seen is "double happiness" (*xuangxi*), which is made by doubling the single character for "happiness" (*xi*). The symbol was commonly associated with marriage celebrations and with good times generally. This ceramic ware served more than utilitarian purposes, as the simply made and familiar rice bowls, ceramic spoons, teacups, and food storage containers materially and psychically linked the workers to home and hearth.

Despite the seeming abundance and uniformity of material objects, an individual worker occasionally would try to identify an item as his own by "pecking" his name or a unique symbol into the thin glaze. Sometime in the late 1860s, a Railroad Chinese at the summit used a sharp implement, perhaps a nail, to carefully mark his rice bowl with a well-formed character, *xing*, the word for apricot. At some point the bowl was broken, or perhaps it no longer served his needs and he discarded it, to be found 150 years later lying right on the surface of the ground.

Material objects also tell us a great deal about the immaterial, spiritual concerns of the Chinese migrants who worked on the Central Pacific Railway. Chinese were deeply spiritual and believed in the ubiquity and influence of ghosts and spirits. Ghosts could be responsible for much of the misery of life. They might cause accidents, illness, and even death. In more formal religious terms, the Railroad Chinese believed in a variety of local Siyi deities and aspects of Buddhism and Taoism. Great historical personages could also become demigods. Religious rituals to honor ancestors and appease spirits structured the rhythm of life in southern China, and the Railroad Chinese continued their traditions in California. They built temples and altars everywhere they went as soon as they arrived. Though there are no direct descriptions of religious observances by Railroad Chinese while they were living along the construction line, observations about their practices in San Francisco and other towns in the late nineteenth century are common. The reports from different locations and times describe very similar practices.

Figurines and images of the same deities existed in all the Chinese temples spread throughout California. Among the most common were the fierce lord Guan Gong, derived from a Han dynasty general and possessing courage, strength, and integrity, and Guan Yin, the goddess of mercy and compassion. Worship and respect for departed elders also held a central, almost daily place in Siyi lives. Incense, candles, figurines, and symbolic worldly items such as food and money for use in the afterlife filled altars, including some simple ones constructed in worker camps. Worship was conducted largely without formal clergy or spiritual authorities. Some Railroad Chinese may have performed rituals for their ancestors at the end of every day. But it was the elaborate Chinese festivals that caught the attention of non-Chinese who tried to make sense of the emotion, music, rituals, food, incense, and fireworks that periodically overwhelmed the California towns inhabited by Chinese.

Gui jie or *zhong yuan jie,* the Hungry Ghost Festival, which occurs on the fifteenth day of the seventh lunar month (mid- to late August) was an especially important one. Loud, raucous, scary, and playful, the festival occurs over several days, culminating in a great evening event. It held special cosmological and existential significance for the Railroad Chinese as the festival sought to appease despondent spirits stranded in the netherworld. They had received no proper burial or had died tragically, and thus could not eat (in Chinese tradition, souls still need to eat, which is why altars always have food) or enjoy restful peace. They were rootless, homeless. Railroad Chinese knew many from among themselves who had perished under tragic or unfortunate circumstances, including while working to build the CPRR.

In mid-August 1868, Railroad Chinese, perhaps Hung Wah himself, participated in *gui jie* in Grass Valley, a town close to the rail line. In the 1860s it had established itself as the spiritual center for Chinese in the surrounding gold mining country. Local Chinese had built temples for worship and for conducting the annual festivals that structured the Chinese year. Hung Wah may have known about the event weeks or even months in advance, as local leaders would have begun fund-raising for the activities in midsummer. A subscription of twenty-five cents would provide a Railroad Chinese special access to ceremonies. There would be plentiful food, cultural performances, and rituals performed by priests from San Francisco. In early August, local Chinese would have begun to practice their musical instruments for festival performances; the white population could not have avoided hearing the loud and unusual sounds in the evenings. Special pavilions and stages were constructed to hold elaborate presentations that had little in common with familiar Christian practices.

Entering town, Hung Wah would have quickly encountered its Chinese quarter all lit up with a multitude of oil-burning lamps, Chinese lanterns, and candles. Lights and hundreds of colorful paper images of wild animals, devils, and gods decorated the streets. After sunset the unhappy ghosts were to come up from the world below to wander the land and molest the living. Small fires were fed with ritual paper items made in the form of money and valuables to appease the spirits. The local Chinese temple was festooned with rich tapestries, decorations, and calligraphy with propitiating inscriptions. Elaborately detailed, constructed deities large and small abounded: some ten feet tall, ferocious and threatening, others showing a benevolent demeanor. A huge god reigned over his court. Frightening images of displeased ghosts appeared everywhere, with long, thin necks because they were unable to eat on account of their misfortune. Flickering light from altar candles and lamps exaggerated their threatening features and made their shadows dance. Heady incense and smoke filled the air and disoriented the unaccustomed visitor. Spiritual leaders were dressed in white robes with hoods made of light blue satin covering their heads. They engaged in long, mesmerizing incantations, while discordant music from Chinese reed and string instruments, cymbals, and drums filled the air. Chinese men sang in a mournful nasal falsetto.

A reporter noted that the whole scene was "brilliantly illuminated" and "festive," with the "strange and weird music" heard throughout the entire city all day and night. In a special display stall, a woman sat, her face covered with thick white makeup as she wept tears of red blood for the wickedness of the human world. A noble white horse inhabited one stall; in another a ghoul held forth in court. The music, rituals, offerings, and decorations aimed both to please and to distract the wandering ghosts. Colorful paper boats, both miniature and full-size, might be brought to a nearby river or spring, where they would be set on fire and sent off to the netherworld. And then there was food, always food. Food was left for the ghosts and deities, and the general public, Chinese and white, was well fed too. Long tables groaning with roast pig, chicken, and other Chinese specialties ran down the street through the center of town. The festival ended with the dispatch of a big demon, his manifestation draped with firecrackers and a rocket placed along his spine. The local community assembled their own fireworks from black powder, the same kind used on the railroad. These were ignited, blasting him to pieces and sending his remains into the sky. The world of the living was rid of him for another year, the ghosts propitiated. As one white American who witnessed the festival wrote, "I have crossed the Sierras and passed safely around 'Cape Horn' and attended services in the Mormon Tabernacle, but none of these sights were so wonderful as the Chinese camp meeting."

The rituals of *gui jie* held a much deeper meaning than the viewer then could have known. For Chinese, more tragic than dying in a foreign country, was to die and not have one's remains returned to ancestral soil. Becoming "an abandoned soul and wild ghost" (*guhun yegui*) was a fate worse than death itself. One would be tormented for eternity, bereft of proper interment and spiritual succor from one's descendants. The Ghost Festival was meant to appease and distract such suffering spirits.

Old-time Chinese Americans to this day continue to recount haunting stories of death long ago in the mountains of California. One story tells of places in the Sierra where, when the night is dark and cold winds blow, one can hear the wailing ghosts of Chinese railroad workers who died during the construction effort. They are lost, suffering, and still seeking a way home to find eternal peace. Others who died had their remains returned, and they are content, but these forlorn spirits are the ghosts of those whose bones were never found, never repatriated. It is in the bones where the soul resides. The forsaken ghosts are doomed to wander Gold Mountain forever. They will never return to their home villages to rest among kith and kin. The Hungry Ghost Festival is the time to comfort them.

And what comfort some of these tragic spirits would need.

6
THE SUMMIT

my brother and i
he barely 20 and i, 25 had survived harsh winters
digging under tunnels of snow
lowered in baskets
we chopped holes in granite cliffs
setting dynamite
that tore a road out of sheer rock
many of our friends died

— FROM ALAN LAU, "WATER THAT SPRINGS
FROM A ROCK," 1991

ON A SULTRY FOURTH OF JULY, 1866, THE CITY OF SACRAMENTO
celebrated the ninetieth anniversary of the American Revolution in
grand fashion. Special activities around the city began just past midnight with ringing bells, exploding fireworks, and illuminated displays,
some with Chinese paper lanterns. Then, at 9:00 a.m., as a formal parade started to march through town, a long Central Pacific train pulled
into the city's station, carrying 1,600 passengers from Newcastle, Auburn, Dutch Flat, and other points east along the line, according to
news reports. Among those who enjoyed the pleasant train ride — and
a warm welcome from the Sacramento spectators — were scores of
Chinese railroad workers. Wearing their work clothes, they rode in
the parade as part of the CPRR procession in seven horse-drawn carts,
standing and sitting amidst wheelbarrows, picks, and shovels. A banner
proclaimed, "Pacific Railroad Laborers Ho for Salt Lake, 1876." Spectators warmly welcomed the CPRR unit, and a local reporter noted that

the highly visible Chinese in the contingent were worthy representatives of "the army" that was then laboring in the Sierra.

Charles Crocker addressed the gathered crowd. He proudly announced that "the iron horse was now puffing his nostrils at an altitude of over 3,600 feet above the level of the sea" and was within twenty-three miles of the summit. If all went well, he optimistically predicted, the line would reach the eastern side of the Sierra by January, and in two years the line would arrive at the Great Salt Lake. Just how significantly he had underestimated the challenges of getting through the summit and the deserts of Nevada and Utah, Crocker could not yet know.

Huzzahs to the republic and its noble ideals rang out throughout the celebration, which highlighted the victory of the Union in the Civil War, which had concluded just a year earlier. Speakers hailed the end of the curse of slavery and urged support for freed people and their welfare. Speakers reminded audiences that black and white soldiers had fought together and that "all men are created free." In San Francisco, where the largest celebration occurred, one prominent orator called for liberty for all, explicitly including "negroes and Chinese."

The Railroad Chinese were becoming recognized, and honored, as the builders of the "grand Pacific Railroad," which was "belting East and West together in one fraternizing tie," as one speaker put it. According to the Six Companies in San Francisco, approximately one quarter of all the Chinese then in California, 58,000 in total, were employed by the CPRR or on "other public improvements." In fact, the terms "Chinese" and "railroad worker" were becoming synonymous, and the possibility that Chinese could be accepted as a worthy element in the still emerging American nation seemed real indeed.

By the time this Independence Day celebration took place, the CPRR line actually extended as far as Dutch Flat (3,144 feet in elevation), sixty-seven miles from Sacramento. From there, the army of thousands of Railroad Chinese, using hundreds of twenty-five-pound kegs of blasting powder every day, continued to make steady progress up and up through locations with picturesque names like Green Bluffs (seventy-one miles from Sacramento), China Ranch (seventy-six miles), Blue Canyon (seventy-eight miles), Lost Camp (eighty miles), Emigrant Gap (eighty-four miles from Sacramento and 5,200 feet in elevation), and then, in late November, Cisco, ninety-two miles from the starting point at almost six thousand feet above sea level. The town boomed as a key base for railroad operations farther up into the Sierra. The company constantly ran one hundred locomotives and hundreds of cars along the completed track to bring materials, supplies, and workers to the different construction sites where work continued concurrently. From Cisco as the terminus, pack animals and human labor had to transport construction materials and supplies off-loaded from the train up into the high elevations and beyond.

The dramatic contrast between the beauty of the land and the ferocious efforts of the workers to push the line forward touched the company's usually no-nonsense chief engineer for tunneling, John R. Gilliss. In a report several years later to other professionals, he vividly recalled one special experience. One evening in late 1866 after snow had fallen, he went for a walk in the summit area. The path was "strangely beautiful at night," he said. "The tall firs, though drooping under their heavy burdens, pointed to the mountains that overhung them, where the fires that lit seven tunnels shone like stars on their snowy sides." As Gilliss described it, "the only sound that came down to break the stillness of the winter night was the sharp ring of hammer on steel, or the heavy reports of the blasts." The Railroad Chinese night shifts were hard at work in those tunnels.

In a formal report about the company's work in 1866, CPRR president Leland Stanford, whose prose was usually turgid and uninspired, described the impressive progress in uncharacteristically forceful and evocative ways. The construction work, he emphasized, was "the most difficult ever yet surmounted by any railroad in the United States, if not in Europe," and with no exaggeration, Stanford called the effort "a herculean task." The geography was imposing. Track had to be laid over country that was "rugged and rocky, upon a steep mountain side, and up by deep ravines, requiring a continued succession of deep cuts and high embankments, many of which had to be protected by heavy stone walls." Moreover, "large and long culverts of stone" had to be built "to pass the torrents of water which fall in the mountains." Rock of the "hardest kind" was required for building these projects.

Ever watchful of the budget, Stanford also stated that the work was costly, as the company had to pay in gold for "all labor." He was referring, of course, to the Chinese. Still, the advance had not been as great as hoped because of the inadequate quantity of black powder on the West Coast and the company's "inability to procure as many laborers as we wished and expected." (All the powder made on the West Coast at the time came from the California Powder Works near Santa Cruz, which began operations in 1864. Here too there was a Chinese connection: all of its 275 workers were Chinese.) The company had wanted to hire as many as fifteen thousand workers but succeeded in attracting only ten thousand, for there were other job opportunities for them. Those who had signed on to the CPRR were "kept constantly at work during the spring, summer, and fall months." Through the current winter, the company, according to Stanford, continued to employ six thousand men, with thousands of others furloughed until the spring. With the summit still more than fifteen miles beyond Cisco, the company was trying to arrange to bring on twenty thousand workers to assault what he called "the hardest of granite, ironstone, and trap" during the coming year before yet another winter set in. Railroad Chinese were responsible for completing almost all of the work Stanford described. The company's very existence had become dependent on them.

While Stanford wrote his report in the comfort and security of his home and office in Sacramento, thousands of Chinese were then living in caverns excavated beneath snowdrifts so they could continue to work on tunnels through the granite. Thousands of others worked east of the summit in what was called Truckee Canyon, where the winters were less severe but the work was still dangerous and daunting. Dense forests blocked the route. Workers had to fell and then blast out the stumps of huge pines, up to eight feet in diameter. The frozen-solid ground defied the graders. All materials, including locomotives, train cars, and tons of iron, had to be hauled over the summit on sleds to supply workers eastward. But tunneling at the summit was the most perilous of all the construction challenges in building the railroad. The assignment bordered on the inhuman and required superhuman effort to complete.

The decision on how to get the line through the towering Sierra was not easily made. Would the line roughly follow the dramatic surface contours of the mountains, through multiple tunnels that had to be carved through solid granite? A train would have to wind through the canyons, snake along jagged cliffs, traverse steep ravines, go up and down sharp inclines, navigate twisting switchbacks, and pass through mountain tunnels. Workers would face years of scorching summers at high altitude and horrendous Sierra winters. The line would have to go right through the area where the doomed Donner pioneering party was snowbound for almost four months. Stranded, some in the group had resorted to cannibalism to survive. Knowing this history, the CPRR leadership at one time seriously considered the possibility of avoiding those dangers by boring a *single* tunnel all the way through the Sierra! As envisioned, it would have been five miles in length, thirty-two feet high and sixteen feet wide, as much as one thousand feet below a surface route. The entry point would have been south of Donner Summit and the exit at Cold Stream on the Nevada side. It was estimated that the tunneling would cost $1 million a mile in mid-nineteenth-century U.S. dollars. There is no indication whether the company gave much consideration to what the workers would have faced laboring in that endless monstrous tube. The company eventually opted for the least bad of the options. It rejected the five-mile tunnel idea and decided on a surface route that still required fifteen shorter excavations through the mountains.

Railroad Chinese had bored five tunnels before they reached the greatest challenge, Tunnel No. 6, or Summit Tunnel, located 105 miles from Sacramento. Seven other tunnels follow over the next eight miles. Two more lay farther east near the Nevada border. Most of the tunnels were not straight but curved, which made the challenge even more demanding and difficult. Tunnel No. 13, for example was 870 feet in length with a sharp curvature. When the bores that had been started at either end met in the center, they were just slightly parallel, only two inches from meeting head-on. The competing Union Pacific had only four tunnels to excavate, and they were much shorter and went through less dense material. The total length of the CPRR tunnels was three and a half times the length of the UP tunnels. But most of the CPRR tunnels required no framing with timber, as the rock was absolutely solid. In all fifteen tunnels, the "laboring force was entirely composed" of Chinese, except for a handful of whites at one tunnel. The Chinese in the summit area numbered up to nine thousand, according to engineer Gilliss, who praised the Railroad Chinese, calling them "as steady, hard-working a set of men as could be found."

Of the many daunting construction accomplishments of the Railroad Chinese, boring the Summit Tunnel occupies the apex of them all, not just in geographic location but in difficulty, too, because of its length, the weather, and the stubbornness of the rock. It was the most imposing obstacle to getting through the Sierra. Located at the Sierra crest and paralleling Donner Pass, the tunnel eventually stretched 1,659 feet, almost a third of a mile, or more than five football fields in length. It was sixteen feet wide, twenty-three feet high, and, at its deepest, 124 feet below the surface. Adding to the challenge, the tunnel sloped thirty feet in elevation going west to east. It took more than two years of constant work to excavate and lay tracks. Chinese worked in it and other tunnels simultaneously.

The company had workers begin construction on the tunnel in the fall of 1865, but early snow stopped the effort. After warmer temperatures made work possible again, Railroad Chinese resumed their effort and attacked the tunnel's two end points, the west and east portals. Because progress would have measured just an inch or two per day with the use of nothing but hammers and chisels, workers used blasting powder to crack the rock and then remove it. Considerable variation in skills, experience, and ability distinguished the many Railroad Chinese, but only the best among them worked at Summit Tunnel. Hundreds of them became the company's elite soldiers.

Thirty to forty men constituted a gang that worked under a white supervisor at each portal. In turn, the gang was divided into multiple teams of three. One member of the team would locate a seam, crack, or crevasse in which to start a hole and then position a three-, five-, or six-foot-long steel pole drill that had a flat, flared tip. The two other team members, wielding eight-pound sledgehammers, pounded the top of the drill. The bit would then be rotated a quarter turn to go deeper into the stone. Bang, bang, and another quarter turn. The process, sometimes known as "double jack" drilling, required close teamwork, skill, care, and endurance. It was unbelievably laborious: teams could drill just three holes, two and a quarter inches in diameter, two and a half feet deep, in an eight-hour shift. The teams were on two staggered levels in the tunnel bore. Four or five teams of men worked at the rock face on the upper level, called the "heading," while other teams below them stepwise on the roadbed level, the "bottom," carried out the broken rock. Working on two levels made scaffolding unnecessary and removal of debris more efficient.

Imagine the noise, vibration, fatigue, and monotony but also the hellish confinement in those tunnels, lit only by oil lamp or candle-light! The air was thick with rock dust, acrid fumes lingered from previous explosions, water dripped and flowed from fissures in the cold rock, and sharp, heavy icicles hung down in the winter. Air temperature ranged from cold to frigid. Rock fragments flew through the air and into eyes and mouths. A moment of distracted attention, mistiming, or simple error and there would be a smashed hand, arm, or fingers. Work in that great dark maw of the mountain never stopped, as three shifts of eight hours each covered a twenty-four-hour day throughout the entire year.

Work continued nonstop through the summer and into the fall and winter of 1866–67, which was one of the worst on record. Forty-four snowstorms from November 1866 to May 1867 left immense quantities of snow. In an understatement, E. B. Crocker reminded an impatient Collis Huntington in New York that the summit "is a rough place in a storm." The heaviest blizzard of the season lasted from the eighteenth of February to late on the twenty-second and left six feet of snow. Another storm lasted two weeks. Removal of the snow from the track and roadbed required hundreds of hands.

When the drifts were too massive, the workers had to carve out caverns beneath the snow to live and work in the Summit Tunnel and others. A maze of caverns cut through the snowdrifts, connecting living spaces, different tunnel entrances, and work areas. It was an unheard-of existence but one required by the company in order to keep the work going through the terrible winter. Tunneling, which was the most time-consuming task, had to continue without interruption to stay on the construction schedule.

Going to the face of the tunnel's bore, Railroad Chinese used their drills and hammers to open up holes in the granite, filled them with explosives, a fuse, and clay, hay, or sand, and packed them tight. The fuse would be lit, workers fled the cavern, and a blast would follow like that from the mouth of a huge cannon. Explosions cracked the hard rock and produced thick, burning smoke that had to dissipate before removal of the heavy debris and drilling could resume. The thundering blasts shook the very bowels of the Sierra. Not all the completed drill holes in the tunnel were used, however; many can still be found intact today in tunnels and surrounding rock. Existence, let alone grueling work, in that foul-aired, dark, freezing cavern defies comprehension.

Alfred Hart captured many images of the Railroad Chinese while they worked in the summit area. His work shows us the ruggedness of the land but also lets us see on occasion individuals, unlike in earlier photos where the workers appear as a largely indistinct mass. In "Laborers and Rocks. Near Opening of Summit Tunnel" (below), for example, a half-dozen Chinese seen at close range are breaking down boulders with drills and sledgehammers. They dress similarly but not identically. Some wear leather boots and dungarees; others wear light cotton tunics. Their sunhats vary in style.

In a dramatically contrasting scene, in "Snow Plow. At Cisco" (opposite), Hart depicts a Chinese man, in a Western-style hat, standing before a huge snowplow to help establish the size of the machine and the towering drifts of snow that still blanketed the land's surface as late as May. "Constructing Snow Cover. Scene Near the Summit" (opposite) shows construction of part of the miles of snow sheds that were erected to protect the line. Though Chinese probably accounted for a small proportion of the skilled carpenters, one Chinese fellow, perhaps a helper, stands off to the side, staring at the camera. He moved slightly, though, creating a ghostly effect.

Two of Hart's most aesthetically appealing images from the summit area show a more temperate side to the climate, and also feature standing Chinese as central elements in the frames. Now known popularly as "Tea Carrier," which Hart named "Heading of East Portal.

Tunnel No. 8, from Donner Lake Railroad, Western Summit" (below), the photograph captures a Chinese man carrying tea to his compatriots in a jug suspended from a shoulder pole. The jug is recycled ceramic and may have held foodstuffs from China. He stands alone, face obscured in shadow, wearing tall leather boots, a tunic, and a sunhat. A conifer bravely reaches out of the cliff above him. The scene is at the same time daunting, with the hulking, immovable mountain resistant to its violation by humans but also with broken rock all around that serves as evidence of a fierce battle.

In "Coldstream, Eastern Slope of Western Summit" (opposite), three Railroad Chinese stand at the edge of a crystalline pond high in the Sierra. It is summer or fall, with no snow visible on the ground. One of the men is in dark, loose garb with a bowler hat and possibly his queue hanging down his front. Might he be a contractor or even a gambler? He does not look like a laborer from the line. A second man is observing the scene and wears what appears to be a butcher's or cook's apron and leather boots. The third and most visible Chinese is a water carrier, with what appear to be a small barrel and a can suspended from a shoulder pole. He stands on a wooden dock, about to dip his containers into the clear water. Behind the group is the back of a wooden structure. A broken wooden wheel and other cart parts lie abandoned on the ground, suggesting that the site was a long-term

worker encampment. This photo illustrates the many different roles
Chinese played on the line and the specialization of their labor.

Many of Hart's photos capture the spectacular beauty of the mountains and the colossal scale of the completed work and its surrounding environment. One example is "Donner Lake, Tunnels No. 7 and 8
from Summit Tunnel, Eastern Summit in Distance" (next page, top),
taken above Tunnel No. 6, which shows us completed work in carv-
ing out the roadbed. The track is not yet laid, which dates this to before June 1868. Two other tunnels are visible. A party of well-dressed
men and women stand atop a constructed embankment and take in
the commanding view but are careful to stay safely back, away from
the precipice. What would a Railroad Chinese worker forging the iron
road in that unfamiliar landscape have felt or thought as he stood and
took in the majestic vistas so far removed in distance, climate, and environment from his home in the alluvial plains in semitropical southern China? Would he have been able to enjoy the magnificence of the
high country, or was it a place he would simply have wanted to quit as
quickly as possible?

Close to where he took that shot, Hart also photographed the area
on top of Tunnel No. 6 in "Shaft House over Summit Tunnel. American Peak in Distance" (next page, bottom). He shows the barrenness

of a landscape unable to support much plant life. In the middle of the frame he includes the buildings around a vertical shaft that extended down to the midpoint of Tunnel No. 6 and housing for the workers.

In one of his most stunning images, Hart captured the interior of the uncompleted Summit Tunnel (opposite). Using an unknown light source, Hart tries to expose the guts of the dark, cavernous bore.

The effect is eerie and harrowing in the confinement of the mountain's bowel. At the far end of the tunnel, one can dimly see the two work levels, the "heading" at the top and the "bottom" on the roadbed level.

Photography, especially outdoors, was strictly limited by the technology of the time. Photographs are often static, sometimes lifeless scenes. Other visual artists, however, could create depictions of the railroad project with greater variety, energy, and imagination. They could suggest movement and human activity. The work of the illustrator Joseph Becker (1841–1910), for one, gives us views of the Chinese that would have eluded a photographer. Becker, who worked for the popular *Frank Leslie's Illustrated Newspaper* for forty-one years, was one of the most successful illustrators of the nineteenth century. After working on Civil War scenes for the periodical, he was sent to the Far West to create images that would accompany a special feature on Chinese, later published in a series of installments with the title "The Coming Man." Editor Leslie wanted to "scoop" his competition with extensive reportage and depictions of this population, a subject of great curiosity because of their work on the Pacific Railway. It would be the first major feature on Chinese in America by a national publication.

Becker spent six weeks observing Chinese and drawing them, and *Frank Leslie's* reproduced many of his works. One fascinating piece, "A Chinese Camp-Scene on the Line of the Central Pacific Railroad — 'The Coming Man' Preparing His Evening Meal" shows a busy encampment, which includes men walking about, setting up a tent, and eating with chopsticks from rice bowls and a large common platter of food. Another, holding a long spatula, is cooking. A covered wok may have contained steaming or stewing food. Another one holds numerous whole fish frying, releasing a tantalizing aroma. Laundry flutters in the background. Another illustration shows the interior of a sleeping quarter. Captioned "Chinese Tent Scene, on the California Pacific Railroad," it depicts Railroad Chinese settling in for the evening's rest. One is smoking, and a lone candle illuminates the tent. Clothes hang down heavily. (These images appear in chapter 5.)

One of Becker's best-known images is "Across the Continent: The Snow Sheds on the Central Pacific Railroad" (above), which shows Chinese with tunnels and snow sheds, the accomplishments of their labor. They are hailing the arrival of the train. Snow remains on the ground.

A small cache of informal Becker sketches that never made it into print allows us to "see" Railroad Chinese in different ways. One depicts many Chinese workers alongside the track with a steam engine rapidly approaching. Chinese scramble to get out of the way. The active mass of workers contrasts with the beautiful scenery of trees and snow-covered mountains in the background. Another sketch, seemingly from the same area, shows a Chinese encampment, but instead of tents, this gathering includes modest structures, some with chimneys, indicating the camp was not temporary. Men are moving about, gambling and cooking (above, left). Another image is titled "Chinese Porters for Railroad" (above, right). Though it is cartoonish, as was much of the work of other non-Chinese artists at this time, who had great difficulty rendering Chinese features, it is one of the few complete depictions of Chinese, relaxed and chatting with one another in the middle of snow season in the high country. It presents a moment of human interaction captured many years ago. One can only imagine what sketches Railroad Chinese made in their spare time. There surely must have been an artist or two among the thousands. How might they have rendered themselves and the landscape?

Conditions in the High Sierra were as deadly as they were beautiful, but the railroad workers straining to break through the summit had little opportunity for rest or contemplation. In its relentless drive to compete with the Union Pacific, the CPRR was pushing them harder and harder. And as the work grew more difficult, the solutions for overcoming the challenges of the Sierra became more extreme.

For a short while, the company had workers use the newly invented, and controversial, explosive liquid nitroglycerine. It had several distinct advantages: it produced much less smoke than black powder, was eight times stronger, required smaller drill holes (one and a quarter inches in diameter), and cracked rock in ways that made removal of debris easier and faster. It was more cost effective for the company, but there were also clear problems with its use. Many feared its instability and unpredictability, especially after a horrendous accidental explosion leveled a Wells Fargo building and rattled the ground beneath downtown San Francisco. The CPRR itself experimented with it in April 1866, but an explosion obliterated six workers who were handling it. The company then tried to manufacture the explosive on site in a small factory near Donner Lake. Chinese workers had to hand-carry vials to the tunnels, where it was used for a few months in mid-1867 in Tunnels No. 6, 7, and 8. But its use was also a touchy business: nitroglycerine froze at just 45 degrees Fahrenheit, which required workers to heat it oh so carefully so it could be poured into the drill holes. It also needed a blasting cap to set it off. Accidental explosions were always feared. The company soon ended its use, not because of its danger but because of patent restrictions placed on it by its inventor, Alfred Nobel, and government restrictions on its use and transportation.

Wanting to make progress with the tunneling as fast as possible, company engineers came up with an extreme solution: they ordered the workers to sink a vertical shaft, eight feet by twelve feet, from the surface at the top of the mountain down toward the calculated halfway point of the tunnel. On August 27, 1866, Railroad Chinese began the work. They were able to dig down just one foot a day for the first thirty feet, before removing debris slowed the effort to just seven inches a day. After eighty-five days of work, they finally completed a shaft more than seventy-two foot deep. Men and debris traveled up and down on a lift run by an old steam engine. At the bottom, workers widened an area from which they could attack two "inner" faces of the tunnel. As this inner tunneling lengthened, workers laid temporary tracks for carts carrying broken rock loaded at the faces. They pushed the carts to the shaft's base, where the carts were hoisted out with their heavy loads. With simultaneous work at *four* faces, workers were then able to carve out approximately four feet of rock per day. The company constructed a wooden building to cover the top of the shaft so that work could continue year-round (see p. 129).

Progress was expedited. The Summit Tunnel was nearing completion. And then, suddenly, the work stopped.

7
THE STRIKE

The strike began.... The men who were working at that hour walked out of the tunnels and away from the tracks. The ones who were sleeping slept on and rose as late as they pleased. They bathed in streams and shaved their moustaches and wild beards. Some went fishing and hunting. The violinists tuned and played their instruments. The drummers beat theirs at the punchlines of jokes. The gamblers shuffled and played their cards and tiles. The smokers passed their pipes, and the drinkers bet for drinks by making figures with their hands. The cooks made party food.
— MAXINE HONG KINGSTON,
China Men, 1977

IN JANUARY 1867, IN THE MIDST OF A TERRIBLE WINTER, CPRR legal counsel E. B. Crocker sent Collis Huntington, who was ensconced in New York City raising capital for the railroad project, a troubling report on the company's condition. Crocker aimed to disabuse Huntington, who watched the budget closely, of the idea that the company could significantly shrink its costly workforce during the winter months. "It can't be done," Crocker reported, if there was a chance of reaching the critical juncture of Truckee at the summit as planned. "If we reduce our force below what it is now, we shall have to discharge our best foremen, and they will get scattered & when we want them again they can't be had, & the same of the chinamen, they will get at work mining & it will be doubtful whether we can get them when we want them." Crocker's account makes clear that the Railroad Chinese were neither tractable nor bound, as critics objected, but independent and free to take advantage of options more attractive to them than work on the railroad.

Crocker further emphasized that since the company required organization, being "thorough & complete is of the first importance." The current workforce had taken months to assemble, train, and settle. "It is a big job of itself to get several thousand men properly camped, proper foremen selected, & each man appointed to his peculiar duties so that all goes off right." Crocker wanted Huntington to understand that the company could not "discharge a man. It will ruin all our future hopes." Indeed, "it will be fatal," he bluntly told Huntington. Returning specifically to the Chinese, Crocker wrote: "We had hard work last summer & fall to get chinamen to work in this hard rock & they kept leaving rather than do it. What men we have now are trained to hard rock work, & we can depend on them. But we cannot rely on new men to stick to it. We have a big job before us in those long deep rock cuts at the Summit, & we are preparing to rush it as soon as we can get at it." The company got 50 percent more work from the experienced crews than with "new men," Crocker argued. Many Railroad Chinese were now veteran and tested workers, not just strong backs.

Leland Stanford, CPRR secretary E. H. Miller, and Samuel Montague, the chief engineer, publicly expressed views similar to what Crocker wrote privately. In a report to the board of directors, the company officials summarized the work that had been completed in 1866 and the goals for 1867. They praised the Chinese workforce but worried that its numbers were insufficient. Only six thousand men were at work because of the dreadful winter conditions. For the coming year, the officials indicated that with the magnitude of very difficult work that still lay ahead and the brevity of the open-air construction season at the summit, the company needed a "large force, probably twenty thousand" to advance the project before the next winter. In order to meet this huge need, the company commissioned a "Chinese artist" to draft a handbill in Chinese to advertise the availability of work for the CPRR. The craftsman made a woodcut of the advertisement and produced five thousand copies, which were to circulate "all over this state & in China." (We are not sure what the flyer actually said, as no copy of it has been found. Company officials themselves were not confident about what was in it. Crocker confided to Huntington that no one ever translated the Chinese text back into English. The "Chinamen all understand it," he wrote, "but it is hard for them to translate it back into English.") Company officials did not seem to realize that their flyer, while it advertised opportunity, also implicitly acknowledged the critical importance of the Chinese workers it then employed. The company's linguistic, as well as labor, dependence on them would not go unnoticed. Recruiting new workers all the way from China would take months, and Chinese workers in California were already largely employed. The labor market was very tight, and company officials possessed extremely limited understanding of what Chinese were thinking and talking about among themselves.

Work, income, and risk were all highly structured, integrated, and hierarchical on the CPRR. The top officers of the company assumed high financial risk and eventually became enormously wealthy. Working in their offices, they faced little bodily risk. Huntington spent most of his time living comfortably in New York City with his wife, his lover and future wife, and family, first in the luxurious Metropolitan Hotel and then in a "modest" three-story mansion he purchased on Park Avenue. Stanford had his own mansion in Sacramento, which he acquired when he was governor. Hopkins and Crocker also resided most of the time in Sacramento, though Crocker, as the head of construction, frequently went out on the road to inspect, supervise, and even personally pay workers on occasion. Field construction boss Strobridge lost an eye to an errant explosion early in the effort, but he and his wife and children lived together in the security and comfort of a specially outfitted railcar, part of a "camp train" that followed the route, and which appears to have housed many of the CPRR's white workers; the camp train contained, it was reported, eating and sleeping quarters for five hundred men. This ten- or eleven-car train contained a "hotel, telegraph office, store, kitchen, sleeping quarters and a 'home that would not discredit San Francisco,'" as one journalist described it. Attached to the train were several platform cars that served as work areas for carpenters and for laborers constructing a telegraph line that ran along the rail line. At key stations on the route, the company established telegraph offices from which they communicated with those behind them and ordered supplies and provisions.

Strobridge, the company leader with whom Railroad Chinese had the most direct personal contact, lived in a forward car in the camp train. He had an office and private quarters, "neatly fitted and well furnished." Attached was "an awning veranda, with a canary bird swinging at the front door," according to a reporter. There, Strobridge spent time with his family and received visitors. His wife accompanied him on the camp train from beginning to end of the construction project. On occasion the Strobridges and their children enjoyed outings in the mountains, including boating on spectacular Donner Lake at the summit. The contrast between their highly visible domestic arrangements and the living conditions of the workers near at hand could not have been starker.

The contrast between the working conditions, type of labor, and wages of the Chinese and white workers on the CPRR could not have been starker, either. White men filled the skilled occupations such as carpenter, blacksmith, and tree-cutter almost exclusively. Others were supervisors over the Chinese. Some whites, to be sure, were also line workers, notably the layers who handled the iron rails; but the overall work duties and living conditions of the white rail workers compared to those of the Chinese rail workers mirrored the pervasive racial inequality of American life at the time.

Once, to satisfy their curiosity and to try to squeeze as much work as possible out of their employees, the company directors arranged a competition between Railroad Chinese and workers from Cornwall, in England, who enjoyed the reputation at the time of being the best miners in the world. The CPRR had recruited them with high wages away from mines in Nevada to tunnel at the summit. Chinese and the Cornish were set to work at opposite ends of the tunnel. After measuring the completed work at the end of the day over several days, the company discovered, to its surprise, that the Chinese had advanced farther than the Cornish team. In public testimony in 1877 before a special United States Senate committee investigating Chinese immigration, Charles Crocker reported that the competition was "hard work, steady pounding on the rock, bone-labor," but "without fail," the Chinese "always out-measured the Cornish miners" in the amount of cut and removed rock. Crocker maintained unequivocally that "the Chinese were skilled in using the hammer and the drill," and in terms of their attitude, they were "very trusty," "very intelligent," and they lived up to their contracts. In sum, Crocker conceded that compared to "white men," the Chinese displayed "greater reliability and steadiness," and with their tremendous "aptitude and capacity for hard work," they had "worked themselves into our favor."

All whites, including the line workers, received significantly higher wages than the Chinese. This pay disparity can be seen on the November 1866 payroll sheet for what appears to be one work camp, "Summit 51 'A,'" of Charles Crocker's construction company. Alongside Euro-American names, listed with first and last names, followed by "occupations" such as foreman, blacksmith, or driver, Chinese names are listed as Ah Tom, Ah Keale, Ah Nou No. 1, Ah Nou No. 2, Ah Tom No. 2, Ah Kow, Ah You, and Ah Sam. (The diminutive "Ah" commonly precedes an effort to spell what presumably is a Chinese surname; several of these men may have been related, perhaps even brothers.) The occupation of all of them was "waiter," and they were paid only sixty-six cents a day, much less than the one dollar paid to Chinese construction workers. The total pay that month for the men just named ranged from $3.96 (for a fellow who worked only six days) to $25 (for those who worked thirty days). The sums were far less than for those with Euro-American names (some of whom may have been African American). Most of the "foremen" received in total between $60 and $90. A per diem fee for board was deducted for several of the Chinese and two of the others. The Chinese waiters likely served food to those who lived at Summit Camp, a pivotal location for the railroad at the highest elevation of the project, which was occupied for four years. Lower down on the same payroll sheet we find the name of Ah Gee, a "helper," who was paid a dollar a day for twenty-three and a quarter days of work and had $3 subtracted from his pay for board. He may have "helped" Ah Ming, who is listed as a blacksmith and was paid $1.53 per day for fifteen days of work. He had $2 taken from his pay for board. Most of the blacksmiths with Euro-American names earned $2.50 a day with nothing deducted for board. Though the Chinese names as listed are almost no help in trying to identify specific individuals, the record still provides interesting insights. Those with Euro-American names clearly received substantially higher pay than did Chinese, who themselves performed different types of work, were paid at different rates, and kept different schedules.

While the Chinese men listed on this payroll were waiters, even those who did dangerous work could not expect to be paid anywhere near the level of white workers. Indeed, in an inverse relationship, the Railroad Chinese received the lowest pay but bore the greatest risk to life and limb. Whites and Chinese lived and usually worked in highly segregated settings. African Americans, Native Americans, Mormons, and European immigrant men, Irish and others, also worked along with Chinese and "Americans," presumably native-born whites, who usually refused to work with Chinese. Very little is known about the experiences of these groups and their interaction on the CPRR. Consistent with capitalist practices at the time, company leadership appears to have paid little attention to the welfare of the workforce, other than to see that they completed the needed work. Lewis M. Clement displayed this disengaged attitude once when he was asked about Chinese workers, bluntly stating that he "never took any particular interest in them, never cared about them so long as we got the work done."

The extant evidence we do have provides only a general and sometimes conflicting picture of the pay differences among the wage workers. Although race was a basic factor, with whites always receiving higher pay even for the same work, differences in job assignments also accounted for pay differences. Chinese tunnelers, for example, received more than Chinese waiters.

Arthur Brown, the engineer overseeing wood construction, recalled a few years after work was completed that his white carpenters, probably in 1867–68, were paid $4 a day and foremen $3.75 a day, with board included in their compensation. "Laborers," presumably Chinese, were paid $2.25 to $2.75 a day, but the cost of their board was deducted— from forty cents to $1.25 a day, according to different sources. Engineer Clement said that white wood-choppers were paid $40 a month, with their board included. Chinese timber workers received $30 a month and paid for their own provisions. Clement also noted that provisions up in the high elevations were expensive, as they all had to be packed in by mule or pack trains. There was a constant strong upward pressure to raise the pay of white workers, recalled Clement, as they could always secure better wages elsewhere, even twice what the railroad could pay them, and they still tended to run off to the latest gold strike where they hoped to strike it rich.

Tunnel engineer Gilliss also provided information on wages. He placed the pay of Chinese tunnel workers at $30 to $35 in gold per month, out of which they had to pay for their board. At Tunnel No. 6, the Summit Tunnel specifically, Gilliss calculated that Chinese received $31 per month, without board; white foremen received $120 per month, along with their board; and blacksmiths received $115 per month, with board. In comparison, white laborers on the Union Pacific, according to Gilliss, were paid $3 to $4 *per day* in currency, or between $78 and $104 per month.

Before the Senate committee on Chinese immigration, Charles Crocker and James Strobridge testified about their experiences with Chinese labor on the CPRR. Both expressed high regard for the Chinese, and though they expressed a racial preference for hiring whites, the two maintained that Chinese were as good as the best white workers. Crocker, who claimed to have been a committed abolitionist from his youth, insisted that Chinese were free agents, and in no way "servile labor" that "degraded" whites, as in the slave system in the South. An employer in California could not work a Chinese unless he was hired and paid properly, he testified. As head of construction overall, however, Crocker had only a general overview of his workforce and was not even sure how many Chinese he had employed—perhaps ten thousand at the high point, according to his estimate. When they worked for the CPRR, Crocker said, the Chinese grouped themselves into teams, with one among them being the "headman." The company paid him, and he in turn distributed the wages among the others. Whites were paid individually. The company paid Chinese $35 a month, he recalled, or about $1.25 a day. They spent approximately forty cents a day on provisions purchased from the company store.

Strobridge confirmed the amount of the pay differential between Chinese and white workers. And like Crocker, he expressed respect and appreciation for the self-discipline of Chinese and their work ethic. In contrast, he cited the record of UP white workers who frequently went on strike or disrupted work, including even in the days just before the two lines met at Promontory Summit in Utah. UP workers even physically detained company vice president Thomas Durant because of his nonpayment of wages. Chinese workers, Strobridge observed, never behaved in such a way, even though "sometimes we did not pay for two months and perhaps more." They were never "docile," Strobridge testified: "I do not think the Chinese are any more docile than white-men." White workers after getting paid, he said, often "will get drunk," and "that is when trouble comes with them." Chinese, by contrast, were exemplary on and off the job. Carefully choosing his words before a panel of U.S. senators who believed that the company, in deliberately hiring lower-paid Chinese, was damaging the interests of the white population, Strobridge argued that Chinese workers still "would be preferable" because "we have less difficulty with them."

Strobridge's frank assessment of the quality of Chinese workers irritated the committee members, but his testimony also reinforced their anti-Chinese hostility. The senators suspected that the railroad men favored Chinese simply because of money: Chinese labor cost less. At the end of their time with Strobridge, one member bluntly asked: Wasn't the issue about the Chinese simply about their pay? Wasn't their labor "about thirty-three per cent cheaper to the contractor than the white labor?" Strobridge responded, going further: "It is much cheaper. Their board is an important consideration." Earlier in the hearing, Crocker had said almost the same thing when he was asked, "Did you make more money out of [employing Chinese] than if you had employed white men?" Crocker simply replied, "I think I did."

There is no question that Chinese received significantly lower pay than did white workers in the same job categories and far less than white supervisors, blacksmiths, teamsters, hostlers, and other higher-paid positions. Few Chinese filled what were considered to be skilled positions. Anti-Chinese politicians cited the wage differential as obvious evidence of the avarice of the railroad barons, who gained immense profits by not hiring white men. In their view, Chinese deprived deserving whites of work. Railroad company officials defended themselves by saying that although they preferred to hire as many whites as would take the work, the numbers fell dramatically short of need. Moreover, they argued, hiring Chinese actually created more and higher-paying jobs for white men, for, without Chinese, the railroad enterprise would not have been able to succeed. Instead of employing only several hundred white men as laborers, the CPRR, it was argued, was actually able to hire several thousand white men in higher-paying positions because of Chinese labor.

From the viewpoint of Railroad Chinese, though the wage differential based on race was glaring, and racial prejudice was openly practiced, they knew that the wages they received were many times greater than what they could earn in the Pearl River delta as farmers or labor-ers. Physical risk, even the risk of death, was exceedingly high, but so was their gain relative to what they could make in their home villages.

The power imbalance between Railroad Chinese and their white co-workers on the CPRR led to acts of resistance large and small. Some-times these could be as minor as a prank at the oppressor's expense —an act that acknowledged but also slyly subverted the inequalities between white and nonwhite workers. The Siyi people can be a gar-rulous lot, after all. In the camps where they resided, and around the after-dinner fire, they might have exchanged the latest news or stories about the stupidity of white supervisors or about the crazy company building the railroad through such impossible territory. One such tale, handed down by Chinese Americans through the decades as they re-counted the lives of their ancestors from those times, and recorded by a community historian, goes roughly as follows.

A Chinese cook once worked for a crew of white railroad workers. He was mild-mannered and worked hard but became the butt of their pranks. As told by an old-timer, Moon Lee, whose father and grand-father had been Railroad Chinese, the whites harassed the cook "by sneaking into his tent and tying knots in his pants legs and shirt sleeves. The cook did not make any fuss but just rose earlier and patiently un-tied the knots and got on with the food preparation." The story seems to emphasize the stereotype of the long-suffering Chinese, until it takes a surprising turn. Moon Lee continued: "One day, after a particu-larly savory dinner, the ringleader, ashamed of the tricks, gathered his gang around him and informed the Chinese that hereafter he was their friend and no one would harm him. The Chinese cook's eyes bright-ened." He called out with a smile, "All-li my flens, now I no pee in the soup!" What howls of laughter this subversive act provoked through the years!

The consolations of a joke at the white man's expense that was shared around a campfire would not have diminished the very real eco-nomic inequities that the Railroad Chinese endured. Derisive laugh-ter might provide a measure of psychic comfort, but stories like this one would also remind them of their penurious social and economic status. And it was always income that was paramount in the minds of the Railroad Chinese: it was the entire reason why they had come to America in the first place.

But what did Hung Wah and thousands of other Railroad Chinese do with all their hard-earned pay? Unlike workers on the Union Pacific, who received their pay in paper currency, Railroad Chinese insisted on receiving gold coins. They were familiar with and trusted gold and silver, the other precious metal they knew. Paper currency was just paper to them. The coins probably came from the federal mint constructed in San Francisco in 1854, which processed California gold that Chinese miners themselves had helped gather. Did the Railroad Chinese stash the coins in hiding places in their campsites? Did they carry them on their person as they worked? Did they entrust the gold to contractors for safekeeping? Did they periodically transport it to towns where a Chinese merchant or a branch of Wells Fargo, one of the early banks in the West, held it for them? We have no record of where this immense amount of money was kept safely for future use, including for sending remittances back to families in China who were becoming increasingly dependent on the income. It is ghost money.

Chinese folklore is full of stories of the righteous bravery and honor of an upright general or official who was wrongly treated but finds a way to gain redress and make things right. An actual episode in 1867 in California inspired a populist version and remains one of the most outstanding and intriguing of the many dramatic moments that punctuate the CPRR construction effort — the mass collective action taken by thousands of Railroad Chinese in June 1867. It is known as "The Strike" and was the largest, or certainly close to it, workers' strike against a private employer to take place in America to that date. And it was undertaken in the most difficult of conditions. Despite its significance, historians have paid only occasional and limited attention to understanding it. Respected studies of the American labor movement do not always even acknowledge its existence. This erasure is emblematic of the obscuring of the Chinese in the country's record generally and helps perpetuate the one-dimensional view of the Chinese in nineteenth-century America as marginal at best or simply a tractable, victimized workforce devoid of personality and agency.

When the strike is mentioned in historical writing, the story usually emphasizes the desperation of the Chinese. The workers, it is said, were driven to act because of the horrible conditions of their work.

Crocker, years later when he was interviewed about the episode, boasted that it was his toughness and resolve that forced the Chinese to return to work. The strike "failed" in achieving its demands, in his telling. His account, the prevailing one, is the familiar trope of an employer breaking a strike because of his determination to maintain full control and authority. The actual story of the 1867 strike, however, is much more intriguing.

Insights into the thinking of top company leadership as found in their private correspondence and other documentation offer a picture substantially at odds with Crocker's self-congratulatory version. The company actually had little understanding of what it faced in the standoff with the Chinese, whose leadership, organization, thinking, and aims were a complete mystery to the CPRR. Its management never did understand why the workers acted when they did, what their purposes were, and the reasons for their decision to end the strike. It all remained incomprehensible to Crocker and the rest of the company leadership even after the workers returned to the line.

The Railroad Chinese had certainly wanted change, but they acted to take advantage of their relatively strong, not weak, position. The company was in shaky financial condition, and it was no secret that it had become fully dependent on Chinese labor. Without it, the company would flounder, and perhaps even crash. Thus, it was the company's vulnerability, not desperation among the Chinese, that lay at the heart of the strike story. This is clear from letters the principals sent privately to one another beginning in early 1867 and then throughout the strike in June.

In early February of that year, E. B. Crocker again wrote Collis Huntington about continuing labor needs. There were just not enough men to work in the Truckee area. One reason was that the Chinese, far from being subservient and at the beck and call of the company, were away celebrating the Chinese New Year, the most important festival for Chinese. Fortunately, Crocker wrote, the holiday "is just over" and "we look for them to be coming along from [it] pretty fast." But the company still had far fewer workers than it needed, and it is clear that the Chinese were not a workforce at the mercy of the CPRR. They had their ways too, and the company had become reliant on them. Crocker reminded other company leaders about the superiority of the Chinese tunnelers compared to the Cornish miners. The Chinese "beat them right straight along—day in & day out." The Chinese "can't be beat," and they cost about half as much as white workers, too.

In early April, independent news reports publicly disclosed the CPRR's continuing efforts to increase its workforce; it was "offering work to any number of Chinamen." Company agents had combed through the mining regions of California to find willing and able Chinese and hoped that up to twenty thousand of the "prospective unbleached American citizens" would join the construction effort within the month. Such wild optimism would not be realized.

A month later, Crocker expressed frustration and some concern in his letters to Huntington. The weather remained challenging, with heavy snow as late as April making progress difficult. "Providence seems to be rather against us," Crocker confessed. But there was hope on the horizon: "The prospect seems favorable for getting a large force of chinamen," he wrote on April 27. On May 16, he noted that their work on the line had also impressed others who had come to inspect the construction effort. "Several of our largest Capitalists have been over the road recently," wrote Crocker, and "they all express their astonishment at the magnitude of the work already finished, and at the comparatively low cost. The cheapness is due in a great measure to the low price of Chinese labor. It is opening the eyes of our business men to see the readiness with which this class of cheap labor adapts itself to the construction of railroads." Awareness of the obvious value of Chinese labor in both cost and productivity was moving beyond the CPRR leadership. Chinese themselves were not unaware of the importance of their own labor power.

A week later, Crocker again expressed concern over continuing problems in advancing the construction. Snow still impeded work between Cisco and Truckee. And "another difficulty begins to appear—a want of men," he wrote. The company was still "scouring the state" for workers, "but they come in very slow." The problem, according to Crocker, was that Chinese were finding other, more attractive opportunities. "The truth is the Chinese are now extensively employed in quartz mines & a thousand other employments new to them. Our use of them has led hundreds of others to employ them—so that now when we want to gather them up for the spring & summer work, a large portion are permanently employed at work they like better." Ironically, the qualities of the Chinese workers that the company so valued and publicly praised were making them highly desirable to other employers, and unavailable to the company.

The press noted the movement of Chinese, not just away from railroad work but out of the state of California altogether. In the first half of 1867, the *Daily Alta California* reported, thousands of Chinese had departed for work in Idaho, Montana, and Nevada, where wages were known to be higher. Another issue privately worried company leaders. Leland Stanford wrote to tell Mark Hopkins what he had learned from a friend and from his own personal Chinese contacts: that there was widespread unhappiness among the Chinese workers contracted under "Sisson," likely referring to the Sisson, Wallace Company. Stanford does not say why the Chinese were unhappy with Sisson, but it was not good news.

Within days of writing to Huntington in mid-May, Crocker and the other principals took the radical step of *voluntarily* raising the wage rate of the Chinese by more than 13 percent to attract more workers. Crocker explained to Huntington, who kept a close watch on the company's purse strings, why they had to act: "The question whether we can get all the chinamen we need is very important, & we have concluded to raise their wages from $31 to $35 per month & see if that will not bring them." The company, which had been paying Chinese half as much as white workers, hoped that increasing pay would also stop Chinese from leaving the line for work elsewhere. Crocker bluntly predicted that the company would "find that our supply will be short unless we do something." With the wage hike, the company estimated that its Chinese workers would make $10 more a month than in mine work, a premium of 40 percent. The preemptive wage increase, however, had only limited and disappointing success. Hopkins soon informed Huntington that it would be "impossible" to continue the work without the Chinese, and even with the pay raise, they "are coming in slowly."

In early June, E. B. Crocker's anxiety about failing to reach construction goals in the Sierra because of "the scarcity of labor" appears to have heightened. He wrote Huntington that the Chinese workforce was "not now increasing & the season has come when it ought to increase." The Chinese were being drawn elsewhere where their work was "lighter than ours . . . [E]verybody is trying them & now we can't get them." The company still hoped that the wage increase would attract more workers, but Crocker was not at all confident. "We fear we shall not be able to get this large force [into the Sierra], but intend to do the best we can." Crocker ended his sober letter by reiterating his deep concern to Huntington: "The future is rendered more uncertain from the scarcity of laborers, & the extent of this scarcity we do not know now." Desperate, the company appealed to the federal government to send "5,000 negroes to work building the road." The news went public, revealing the dire circumstances of the company. Its severe labor needs were open and obvious.

Then, on Wednesday, June 19, a massive accidental tunnel explosion occurred a mile north of Cisco. According to a news report, it took the life of a "white man Burns, having a wife and family at Cisco," and "five Chinamen," who were "blown up" and "horribly mangled." The thunder from the disastrous explosion reverberated for miles up into the foothills, heard no doubt by the omnipresent Railroad Chinese.

On June 24, at the height of the construction season, precisely when the company most hoped to make rapid progress, three thousand Railroad Chinese, in a fully coordinated and informed effort, put down their tools and refused to work. From Cisco to Truckee, almost thirty miles, Chinese at scores of sites and in hundreds of teams stopped working in unison. One news report called it "the greatest strike ever known in the country."

In this bold act of resistance, the strikers may have been inspired by a smaller labor stoppage by fellow Chinese railroad workers in California nearly a decade prior. It was said that in 1859, an unscrupulous Chinese contractor withheld the wages due 150 Chinese who were working on a rail line near Sacramento, before the CPRR. They rebelled, attacked the contractor's assistant, and threatened him with violence. The frightened clerk took refuge in the station house and was saved only by the arrival of the local authorities. Through the years, Chinese workers, long after the incident had passed, likely told and retold this story of strength through collective action.

If the Railroad Chinese were influenced by recent history, the CPRR was blind to it. The company was completely unsuspecting and unprepared for the sudden mass action. The strike involved "all" the Chinese in the summit area, according to Mark Hopkins. It was disciplined and methodical. How they planned, communicated, and coordinated with one another, however, is not known at all. A news report at the time spoke of a flyer that circulated among the Chinese just before the strike, but considerable deliberation and planning must have taken place long in advance of the walkout. Reaching unity in purpose, in specific demands, and in the timing of action among three thousand workers spread along miles of construction work and living camps was a stunning accomplishment.

Why the Railroad Chinese chose the specific date to go out is also unclear, but Chinese cosmology is likely to have played an important role. Chinese did not undertake any major life actions without divining heaven and earth. The strike began just days after the summer solstice, the longest day of the year and the peak time for male energy, as the sun represented this male energy and the moon female energy. It was thus the time for action and struggle that also corresponded with what may have been the strongest bargaining position the Railroad Chinese had ever occupied, for if the CPRR did not get through the Sierra summit soon, it faced financial ruin. The reported Chinese flyer may actually have circulated on the day of or the day after that year's solstice, late evening on Friday, June 21, and just days after the Cisco tunnel explosion. It was the Year of the Rabbit, according to the Chinese zodiac. Saturday and Sunday may have been used for final communication and organization. The actual strike began on June 24, Monday, the start of the workweek.

The exact demands the Chinese advanced are not entirely clear, as we know them only from English-language news accounts, which themselves are not fully consistent. The basic demands appear to have been wage parity with white workers, which meant an increase in wages to $40 per month, reduced workdays from eleven to ten hours in the open (some news reports mentioned a demand for an eight-hour workday), and shorter work shifts in the tunnels. The *Sacramento Daily Union* also reported that the workers protested "the right of the overseers of the company to either whip them or restrain them from leaving the road when they desire to seek other employment," though this claim is not corroborated elsewhere, and it was well known that Chinese workers regularly left the line for other employment. The strike apparently was not the first or last work stoppage by Chinese. According to the memoir of an associate of Strobridge, the construction boss had dealt with Chinese refusing to take shifts in Summit Tunnel work several times before the strike.

An agitated Strobridge wired Charles Crocker with news of the walkout: the "chinamen have all struck for $40 & time to be reduced from 11 to 10 hours a day." White workers reportedly continued to work. Crocker rushed out from Sacramento to go to the line and handle the matter personally. He and the other principals of the company immediately saw this confrontation as a showdown. Hopkins wrote Huntington that if the Chinese "are successful in this demand, then they *control* & their demands will be increased." He still wanted to believe, however, that the situation "will be controlled by us." He reminded Huntington that "when any commodity[?] is in demand beyond the natural supply, even Chinese labor, the price will tend to increase." Hopkins also expressed hope that five thousand freedmen would soon join the company workforce to use against the Chinese. They never arrived.

The Chinese strike continued, with the workers peacefully encamped and living on gathered supplies. On June 27, E. B. Crocker wrote again to Huntington and tried to explain what was going on from his point of view. "The truth is they are getting smart," he confessed in a remarkably revealing comment. It was known that the company was facing an acute labor shortage and "the prospect has been that we were not likely to get what we wanted." He acknowledged, "Who has stirred up the strike we don't know, but it was evidently planned and concocted." And most concerning to Crocker were the implications of this confrontation: the company "cannot submit to it —for they would soon strike again, & we would always be in their power." Crocker, in desperation, asked Huntington to get as many new workers as possible to come out. "The only safe way for us is to inundate this state and Nevada with laborers, Freedmen, Chinese, Japanese, all kinds of laborers." The company could put five thousand of them to work immediately.

E. B. Crocker wrote to Huntington again the very next day to report that his brother Charles had met personally with some of the leaders of the Chinese workers, including possibly Hung Wah, and informed them in no uncertain terms that the company would not pay more than $35 a month. He claimed that Charles had conversed directly with the Chinese in their "language," apparently a pidgin. Labor contractors, headmen, and workers all seemed to be united. No divisions among them at this moment were evident to company leaders.

In a stunning expression of militancy and a demand for equality, strike leaders told Charles Crocker, in his words, "Eight hours a day good for white man; all the same good for Chinaman." But Charles would not have it and supposedly told the strikers, "John Chinaman no make laws for me; I make laws for Chinaman. You sell for $35 a month, me buy; you sell for $40 and eight hours a day, me no buy." Taking a hardline position, in his view, was "the only way to deal with them." E. B. Crocker confided to Huntington that "this strike of the chinamen is the hardest blow we have had here . . . If we get over this without yielding," the shaken Crocker wrote, "it will be all right hereafter," but the outcome was completely uncertain. He again urged Huntington to "do what you can to get laborers sent here from the East." Hopkins also pressed Huntington once more to bring freedmen out to California. "A Negro labor force will tend to keep the chinese steady, as the chinese have kept the Irishmen quiet." Making use of racial and ethnic differences within the workforce had become a familiar employer weapon.

When histories mention the strike, the cited evidence comes largely, and unquestionably, from Charles Crocker, a problematic source. He later praised the Chinese for their discipline and orderliness during the strike, which is consistent with his observations elsewhere and reinforces his reputation as commander over his workforce. But other evidence sharply contrasts with the commonly circulated image of compliant Chinese. A brash young visitor from France, Comte Ludovic de Beauvoir, who was then touring America as part of a voyage around the world, personally witnessed the strike and saw that the Chinese were far from quiet. After describing the daunting work of building the railroad and the indispensability of the Chinese workers, de Beauvoir reported that the Chinese, while retaining many aspects of their traditional social organization and culture, had also quickly learned, in his opinion, "the worst part of Anglo-Saxon civilization," and that was the "strike." Why he thought Chinese independently knew nothing of collective action is unclear, other than that he himself was ignorant of Chinese life. But because the company refused to comply with their demands for a wage increase, he wrote, the Chinese "left their pickaxes buried in the sand and walk around with arms crossed with a truly occidental insolence." The French visitor included an etching of these rebellious Chinese that is sharply at odds with American images of inoffensive Chinese. De Beauvoir's depiction is of men who were arrogant and swaggering, evidently feeling very much empowered (below).

Then, after a week, the strike ended. The company had lost eight precious days of work. E. B. Crocker described to Huntington what he believed had transpired—the Chinese labor agents themselves had stopped supplying the workers with goods and provisions, and "they really began to suffer"—though Charles Crocker later claimed that he was the one who had had the food supplies stopped. "None of us went near them for a week," E. B. Crocker confided to Huntington. "We did not want to exhibit anxiety." This most telling comment reveals the very real private apprehension of the company leadership and their fear that they could not keep it secret from the Chinese. But then, Charles Crocker, E. B. Crocker wrote, "went up, & they gathered around him & he told them that he would not be dictated to, that he made the rules for them & not they for him." He also said that if they returned to work immediately, the company would not dock their wages for striking. If they refused, they would get no pay at all for June. The parties negotiated, with the Chinese asking for some concession in the length of the workweek or even a small increase in pay, but Charles Crocker still refused to budge. His position, according to E. B., was clear: by standing firm then, the company would prevent future strikes. Most of the Chinese decided to return to work, though some did not and threatened, it was alleged, "to whip those who went to work & burn their camps." Divisions among the Chinese had emerged, but Charles Crocker promised to protect those who resumed work. He pledged that his own security force would "shoot down any man that attempted to do the laborers any injury." He also had the local sheriff and armed guards on hand to ensure that there would be no fighting among the workers. It was a tough negotiation. The strike had completely exhausted Charles, according to his brother. They knew it had been a showdown.

The company never learned who organized and led the strike. Hopkins privately and wildly speculated that "chinese gamblers and opium traders" who were prohibited from the line had instigated it. That thousands of Chinese would have listened to such elements is improbable. But Charles Crocker wondered if agents from the UP were responsible for the unrest in an attempt to gain an advantage in the competition with the CPRR. One news report declared that "Designing White Men" were responsible for "instigating" the unrest. Again, these were dubious explanations. Company confusion about the Chinese and their action clearly reigned. The company did not even listen to itself: the letters among the principals show that they had a good sense of why the Chinese struck. The workers and the principals both knew that the labor shortage had placed the company in a difficult position. The strike exploited the CPRR's vulnerability. The Railroad Chinese, as E. B. Crocker had acutely observed, "had gotten smart."

Historical accounts that rely on Charles Crocker's public version of events reproduce a story that every boss tries to construct when confronted by worker adversaries: the employer must be unrelenting toward the challenge to authority and appear to be in full control. The message was critical to send to strikers but also to the curious public, including investors, who might have wondered about management control and the financial prospects of the company. The CPRR, highly dependent on public funding and private investments, was itself deeply invested, literally and figuratively, in its public image as an enterprise in sound condition and on track in its construction objectives. Charles Crocker had compelling reasons to appear tough and diminish the position of the Chinese. As the company knew, this was not just a showdown with the workers but also a make-or-break fight for its reputation and its very existence.

Though the company did not concede to the strikers' demands, it would be a mistake to conclude, as most historical accounts do, that the Chinese "lost." The workers, in a well-coordinated effort involving thousands, spread over miles of the train line, had defied the company, and it is clear from the internal record that the Chinese collective action had deeply shaken the principals. They had also gotten bad press. The company leadership would not forget the confrontation and realized that the workers could never be taken for granted. What is more, it appears that the company also quietly improved pay following the strike, at least for skilled and experienced Chinese workers, over the subsequent months. Wages for them went above $35 a month. Three years earlier, when Chinese first began working on the CPRR, their pay had been $26 a month. For some, it jumped 50 percent higher.

Did the Chinese themselves see the strike as a failure? Again, we have no firm evidence, but they could have believed that the effort itself, and not necessarily achieving its demand, was the important thing. The strike might be understood as being as much, or even more, a clash of cultural logics rather than an incident seen in standard Western labor-management terms. Collective action could be an important expression of will, a matter of achieving "face" and self-respect. The specific outcome was less significant than the act of defiance itself.

The self-discipline and organization of the striking Chinese did in fact favorably impress the railroad leadership. Sometime after the strike ended, Charles Crocker spoke about the conduct of the strikers. His words actually revealed a respect for their resolve and manner, for, unlike others, who would descend into "murder and drunkenness and disorder," Crocker said, the Chinese were entirely different. For them, it was "just like Sunday all along the work," which the no-nonsense Crocker meant as a compliment to their sobriety and seriousness. There was no violence or carousing. The Railroad Chinese, in protest as at work, were earnest and self-respecting.

After the strike ended, work resumed quickly to the satisfaction of the company. On July 6, E. B. Crocker reported to Huntington that "the Chinese are working harder than ever since the strike," and he thought there would be no further troubles. He believed they had been embarrassed by the whole episode, though he gave no specific evidence to support his comment. Significantly, recent arrivals from China were coming in good numbers. "Matters here begin to look more encouraging," Crocker wrote. "There is a rush of chinamen on the work. Most of the fresh arrivals from China go straight up to the work. It is all life & animation on the line." This last comment suggests another reason why the Railroad Chinese may have struck when they did. That the company's effort to recruit workers in China was achieving success was likely well known. Many new workers were on the way, and their arrival would weaken the bargaining position of those currently working. Best strike before the newcomers came on line.

Three weeks after the end of the strike, the company appeared pleased with the situation. E. B. Crocker reported that he was happy to show visiting officials from Washington that "construction [was] progressing rapidly." The "heavy work" toward the Summit Tunnel "is well started & as fast men come on they are put upon this portion." At the summit, the tunnels were nearly "all worked out during the winter," and now the men were "working upon the open cuts & the rock is rapidly disappearing." The work in the Truckee Canyon was nearing completion in excellent shape. And perhaps most important, "the laborers are working well" and seemed satisfied with their wages. Moreover, new recruits were arriving "from China in large numbers. The greater part of them immediately go to work on the railroad," and "the prospect is that we shall soon have all that we can work to advantage." Crocker reported that a federal official, a Mr. Johnson, "was highly pleased with the character of the work, & all he saw & his report to the Secretary of the Interior will be all that we can ask."

Railroad Chinese finally punctured the mountain on August 3, 1867, allowing "daylight," or rather really just air, to break through the long, dark tunnel, though more months of steady work, including through a second terrible winter, were needed to complete the excavation, form the roadbed, and lay track. Passenger trains would not safely pass through the tunnel until June 1868. "A wonder" is what the *Daily Alta California* declared Tunnel No. 6, or "The Great Bore," in November 1867, when the work was finally done. California should "well be proud that such a triumph of labor and skill has been executed in our own State and country."

THE STRIKE • 159

The labor crisis appeared to have ended—but then in the fall, E. B. Crocker again reported to Huntington that workers were not joining the line as quickly as before. "We have barely got men enough" to finish the work between Cisco and the summit, he wrote. Moreover, "a great many chinamen went back to China" recently. Among them were several of the leading Chinese labor contractors who had been supplying workers. Before they left, however, they said they would encourage "a large immigration to come over & work on the road next year." Crocker optimistically expected that they would "induce thousands to come over." Other agents of the company, and the Chinese handbills, would also follow up to attract further numbers, and the company worked with the steamship companies to offer "favorable arrangements" to bring workers over. "We want 100,000 chinamen here," Crocker declared, "so as to bring the price of labor down." Huntington replied that he was in full agreement about encouraging immigration but went even further: "I like the idea of your getting over more Chinamen; it would be all the better for us and the state if then should a half million come over in 1868." The entire population of the state of California in 1860 was under 400,000.

In important respects, "The Strike" resembles the prototypical modern workers' collective action. Employees presented demands to their employer for improvements with remarkable coordination and discipline that threw company officials into consternation but also earned their grudging respect. The strike also bore features of Chinese historical social action. They timed their action to correspond with an auspicious cosmological moment, and they conducted themselves with dignity. The long aftermath of the strike is also telling. Chinese workers on later railroads and other construction projects resorted to work stoppages and other disruptions of work with notable regularity. In August 1869, Chinese workers near Stockton, California, stopped working because of nonpayment of wages. In the 1870s, a thousand Chinese worked in the Santa Cruz Mountains, south of San Francisco, building rail lines for transportation to the coast and for exploitation of timber resources. As they had done on the Transcontinental, they graded, tunneled, and laid track. Many were probably veterans of work on the CPRR. During four years of labor, they impressed their employers as hardworking and honest but not docile. When mistreated or abused, the Chinese workers responded to defend themselves, sometimes violently, as reported in the local press. Memories of "The Strike" must have been strong. Chinese workers elsewhere regularly used work stoppages as a weapon. In 1875, three thousand Chinese workers in the Tehachapi Pass near Los Angeles struck over mistreatment. They had become veterans of class struggle. Action did not always have to end with achieving a material result. Sometimes it was enough to make a statement and display a righteousness that would one day be remembered and honored.

Observers who came to see the work being done by the Railroad Chinese in the High Sierra were not always respectful of the workers themselves—but they were uniformly impressed by the results. In the fall of 1867, Robert L. Harris, a green easterner and future railroad engineer, traveled along the CPRR construction route and left a memorable record of what he witnessed. Harris rode the line from Sacramento to Cisco and then hiked for the next three days up and over the summit. He found the scenery sublime but the ravines and steep cliffs terrifying. He encountered Chinese workers everywhere and in one instance stumbled across a crew of sixty who were scrambling for safety, just because, it seemed, of a few loud reports eight hundred feet away. He scoffed at the "frightened haste of these stupid fellows," as he put it, for running from noises he thought inconsequential. But then a white foreman quickly pulled Harris under cover just as a "*big* blast" boomed with "a sound as of thunder." The experienced Chinese knew the earlier noises had been warning explosions. "A young volcano showered its stones in the air," Harris wrote, "rending trees, tearing the ground, and falling about and over our hiding place." He was glad to leave his hiding place alive and uninjured. Chastened, he later arrived at Summit Camp, where he bedded down for the night, and even though he was exhausted, "the dull boom of blasts in the tunnel, three hundred feet distant" awakened him. Chinese workers were still working.

At another location, Harris reported on blasting to clear the route along a perilous cliff. One operation required three massive explosions to destroy a granite outcrop. He watched workers drill down eight feet, and then after several small explosions had widened a seam, they put in an immense load of powder. The huge explosion that followed tore "three thousand tons of granite" from "their long resting-place," he wrote. One seventy-ton boulder settled a third of a mile away. Another rock weighing 240 pounds was thrown clear "over the hotel at Donner

Lake—a distance of two-thirds of a mile." The writer had never seen such destruction and was glad to escape from the ominous tunnels and explosions, despite the stunning scenery of the High Sierra.

E. B. Crocker also visited the summit area in the fall of 1867 and witnessed the Railroad Chinese at work. What he saw made a deep impression on him and he privately shared his experience with Huntington. Crocker wrote that he was "perfectly astonished" to see the great progress in the "hard rock work." The skill of the Railroad Chinese fascinated him, their effort "done up scientifically," in his words. Mentioning no white supervisors or engineers directing the work, Crocker described an episode similar to the one Harris depicted. The Chinese "work the rock up to a face, then go back 3 to 4 feet from the face, put in a hole 12 to 20 feet deep, fill it with powder, which is only powerful enough to 'spring a seam,' cracking the rock enough so that powder can be poured in." Chinese then "put in powder by the keg, from 1 to 50 kegs according to its size. The effect is to blow the greater part of the rock clear over the cliff & out of the way. It is a sight to see these heavy seam blasts go off. It makes the earth shake like an earthquake. But the result is that the rock rapidly disappears & begins to look quite like a R.R. there." Crocker's privately shared account not only provides a vivid sense of the demanding and dangerous work that Chinese completed but also reveals once again how deeply their work impressed company leaders.

After the hard winter of 1865–66, the company principals realized that they needed a radical alternative to protect the miles of laid track and roadbed from heavy snows and avalanches or progress would be delayed by weeks in the main construction season. This realization was sped along by another bout of awful weather. During the winter of 1867–68, snow became so compacted that twelve of the largest locomotives coupled together could not clear the track. Banks of the stuff froze to a depth of ten to thirty feet. The engines backed up and then slammed ahead at the white mass but made only a few feet of progress. The wear and tear on the machines and track worried the company management, and they stopped the frustrating assault. At great expense of money and time, thousands of Railroad Chinese had to use picks and shovels to remove snow and ice before track work could resume.

The company developed a radical idea to solve the problem, and it too would involve Chinese: they would help build miles of snow sheds to protect the line. Arthur Brown, the engineer responsible for the effort, thought the expense of building miles of wood structures was "appalling and unprecedented in railroad construction," yet the company decided there was no alternative.

The previous summer, the company had directed its workers to build test structures that covered five miles of the roadbed. The longest shed was half a mile in length. At the start of the work season in the spring of 1868, the company assigned 2,500 workers, mainly Chinese, to complete thirty more miles of structures. The sheds usually had open sides but with gabled roofs to keep the snow from building up and crushing the structure. Snow galleries were similar but had roofs that slanted up in the direction of the mountain slope so that accumulated snow would slide off. The interior of the sheds measured sixteen feet wide by seventeen and a half feet high to accommodate the trains. The galleries were about the same size but could have wide roofs, some extending a hundred feet or more up the slope of the mountain so that snow could move down the mountain and over the structure. In total, when completed in 1869, sheds and galleries extended thirty-seven miles in length and had used 65 million feet of timber and nine hundred tons of bolts and spikes.

Chinese were linked to this effort in different ways. They graded, dug foundations, and assisted the carpenters. They also helped indirectly. The structures required an enormous quantity of wood, much of it logged and shaped right in the Sierra from hastily constructed mills along the route. They used huge saws to make the planks, and also produced cordwood and charcoal for locomotive fuel. One reporter told of seeing dozens of sawmills and swarms of "laborers of every nationality and hue — Europeans, Americans, Africans and Asiatics (the latter immensely preponderating in number) — engaged in cutting down and preparing the timber for the road." Hundreds of Chinese stayed on as woodworkers in the mountains and in Nevada after the completion of the line.

The company realized, however, that the wooden structures that protected the tracks themselves required their own protection. Winds and snowslides swept away structures or damaged them so badly that the debris created new problems. The horizontal pressure from snowdrifts snapped supports. The snow could move like a glacier with relentless force and carry away trestles and other structures. At some locations, workers erected embankments and walls that extended the slope of the mountain so that snow would slide up over the sheds. In other locations, they built massive retaining walls against snowbanks that could reach eighty feet in height. Engineer Lewis M. Clement reported that at one stretch of the line workers built retaining walls protecting four miles of the track.

The most dramatic example of one of these Chinese retaining walls, which still stands, is located between Tunnels No. 7 and 8 at the summit. A steep ravine cleaved the planned road and it had to be spanned. Railroad Chinese built an immense retaining wall up the ravine to create a roadbed using stone excavated from the tunnels. Begun in the fall of 1867, the work was stopped by winter snows. It resumed early the next spring, though tall snowdrifts continued to blanket the area. Workers bored tunnels under the snow to the base of the ravine, where they brought excavated stone and built upward. Using chisels and a masonry technique employed in China, they hand-cut the granite to make blocks forty to fifty inches long and twelve to twenty inches tall. Smaller pieces fit in the gaps. The whole effort was a giant three-dimensional jigsaw puzzle, with stones interlocking to hold together. No mortar was used. The wall is almost two hundred feet long and seventy-five feet tall and shaped like an inverted pyramid, though deepest at its base set into the mountain. There it is eighty-two feet deep compared to seventeen feet at the top. Hidden from view is a stable rock culvert to divert water. Amazingly, 150 years later it remains not just standing but solid, a marvel of construction. Similar hand-carved rock walls built by Chinese from that era are still found all around northern California today. In 1984 the Truckee-Donner Historical Society named it the "China Wall of the Sierra" and laid a plaque to commemorate the achievement. The wall stands as evidence, according to the plaque, of the "Asian 'Master Builders' who left an indelible mark on the history of California and the West."

Such accolades came at great cost. Company leaders rarely spoke directly about the risks their workers faced, but comments about the construction effort and journalists' reports include many references to tremendous dangers from accidents and horrific working conditions. Engineer Gilliss, for example, recalled the terror of snowslides. During winter in the Sierra, slides were so frequent that work at the surface often had to be suspended. Wooden structures could not provide safety: avalanches swept "over the shanties of the laborers" and buried them. The snowslides were "rapid and noiseless" and would sweep away entire teams of men. He recalled that at Tunnel No. 10, a slide killed fifteen or twenty Railroad Chinese in just this way. (Chapter 10 will examine death on the line in depth.)

A New York reporter recorded his impression on encountering the High Sierra: at Crested Peak, "the rugged precipice towers above you a thousand feet, with its shattered sides looking dreadfully as if they wanted to drop an immense fragment of rock on your head." Nevertheless, "Chinese courage," as he put it, rose to the occasion and attacked the cliffs. In the winter, though, work became "impossible," he wrote. "Avalanches accumulate on crested peak, and breaking away, no one knows when, come crashing down the mountain side." Twenty years after the winters of the late 1860s, Alfred E. Davis, a longtime California businessman and railroad executive himself, tried to describe the frightful winters in the Sierra to those who had not experienced them firsthand in the years before the railroad. Travel through the high country was almost impossible because of the winds, accumulated snow, and the omnipresent dangers. "Great bodies of snow" hung on slopes and avalanched down unpredictably. The challenges to construction at the time were "almost impossible to measure," he said. "Think beyond human calculation."

Even snow at rest could maim. As late as the spring of 1868, many Railroad Chinese refused to work in the summit area because of the blistering intensity of light reflected from the snow. Mark Hopkins privately reported to Huntington that the only Chinese who did work were those, in his words, willing to go "blind & [have] their faces pealed [sic] and seared as though they had been scalded in the face with scalding water." E. B. Crocker reported similarly to Huntington, saying that the "snow had blinded a good many, & we have had to buy up all the cheap goggles in the market," adding, "Think of that. What an item in railroad building." Unsurprisingly, Crocker noted that many of the Chinese harbored "a horror of snow." Despite these conditions, more than five hundred of them went out to remove the snow from the tracks in the summit area. These workers were making their mark, on astonished CPRR officials as in the stubborn granite, proving their determination to push the line through the summit.

8

TRUCKEE

The western states of America are sparsely populated for such a large land area . . . Through opening mines, exploiting wastelands, and constructing railways, cities have been gradually formed, of which the city of San Francisco is especially prosperous. All the former work was dependent on recruiting Chinese laborers and by this opportunity Chinese people could earn their living.

— MEMOIR OF ZHANG YUNHUAN, 1886

THE SUMMIT TUNNEL FINALLY OPENED TO PASSENGERS ON June 18, 1868. Its completion meant that a train could run all the way from Sacramento to Reno, Nevada, a distance of 154 miles, on "the grandest engineering feat ever attempted by man," as the *Alta California* announced.

The newspaper's special correspondent, one of the first passengers to cross the Sierra Nevada by rail, hopped aboard the inaugural passenger train in Sacramento to make the historic journey. His eyewitness account provides a vivid sense of the extreme physical conditions the construction workers faced. Full of excitement and awe, his travelogue is also replete with references to the Chinese laborers and inspires wonder at their experiences in building the line through the Sierra.

The writer describes the changing scenery as the steam-driven train leaves the bucolic Central Valley and passes through the towns of Newcastle, Auburn, and then Clipper Gap. Three hours after leaving Sacramento, the train passes through Colfax and navigates around the infamous Cape Horn. The roadbed is carved into the slope of the mountain, and the train needs to snake along a perilous ledge. "Nervous passengers begin to look around anxiously," the correspondent writes, "peering with evident trepidation down into the depths below," where a branch of the American River flows 1,200 feet beneath them.

At Secret Town, the train reaches 2,985 feet, and peaks appear ahead that are covered with snow. Though it is mid-June, passengers soon see snow covering the ground next to the track and feel the cold air coming down from the mountains. They are thrown back in their seats by the steep climb.

At sixty-seven miles from Sacramento, the train reaches Dutch Flat, and at Shady Run Station, the train reaches the first tunnel, seventy-five miles from Sacramento. It is five hundred feet in length and 4,500 feet above sea level. Plenty of snow still covers the ground next to the track, and soon the train passes through towering drifts, the way cleared by men working with shovels. "Chinamen are swarming all along the road," the writer records, and "they have nearly finished their work in this vicinity and are packing up their traps preparatory to passing on over the summit" into Nevada. At more than one hundred miles from Sacramento, the train enters Summit Valley, at 6,800 feet elevation, and then it reaches Summit Tunnel, 1,659 feet in length. Great banks of snow, ice, and rock still cap the summit at more than 7,000 feet.

At Summit Tunnel, the train must stop. Cars that have jumped the track and other obstacles on the track ahead require the writer and other passengers to disembark and walk carefully through the frigid "Great Bore." Water pours "down in torrents from numberless crevices and seams in the granite walls and roof of the long, dark, cavernous tunnel," adding to the passengers' anxieties over whether they will ever arrive at their destination.

Upon finally emerging in the open, the writer finds many Chinese teams shoveling away the snow and granite rock brought down by winter slides. The travelers must wait hours before the repairs are made on the line and they can return to a train. It makes only halting forward progress, however, with snowslides and rock still needing to be cleared from the track—and with massive snowbanks hemming the train in on both sides. Snow scrapes the sides of the train in the narrow passageway, "the closest fit imaginable."

They pass through more tunnels, ranging from 100 to 863 feet in length, where the writer sees "great masses of solid blue ice, hanging down from the walls like stalactites and stalagmites." Finally, the train begins to descend the eastern slope of Donner Pass on the just

completed rail line. It winds carefully and slowly along the "precipitous mountain-sides," with beautiful Donner Lake below. Because of
switchbacks, seven miles of track are needed to advance just a quarter
of a mile eastward. Pristine deep blue Lake Tahoe comes into view
to the south. Workers are everywhere, cutting trees for the timber
needed for the road. The passing of this first passenger train excites
even the toughened Chinese workers along the route. With the swinging of their broad-brimmed hats "and loud, uncouth shouts," the men
welcome the roaring machine. The report appears to have inspired artist Joseph Becker's work "Across the Continent," seen in chapter 6.

The correspondent returns their greeting. Inspired and impressed,
he praises the Chinese worker, who, "with his patient toil," and with
American energy and capital, "has broken down the great barrier [be-
tween East and West] at last and opened over it the greatest highway
yet created for the march of commerce and civilization around the
globe."

No doubt the author was thinking of sites beyond Truckee, the small
mountain town just past Lake Donner into which his train chugged after leaving the tunnels and switchbacks of Donner Pass. He was certainly looking, too, beyond Reno — the terminus for this train ride, and
a town that had appeared "like magic within a month" after the arrival
of the CPRR. Salt Lake City, in the vicinity of which the competing
railroad companies would join their lines, was still more than five hundred miles farther on, and the great centers of American commerce —
Chicago, New York, Philadelphia — hundreds, even thousands of miles
farther still.

But if the correspondent's imagination was fired by the little town
of Truckee, he could be forgiven. For the settlement — which had been
chosen as a forward camp for railroad workers back when the CPRR
was still climbing into the western foothills of the Sierra — provided
a measure of comfort and security after traversing the intimidating
western slope of the Sierra. It was a place that the Railroad Chinese
would have known well — a place where they could satisfy their fierce
yearnings for diversion and physical release and escape the monotony
and stress of their labor, beyond the few hours after work and on Sunday when they could catch some rest and while away their precious
free time drinking, smoking, or gambling in their encampments. Getting to a town that offered real pleasures — comfortable lodging, good

food, sex, and opium—would have been a blessing. Those diversions and more could be found in the basin below Donner Pass at Truckee.

Truckee lay a few miles east of the summit and near the border with Nevada. Native people had long lived in the area, whose name itself may be that of an Indian chief. Located in a broad basin at six thousand feet in elevation on the eastern slope of the Sierra, Truckee enjoys pleasant weather through much of the year, ample water resources, great stands of timber, and fertile land for agriculture. For travelers coming from the east, the settlement provided welcome relief from the parched Nevada deserts and the arduous trek up the eastern slope. For those coming from the west, Truckee offered respite after crossing through the High Sierra. Close by are Donner Lake, Lake Tahoe, and several rushing rivers. Euro-Americans began to settle there following the Gold Rush, but the town took on more importance after the Comstock silver strike in 1859, as thousands traveled from California through Truckee to get to Nevada. A few years later, the CPRR made it the base of operations for its work on the long stretch between Sacramento and Reno.

Chinese had made up a prominent part of Nevada County, where Truckee is located, as early as 1852, when they formed the largest non-white segment of the population—almost 18 percent of about 22,000 people, a larger number than Native Americans. Most Chinese were gold miners along the Yuba River, which flowed through the county, but there were also many merchants, launderers, farmers, and storekeepers in towns such as Washington, Nevada City, North Bloomfield, and Grass Valley. Some of the worst violence against Chinese in California had also occurred in the region. They were frequent targets for robbery, torture, arson, and murder, highlighted by the brutal killing of Ling Sing in 1854, discussed earlier in this book.

Chinese began to settle in Truckee in the mid-1860s, attracted by the work in the growing timber industry related to the railroad and mining operations in the area. The CPRR line reached the town and made it a base of operations in mid-1868.

Following the arrival of the CPRR line, the Chinese population steadily grew. In winter, hundreds of furloughed workers holed up there to wait out the winter storms until the next work season. Many lived in temporary or abandoned structures. One old barn collapsed under the weight of a winter snow, killing four Railroad Chinese. Others enjoyed the safety and comfort of the China Hotel in the middle of town. Some operated stores, groceries, and other establishments that catered to Chinese. One place was even known as the Oriental Restaurant. Chinese also worked for white residents, providing medical care and other services. From information in the official census of 1870, we know that Truckee was a diverse, multiracial town, with many Chinese, native-born whites, European and Canadian immigrants, a handful of African Americans, including one family with children, and mixed-raced peoples, three of whom are identified as "mulattoes" who were barbers. Four residents hailed from Mexico and one from faraway India. Described at the time as "one of the most populous and bustling places" on the CPRR line, it was a rough-and-tumble hell on wheels, as many of the towns that sprang up along the railroad line were called, with twenty-five saloons in 1868. There, high in the Sierra, it became the location of a major "Chinatown."

Truckee became the center of life for many Railroad Chinese during the construction in the High Sierra and then for years after the line was completed. From the mid-1860s until the 1880s, when hostile whites drove almost all of them out of town in what became the infamous "Truckee method" of expulsion, Truckee had one of the largest Chinese populations in the country. Their presence, which once appeared to be permanent, helped make early Truckee one of the liveliest towns in the state. Today it is a vacation hub, especially for winter snow sports and summer mountain recreation, but there is almost no sign, except in the local museum, that Chinese had once helped establish the settlement and had been an integral and important part of its life. Looking at Chinese life in Truckee provides a sense of the lived experiences of Railroad Chinese when they were not at work.

In 1870, Chinese constituted at least 30 percent of the town's total resident population of 1,580 and 45 percent of its workforce. Other sources estimated the Chinese population as exceeding one thousand. The seasons and fluctuating availability of work made the population count fluid. Hundreds of Chinese on the census rolls were identified as railroad workers, laborers, and wood choppers. They enjoyed a busy Chinese community that included their own opera theater, restaurants, barbershops, teahouses, grocery stores, boardinghouses, fraternal associations, gambling dens, herbal stores, and brothels. Some Chinese lived and worked next door to whites, while others were concentrated in a specific section of the town. A New York reporter who visited Truckee in 1869 described it as a "city of John Chinamen" with "long streets of Chinese laundries, barber stores, ten stores, peanut stands, and nondescript booths," all "adorned" with big signs solely in Chinese. The census also listed four of the town's five doctors as Chinese. The fifth was French. Ah Faw, Sin Wo, Kite To, and Ah Sum were thirty to thirty-five years of age and were trained in traditional Chinese medical practices. Twenty Chinese were listed as cooks, and all, or almost all, of the town's laundrymen, vegetable farmers, and peddlers were Chinese. Others were prominent businessmen, such as Fong Lee, who had already accumulated real and personal wealth in the thousands of dollars and sported a flashy diamond ring on his hand. Chinese labor contractors advertised in the town's English-language newspaper that they could provide any number of Chinese laborers on demand. Almost all of the Chinese residents of the town were male, with just twenty-four listed as female, twenty-two of whom were identified as prostitutes. (It is unclear whether these are self-designations or assigned by another party.) Nine of them were identified as younger than twenty years of age, with Ah Fong and He Low Tow both listed as just sixteen years of age. The oldest was forty, but most were in their early twenties and lived in small groups in the center of town. One household included prostitutes named, curiously, Bling Gouie, age twenty, Bling Ti He, twenty-two, and Bling Gum, twenty-five, possibly all sisters. They lived together with Ah How, age forty, a "wash man." Two white women were also identified as prostitutes but lived at different addresses.

The Chinese prostitutes likely lived, and worked, in ramshackle, hastily constructed wood structures. These were likely sordid affairs, as they usually were in San Francisco's Chinese quarter. Mountain town Truckee held no pleasure palaces where prostitutes dressed in silk, sweet incense filled the air of plush parlors, and customers had lots of money to spend. As in other towns in the rural and mining areas of the region, Truckee's prostitutes had to survive under sorry, even abysmal, conditions.

Most Chinese males ranged in age from their teens to their thirties, with the average age in the mid-twenties. Storekeepers and gamblers were older, in their late thirties and forties. One Chinese male-female couple is listed as married, and an infant, recorded as having been born in California, lived with a Chinese woman described as someone "keeping house." The child's name was Colfax Ah, likely in honor of Vice President Schuyler Colfax, who passed through Truckee in October 1869. He may even have witnessed the marriage of the baby's parents. Chinese naming practices for their children in America favored auspicious names, such as those of political leaders. The youngster's real surname, though, and his fate have been lost forever. Colfax Ah nevertheless appears to mark the beginning for Truckee's Chinese of an American-born and permanent presence in the town. Tax assessor's records show thirty-five Chinese property owners, mostly store owners, grocers, and herbalists. One even identified himself as a jeweler. Evidently there was a market for someone with his skills and goods. More Chinese in Truckee would also soon marry one another in Western legal and social fashion and have children there. Though Chinese continued to expand their commercial activities, most populated the ranks of wage workers at timber and railroad companies. Some even participated in Fourth of July celebrations. Truckee's many Chinese proletarians and store owners formed a highly visible and prominent element in the community, and their future at this key junction of the CPRR appeared for the moment to be hopeful and relatively secure.

As they did elsewhere, Truckee Chinese enjoyed traditional leisure activities such as kite flying, music and singing, and shuttlecock kicking (*jianzi*), precursor of today's hacky sack. Journalists mentioned seeing books for sale in Chinese stores and many Chinese reading during their leisure time. Fictional tales of adventure, desire, magic, spirits, and political intrigue were favorites among Chinese readers. They also wrote letters home and received mail from relatives and friends. Reading these out loud would entertain local friends.

The most common leisure activity for Railroad Chinese was gambling. It had been an accepted part of life in southern China, especially in towns and cities, and Chinese brought thousand-year-old games with them to America. Abundant evidence of such gaming has been found at Railroad Chinese campsites, including discarded six-sided dice, playing cards, dominoes, various forms of tokens including buttons, and small-denomination coins. Some Chinese games required strategy and involved just two or three players, such as dominoes or the board games *weiqi*, or "Go" in the West, and "Chinese chess" (*xiangqi*), which is similar to present-day Western chess. These are lightweight and simple to set up, and could easily be played at a campsite. Games of chance using dice or cards invited wagering, but serious gambling required more elaborate arrangements in the social halls of Truckee.

The most popular game for Chinese in nineteenth-century America was *fantan* (repeated division), which bears similarities to today's roulette. It was simple to play, but captivating with its suspense. A croupier would dump a bowlful of tokens, such as buttons, coins, or even dried beans, onto a square cloth or mat. He would carefully remove four of these at a time with a pointed stick, but before he did so, players numbering as many as sixty would crowd around the table, placing their bets on the number of tokens, from one to four, that would remain with the last removal. Winnings were based on the odds of covering one or several numbers, minus a cut for the house, of course.

Another extremely popular game, still widely played today, was called *baige piao* (white pigeon script), the forerunner of today's lotto, keno, and even bingo. The game's name may have come from the old practice of using homing pigeons to deliver woodblock-printed paper game sheets. These typically listed eighty different Chinese characters arranged in a grid of small boxes. Bettors would black out their choices and return the sheet to the lottery operator, who would draw tokens with characters on them from a container to determine winners, if any. (As the game became Americanized, numbers replaced characters.) It was easily and quickly played and did not require a bettor to be present at the drawing, so any number of people could bet with the use of runners. Odds heavily favored the gambling houses, which made hefty profits off the hardworking Railroad Chinese. Dens could operate all day and night and further separate workers from their savings by selling them other pleasures such as women, food, and opium. Some men became professional gamblers and are listed officially as such on the census rolls. The Chinese-owned gambling dens could also operate behind groceries and other storefronts, making the owners wealthier than selling cabbage.

By the time the Pacific Railway reached Truckee in April 1868, one person who would have been badly in need of its diversions was Hung

Wah. After enjoying a hot hand in the first half of 1866, Hung Wah suffered a devastating reversal of fortune. His numbers appear to have dropped precipitously in the late summer and fall of that year, to just a couple of hundred workers for August and September—a stark contrast to the nine hundred workers he had commanded in July. Then listings for him in the payroll record disappear for the rest of 1866, the last year for which there are extant records.

The drop-off in Hung Wah's business may have been temporary, but another explanation could be that he faced increasing competition from the Euro-American-owned companies that were taking over more and more of the lucrative contracting business. White-owned companies like Egbert, Booth and, most important, Sisson, Wallace accounted for a fast-growing proportion of the workers. In June 1866, Sisson received almost $61,000, which equated to about two thousand workers. An independent businessman in San Francisco named Cornelius Koopmanschap became perhaps the largest individual labor contractor in these years. Little is known about him and his operation, but he was said to have arranged for hundreds, and possibly thousands, of Chinese to come to the United States and work for the CPRR.

Turmoil in his personal life may also have disrupted Hung Wah's business. On the evening of January 9, 1867, his longtime Auburn business partner and friend William McDaniel was brutally murdered in the store he kept across the street from Hung Wah's. McDaniel's wife found her husband's lifeless body with deep cuts to the back of his head and his neck, which severed his spinal column. She reported that she had seen a Chinese man fleeing the scene, though she did not get a good look at his face. A bloody hatchet was found beneath the body, and robbery was assumed to be the motive. The safe was open and partially emptied. Outraged local whites immediately raised $3,000 as a reward for anyone who would identify the perpetrator. Hung Wah personally took the lead among Chinese to raise an additional $1,000, and California governor Frederick Low contributed a further $500 to the reward.

The people of Auburn, whites and Chinese alike, were deeply distraught. The local newspaper described McDaniel as one of Auburn's "best and most estimable citizens." All the town's businesses shut down for his well-attended funeral. Chinese deeply mourned too. McDaniel had been friendly with many of them, and he and his family even lived in the Chinese neighborhood. To honor his death, local Chinese, likely including Hung Wah, commissioned a special large headstone for his grave site. Alongside the English inscriptions on it are Chinese characters honoring McDaniel's memory, chiseled into the marble with skill and care. The marker remains standing in Auburn's old cemetery, a monument to a rare moment of friendship in tragedy in early white-Chinese relations in California.

Within two weeks of the crime, a white resident identified as a former tax collector and self-declared speaker of Chinese provided information to the police about the crime and offered a lurid account. While hidden in evening shadows outside Hung Wah's store, the informant said he overheard men known as Ah Tom and Ah Sing surreptitiously talking about the murder. Ah Sing, identified as an employee of Hung Wah, allegedly disclosed that he had killed McDaniel. The two then separated, with Ah Tom reportedly going to a gambling house and Ah Sing to a brothel. After hearing further incriminating conversations between the men over the next two days, the informant reported to the authorities, who found McDaniel's property hidden among Ah Sing's belongings kept in Hung Wah's store. At Ah Sing's trial, Ah Tom vehemently denied that the conversations ever occurred, but McDaniel's widow testified that it was Ah Sing whom she had seen at the scene, on the basis of his body size and "appearance in these clothes" that he wore in the courtroom. A jury soon found Ah Sing guilty of murder, and the court sentenced him to hang for the crime. Invited by the town's sheriff, twenty townspeople, including Hung Wah himself, witnessed the execution on June 28. Just before a noose was placed around Ah Sing's neck, he reportedly attempted to speak to Hung Wah in "broken English." What was said has been lost to history.

A year later, and one month after the Summit Tunnel opened for business, Hung Wah suffered further misfortune. In July 1868 a huge fire destroyed the entire contents of his shuttered store in Auburn's Chinatown. No one was present or injured. The cause was highly suspect, for, as the local newspaper reported, the "fire was undoubtedly the work of an incendiary." The press did not speculate about what if any connection there might have been between the fire and the McDaniel murder.

Given his string of bad luck, it would not be surprising if Hung Wah had sought comfort in Truckee in the fall of 1868. It had been a tough work season; he would have needed time away from the line and life in the rude encampments there. To get into town, he could simply have hopped aboard a supply train that regularly went up and down the line.

Once in Truckee, Hung Wah would have had any number of options for taking his mind off his troubles. If he didn't go straight to a gambling parlor, he could have visited a barber in the Chinese section of town to have a good shave, shampoo, and bath to remove the accumulated grime from his body. Having a Chinese physician, perhaps Ah Faw, attend to an ailment might be his next stop. While there, he could purchase bags of medicinal herbs and other ingredients from China for tonics he would make back at his camp. With the essentials out of the way, he might visit eighteen-year-old prostitute Ah Fong, who lived right next door to Ah Faw. He might even have paid a bit more to her keeper so he could linger a while longer to enjoy her touch and scent.

Paying for sex probably did not trouble Railroad Chinese like Hung Wah. Even Ah Fong's miserable life might not have given him pause. Prostitutes of all backgrounds and from around the world were everywhere in the West. Other Chinese men, even devout Christians, thought of visiting a brothel as simply "taking a rest."

If Hung Wah happened to visit the gambling house in Truckee, and if fortune smiled on him, he might have treated himself — and perhaps some friends — to a restaurant meal of delicacies such as imported preserved duck eggs (*pidan*), fresh steamed white rice with fatty pork sausage made by a Chinese butcher in Virginia City, Nevada, and just harvested bok choy (*baicai*), grown in town. A little dish of salty, pungent *doufuru*, fermented bean cake and a specialty from Siyi, might have been served as a condiment on the side. He could finish the meal with a hot bowl of "purple soup" (*jicaitang*), made from pork bones and seaweed, which gave it its rich, dark color. On his way back to the train line, he could even have enjoyed a few dried, sweet lychee (*lizhi*) imported from tropical southern China. If he were feeling generous, he could have brought black tea from his home region, packed inside a hollowed-out dried orange peel, back to camp to share with friends. It would have given them a special taste of home — memories to savor in the hard times ahead.

• • •

Towns along the railroad route had many appealing features, but none would have excited the Railroad Chinese so much as the brothels. The reason was simple: there were no women among the thousands of Chinese who worked on the Transcontinental, and very few, other than prostitutes, lived in any of the small towns along the line.

Payroll records, memoirs, and newspaper reportage mention not one Chinese woman working for the CPRR before Promontory. Later census rolls and the records of other railroads name a few Chinese females, including ten who lived in Truckee in 1880 and were listed as working for the railroad in undisclosed capacities, but none appear to have worked during the construction of the Pacific Railway. Physical absence from the line, however, did not mean that women were unimportant or not part of the Railroad Chinese story. They were very much a part of the lived experience of the Chinese workers, fully present in their emotions, dreams, and aspirations, as well as on occasion in their physical lives away from the rail line.

The desperation of Chinese males for contact with Chinese females produced riotous moments such as the incident described by a reporter who witnessed the arrival of almost four hundred Chinese women on board the steamer *China* in San Francisco in March 1869. "Many hundreds" of Chinese men crowded the dock to watch the disembarkation and processing of the women. One by one they were brought up from steerage to the wharf, a teasing performance that only raised the men's level of "excitement" to "its highest pitch." The strenuous efforts of the entire police force were required to control the situation and keep the men away from the women. After disembarking, the women were segregated at one end of the dock and searched for contraband. After they received clearance, police placed them in wagons and carts to take them to different locations in the city. An officer accompanied each vehicle to protect the women, but Chinese men still tried to grab them. Loud, angry arguments that almost broke out into fighting escalated among the competing men as they tried to pull women, and the accompanying police officers, from the vehicles. Not until evening did the scene finally quiet.

Visiting brothels was the crudest interaction Railroad Chinese regularly had with Chinese women, and indeed prostitution was a disreputable and marginal activity in China. The Reverend Otis Gibson, who had served as a missionary in China for a decade before he returned to

America and worked among Chinese in California, held that the level of "chastity" in China was as high as in America and that prostitution was considered just as degrading.

But in America, where the sex imbalance between Chinese men and women was so great, and the ties of marriage and family weak to non-existent, frequenting prostitutes became a common activity for many Chinese men. The large amounts of ready cash they gained from mining and wage work meant they had disposable income far beyond what they ever had in China. In 1868 the Six Companies, which vehemently condemned prostitution for moral, social, and political reasons, estimated the number of Chinese prostitutes in California in the thousands. Other estimates placed the percentage of Chinese female prostitutes in San Francisco from 1860 to the early 1880s in the range of 70 to 90 percent of all Chinese females. The number of Chinese prostitutes in San Francisco in the late 1870s may have been as high as 1,200. The proportion of Chinese prostitutes in the population of small towns in the rural areas could rival that in San Francisco. Approximately 321 Chinese lived in Grass Valley in 1870, and almost all of the thirty-four females were considered prostitutes. In Nevada City in 1870, the census listed more than one hundred Chinese females living in the city, with ninety-four identified as prostitutes. Even allowing for exaggeration of the numbers because of anti-Chinese prejudices that held Chinese women to be immoral and Chinese men debased, the numbers still indicate that a very large number of Chinese women worked as prostitutes.

Life for most of these women, who were often bought and sold by Chinese criminals, was horrible and short. Enslaved as prisoners or sold by impoverished parents in China, indentured young women were brought by traders to America, where they were treated as commercial property. Death by their own hand or from illness took many at an early age. Others found an escape either by fleeing to Christian missions for protection or by buying their way out of their condition. Some married and left the trade. In the 1870s, a young woman in her teens might be obtained in China for as little as $50 and then sold in America for $1,000. These transactions were sometimes conducted as formal business dealings, with women signing contracts stipulating prostitution work as repayment for the loan of money, passage expenses, and living costs. A prostitute could produce as much as $2,500 profit for her owner in a single year.

In the 1870s, for example, an estimated seventy Chinese prostitutes lived in Virginia City, Nevada—almost the entire Chinese female population. Bought in San Francisco for $200, they were resold in the area of the Comstock Lode for between $800 and $1,000. The high point in numbers of Chinese prostitutes in California appears to have been the 1860s through the 1870s, during the construction of the CPRR. After its completion, the number steadily fell. The proportion of Chinese prostitutes in San Francisco in 1860 was almost six hundred out of a total Chinese female population of 681, or more than 85 percent; in 1870 there were approximately 1,500 Chinese prostitutes in a female population of 2,000, or 71 percent, and in 1880, an estimated 435 prostitutes out of 2,000 females, or about 21 percent. In Truckee, Chinese prostitutes declined in number too. The 1880 census lists none. The fall in numbers appears to have been the result of local suppression efforts and federal legislation that specifically targeted Chinese women who were suspected of being prostitutes, as well as a growing number of women who exited the trade and married (sometimes to Chinese railroad workers). From the 1870s onward, records from throughout California show that the number of Chinese, men and women, who married increased steadily.

Though many Chinese men frequented brothels, community leaders forcefully condemned prostitution and the enslavement of women. Prostitution caused great harm, according to an alarmed Six Companies in 1868, when it published an open call to the state to find ways to suppress the activity. Because of the sex business, the organization declared, "the industrious become idlers" and "the rich become poor. Poverty leads to shamelessness; shamelessness breeds lawlessness." Crime, the group maintained, was "on the rise as thievery and robbery occur more and more, causing strife and disorder." Prostitution, literally and metaphorically for the Six Companies, was "a disease for the country." Ruthless criminals who controlled the trade, which was closely linked to opium and gambling, also threatened the authority of legitimate merchants. For all these reasons, the Six Companies wanted California to stop the business entirely and prevent the further entry of Chinese prostitutes into the state.

This public and private outcry against Chinese prostitution elicited much personal testimony from those caught up in the trade. Some came forward to offer moving accounts that exposed the human tragedy; these are among the most numerous first-person reports collected from Chinese about their lives in nineteenth-century America. Even if we allow for an element of sensationalism, the accounts are still heartbreaking. The Reverend William Loomis, a leading Christian missionary among Chinese in America, recorded one unusual report from a man named Chen Ha, who recounted his tragic story on a long poster publicly mounted in San Francisco in 1868. Two years earlier, in 1866, he declared, bandits overran his home village of San. They killed many male villagers and took women and children captive, including his sister Ah Shau. He learned from his father that Ah Shau had been taken to California, where she was forced into prostitution. Chen Ha, tormented by the anguish he imagined she suffered, cried out in his circular: "Alas! Alas! Who that has a sister would endure the thought of her being taken to a brothel? A thousand shames!" Chen Ha, directed by his father, implored his village brethren in America to help him locate his dear sister and return her home. He implored his countrymen to help "rescue her from the torments inflicted by the keepers of the brothels" and "avert dishonor and shame from our native town." Despite valiant efforts, Chen Ha never succeeded in finding her.

A few years later, the moving testimony of Sing Kum, a young woman forced into prostitution at seventeen, came to the public. She had arrived in California as an indentured prostitute in 1871 and over several years was bought and sold four times. "My last mistress," she reported, "was very cruel to me; she used to whip me, pull my hair, and pinch the inside of my cheeks." Unable to endure her life any longer, Sing Kum escaped and took refuge in a Christian mission home for Chinese prostitutes. She later became a church worker. Hundreds of Chinese prostitutes fled to these mission sanctuaries to escape their sexual slavery, and many eventually married Chinese Christians.

Some Chinese prostitutes appear to have had less agonizing experiences. Women sometimes entered into agreements with dealers to prostitute themselves for a period of time, such as four years, in return for a cut of the income or to pay off a debt. Though it is sometimes unclear whether contracts were voluntary and free from coercion, there is evidence that women on occasion could be released from their contract once its terms were met. Afterward, the former prostitute might even become a madam herself, owning other Chinese women.

In the mid-nineteenth century, one woman became infamous in

America in such a way. Ah Toy, who is sometimes identified as the first Chinese prostitute in America, arrived in the United States in late 1848 or early 1849 from Hong Kong at twenty years of age. She was married in China but left for America to become an independent prostitute. Described at the time as tall, English-speaking, and alluring, she quickly gained fame as the most beautiful and successful Chinese courtesan in San Francisco. After a couple of years of this, she started peep shows that catered to white men, opened her own brothels, and allegedly imported many young women from China to work in the business. Reportedly, she traveled to China and purchased young women for $40 each, paid their $80 passage across the Pacific, and then sold them for $1,000 to $1,500. Her notoriety spread to the city's social and political elites, and she sometimes personally appeared in court to argue her case in legal disputes. She eventually retired to Santa Clara County in 1868, where she lived quietly with a new husband, and then after he died, sold clams by the bay. She died in 1928, just three months shy of her one hundredth birthday. But Ah Toy's story was unusual. Violence and degradation characterized the lives of the vast majority of Chinese prostitutes in America.

Outrage among whites about Chinese prostitution and curiosity about Chinese sexuality were closely associated. Official investigations into Chinese morality, including the details of brothel operations, the "corruption" of white boys who went to Chinese brothels, and the physical appearance of Chinese women, sometimes bordered on the prurient. A prominent anti-Chinese political figure in San Francisco claimed at a public hearing that Chinese female prostitutes were actually "insufficient" in numbers "required for the health of the Chinese." From a "hygienic view," Frank Pixley suggested, "they have not their adequate supply," seemingly sympathetic to what he thought were the sexual appetites and physical needs of Chinese men. White journalists and observers often paid special attention to the allure of Chinese women, as they saw it. Ah Toy exploited this white male fascination.

Occasionally, white observers expressed interest in homosexual activity among the largely male population of Chinese who went abroad for work. Immigration inspection agents were asked about evidence of homosexual practices among Chinese who landed in San Francisco. During a U.S. Senate investigation, a visitor returned from China was queried about the "habits" of the Chinese "so far as sodomy is concerned, the connection of man with man." The witness provided little help with the question. Other odd bits of information sometimes appear in the historical record. The 1870 census of Truckee, for example, tells us of a person named Ah John, who is listed as male, eighteen years of age, and living with three older Chinese female prostitutes. Curiously, his occupation is also listed as "prostitute," though this may have been an error. In 1870, as hundreds of Chinese moved to the American South for railroad work after the conclusion of the Pacific Railway, a local newspaper described them to its readership, who were curious about these unfamiliar people. The appearance of one fellow, who might have just come off work on the CPRR, especially caught the eye of the reporter. "We saw one who certainly had the elements of a dandy in him," the journalist wrote. "His cue [sic] was braided in with silk, and so elongated and increased in size that it completely threw his brethren in the shade. He might have vied with almost any lady of fashion in the perfection of his back hair."

Despite the lurid reports on Chinese prostitution and sexuality, the most important connection most Railroad Chinese had with women was with those they left behind in China. Women there who were mothers, wives, or potential mates were an important reason for Railroad Chinese to toil as they did. Their aim was to accumulate savings to send back to families or to establish themselves one day with sufficient resources to marry. Marriage and having children to serve as one's future filial descendants formed the core of their existence. They saw themselves not as autonomous individuals but rather as dutiful family members with obligations to their birth family and their own future family.

Chinese males assumed that they would marry one day, as a wife was essential to produce legitimate offspring, especially males, who would be expected to carry on the ancestral surname line and ensure that the proper cultural and spiritual practices for venerating the dead would be conducted when they had passed on. Peace of mind for the living required at least one male heir. Wives were commonly valued largely for childbearing purposes and as a human resource for the husband and his family. Arranged marriages were the norm in China. Treatment of females was often harsh, even cruel, across class lines, but many personal accounts also tell of affectionate and loving relationships that developed over time.

Wives of farmers typically labored in the fields or in handicraft production, while wives of the wealthy might be pampered but sequestered in loneliness. Many Han families that could afford limiting a daughter's mobility would bind her feet beginning at a young age. The painful practice deformed the foot by curling the small toes beneath the arch but leaving the first toe and heel untouched. In adulthood after years of binding, a woman's foot might be only four inches long, with a broken arch. Dominant norms considered young women with these small "lotus" or "lily" feet, as they were called, more attractive or erotic, and thus enhanced marriage material. Some ethnic groups such as the Hakka and Manchu, and poor families, eschewed foot binding. Their girls had "big feet." Both kinds were seen in California.

There is no evidence that Hung Wah married either in China before he came to the United States or after he arrived, but other Chinese men had wives who remained in the village or were married to them in absentia while they were away. Families hoped the tie of marriage would bind the migrant worker more closely to home and make it more likely that he would one day return. A common practice in the Siyi area was to conduct a marriage ceremony with a live rooster standing in for the groom. The unfortunate bride would accept all the same traditional restrictions on wives and obligations to her in-laws as one who had an actual husband present. A woman who married a Railroad Chinese might live her whole life and never see him. She would be known as a "Gold Mountain wife," might adopt a child or two who were supported by the absent father, and then even die a "virgin widow," as such women were pitifully called. Other young wives might be left behind right after marrying. Laments for their sorry state are heard in many unattributed folk songs originating in the region. One tells the woeful story of a young woman left behind by her husband who goes to America:

> How could you bear parting with me?
> Standing tall and going forward to a foreign land.
> Sailing across the Pacific Ocean,
> Leaving me alone, cold, and inconsolable on my pillow.
> I am young and afraid to sleep alone,

Why should you go and stay abroad?
Yet you still travelled to America,
I regret that we are separated by thousands of miles.
Let me ask you,
How long can one's youthful beauty last? . . .
No matter how much money is brought back home,
You cannot buy back our youth.

The quandary for unmarried male Chinese who came to America was the dearth of potential mates. Though increasing through the years, marriages to non-Chinese remained rare in the nineteenth century. Most assumed, because of their respect for tradition and the separation by race in the United States, that a wife had to be Chinese; certainly it was a given that future life and family meant an eventual return to the village. Chinese women migrants to America, however, were few in number. In the mid-1850s, for example, there were one to two thousand Chinese miners in the Weaverville area in the northern part of California but just four Chinese women. In 1850, more than four thousand Chinese lived in San Francisco but only seven were women. Their number increased to almost seven hundred in 1860, accounting for 37 percent of all Chinese women in the entire country. Even after a decade of immigration, approximately 95 percent of the Chinese in California in the 1860s still were male. The Chinese male-female ratio in California was 39 to 1 in 1850. Between 1850 and 1924, fewer than 5 percent of the Chinese in the United States were female.

Many Railroad Chinese, at least the responsible ones, supported wives and families in their home villages with their ghost money, which they were able to accumulate over time. After paying his living expenses, however, the average Railroad Chinese saved little from his income, especially if he had an opium or gambling habit. Bandits and hoodlums also preyed on Chinese in rural areas because they were thought to have caches of gold or coins they were collecting to send home. Chinese gangsters victimized the workers as well and further reduced the amount of remittances sent home. The Six Companies reportedly rounded up hundreds of them and sent them away in the early 1870s.

The methods used to send money home are still not well known, especially in the early years of Chinese immigration. International banking and remittance systems were in their infancy in the Pacific in the mid-nineteenth century, but it appears that Chinese in America would either take the money back to China with them on their person or have couriers do so. Companies associated with merchants also offered transfer services. Merchant stores in San Francisco and other towns served as proto-banks to hold the money for the workers. Gold was converted into silver, on which the Chinese monetary system was based, especially into Mexican silver dollars. Another less risky way of transferring wealth was to purchase goods or commodities in the States to send back to China rather than sending specie. Very little evidence of gold from America, including coins, is found in China today.

The flow of remittances to China over the years mounted, and sophisticated systems of money orders and funds transfer developed to support it. Many overseas Chinese regularly sent remittances to support parents and immediate families. The funds were also used to construct schools, village halls, and the famous *diaolou* guard towers of the region. Whole new villages might even be constructed with remitted funds. The Siyi region over time became dependent on these remittances, which came from North America, Southeast Asia, Australia, and elsewhere from the workers who went overseas.

Just as Chinese made their mark on California and throughout the United States following their immigration, so too did the Siyi migrants take with them aspects of California when they returned home. The inflow of money into the home villages of the Railroad Chinese transformed the area, but so did the return of the men who brought back foreign-made goods, sometimes items from along the railroad itself, foreign words, new cultural and artistic visions, and new behaviors. These all helped make the Siyi region hybrid and one of the earliest areas of modern China to be linked to the greater world. Examples of this influence, including architectural forms, home ornamentation, handicrafts, and work implements brought back from abroad, can be found today all around the Siyi in homes and museums.

The complexities of the relationships between the Railroad Chinese and their loved ones back in China can also be discerned in the folk culture of the Siyi region itself. One popular art form, known as "wooden fish songs" (*muyu ge*), give expression to heartfelt emotion. Many of these songs reveal the dreams, anxiety, fears, and joys of those who stayed in the villages, but also of those who went overseas for work.

They provide a sense of the actual feelings of the Siyi people. The un-usual name of the art form may have come from the use of wood clap-pers used to keep a rhythmic beat for their recitation. Lyrics, not musi-cal notes, were the important element in these songs or poems, which are akin to what today would be called spoken word. Some singing almost sounded American country-western in style, with high nasal notes and sentimental stories to share. Lyrics collected in the late nine-teenth and early twentieth centuries give voice to a range of emotions, from overblown ambition and sexual longing to lamentations over the separation from lovers, wives, sons, and parents.

Getting to America might inspire special hopes for future prosperity for the family left behind. A child's voice at home calls out:

> *Father, send money back from Gold Mountain more often;*
> *Everyone here is getting new outfits made for the New Year holiday.*
> *The family buys a fat goose to usher in a prosperous new year.*

Blunt and humorous advice is given to parents on selecting the right marriage partner in this song, which also reveals the high expectations laid on those who went to America:

> *Don't marry your daughter to a scholar,*
> *Who would isolate himself to sleep alone;*
> *Don't marry your daughter to a baker,*
> *Who would not have enough time for sleep;*
> *Don't marry your daughter to a farmer,*
> *Whose earthy smell would be repellent;*
> *Marry your daughter to a Gold Mountain guest,*
> *They would come back home with glory and wealth.*

Other songs are more plaintive and told from the position of one who went to America. On a warm, quiet evening, a Railroad Chinese long separated from a lover might have wanted to express his sadness. His song begins on a slightly bawdy note but ends with expressions of missing his true love:

> *The lychee fruit has red skin*
> *And white meat.*

When I put it in my mouth,
It's honey-sweet.
If I could talk to you, my love—
One word repeat—
That would be sweeter far, my love,
Than lychee to eat.

His companions, now stirred, might then have broken out in ribald verse that coarsely recounted episodes with prostitutes. Graphic and crude references to sexual acts, lust and passion, and female and male body parts richly seasoned the country dialects of the Railroad Chinese. Far from the Pearl River delta, there was the possibility of new sexual adventure. One worker might have teased his listeners:

We're guests stranded in North America;
Must we also give up the fun in life?
Girls of the Flowery Flag Nation [United States], all superbly
*   beautiful and charming;*
By all means, have a taste of the white scent while
*   there's time.*
If both sides are willing,
Why not share a dream in bed?
If you betray your youthful vigor and such
*   wonderful delight,*
Just remember, you may return to the old country as a
*   wealthy man, but you won't have this chance again!*

Other, more proper songs beseeched or scolded the young men, separated from the grounding of family and tradition, reminding them to behave, honor their mothers and fathers, and be faithful to wives. In the song "A Letter to My Son," a father invokes the sorrowful image of a loving mother who cried at her son's departure ten years past. She is now "old and weak, like a candle in the wind." The family seldom hears from the ungrateful son and imagines the young man "but gambling and whoring," separated from his wife, who is also filled with "loneliness and unhappiness" and without children. The father pleads with his son to return home soon:

If you want to see your parents, turn around now
Come back home without delay.
If you return home too late,
We may only meet in the after world.
However rich you may be at that time,
You will be facing our tombs alone and with only your sobs.
This letter is too short for me to express my feelings,
It's all up to your heart whether you will listen to me.

In home villages, folk songs also offered a way for women to express their own feelings. One vents the anger of a young wife left behind after just six months of marriage and ends with a sly warning:

At the lunar January lantern show it is crowded;
Men and women are watching the show eagerly.
But I just stay in my boudoir alone, alone in the room.
People are joyful at the lantern festival,
But I'm gloomy with untold complaints.
Thinking long and hard I cannot be relieved
With tears and a desolate mood.
One day if I become shameless,
I will shyly peek at a handsome man.

In songs like this, we see a hint of the tension that must have characterized the relationships between so many Railroad Chinese and their dearest friends and family back in China. No doubt many a railroad worker struggled to reconcile his sincere attachment and fidelity to family with the desire for some momentary comfort and distraction from the hardships he encountered on Gold Mountain.

9

THE GOLDEN SPIKE

The useful and steady Chinese worker became overnight the mysterious Chinaman, an object of unknown dread.
— HUIE KIN, *Reminiscences*

THE LAND EAST OF TRUCKEE CHANGES QUICKLY. UNLIKE THE western slope, where the roadbed rises steadily from the Central Valley up into the summit, the eastern slope drops precipitously into the Great Basin. Contrary to popular misunderstanding, however, northern Nevada, where the line went, is not flat, open country. Nevada, which means "snow-capped" in Spanish, is the most mountainous state in the lower forty-eight states, and the rail line had to wind around the many ranges that run north-south. Thankfully, however, the CPRR could take advantage of river channels in this new terrain, especially the Truckee and Humboldt rivers, as well as gaps through the mountains. The Railroad Chinese would have no more tunnels to bore after they got out of California in the summer of 1868.

Construction work was nevertheless tough, especially in dealing with new climatic conditions. Northern Nevada is high in elevation, with Reno at 4,500 feet above sea level. Summers are scorching, with daytime temperatures easily reaching into the nineties. Winter temperatures can fall well below freezing, though with much less snow than in California, as the Sierra Nevada catches storms coming from the Pacific. In the Humboldt River valley, the thermometer dropped to 18 degrees below zero in early 1869, freezing the ground to a depth of two or three feet. Workers had to use explosives to clear the way for the roadbed.

As the workforce surged forward through Nevada and then into the more even, but no more hospitable, expanse of Utah, work continued on the track that had been laid for miles and miles behind them. The company divided the thousands of Railroad Chinese among many different sites, some all the way back in California, to continue to clear snow and improve the completed work. In Nevada and Utah, the company also had them work simultaneously at many sites on the route. There were no supplies readily available in Nevada, and workers used hundreds of horses and carts to transport enormous quantities of construction materials, food for humans and animals, and water over hundreds of miles of desert. Yet while they were scattered across this immense work site, Chinese continued to be the mainstay of the labor force, as new white workers kept leaving to seek elusive fortunes at the latest gold or silver strike, frustrating company leaders.

In Utah there is high desert. Going from west to east in the direction of the Great Salt Lake, the land steadily rises toward Promontory Summit, which sits at almost five thousand feet in elevation. Harsh climatic conditions mark this grade, called the Promontory Branch of the rail line. Temperatures can range from 28 degrees below zero in the winter to as high as 106 degrees in the summer. With no available water, the soil is parched sandstone, limestone, and quartzites. Scrub brush is about all the vegetation that can survive in this desolate area where the Railroad Chinese continued to build the CPRR to meet the Union Pacific. The leaders of the two railroad companies continued to bicker and maneuver over the actual location of the spot where the two lines would finally meet. All knew that the lines were aiming for the general vicinity of Salt Lake City, and likely to its north, where the land granted by the federal government to the Central Pacific and Union Pacific was most agreeable to railroad construction, but each continued to seek an advantage over the other until almost the last moment.

When the Railroad Chinese broke out of the Sierra in mid-1868, they pushed eastward with energies that had been concentrated in the High Sierra. From Wadsworth, just east of the base of the Sierra in Nevada, they laid track across the deserts and plains at a phenomenal rate. In ten months, from the fall of 1868 until May 5, 1869, when the line reached Promontory, the work crews laid 501 miles of rail line!

Though they progressed more quickly than ever, work in the desert in 1868 and 1869 presented new challenges to the Railroad Chinese. Behind them were mountain tunneling, explosives, snow clearing, and retaining walls in the High Sierra. Railroad Chinese followed the route of the Truckee River as it twisted through western Nevada, but then a forty-mile gap, with no water, separated it from the Humboldt River. In between was brutally dry desert with extreme, killing temperatures. Winds could be ferocious. Many workers lived out in the open in tents, but others appear to have had the protection of prefabricated boardinghouses that the company transported into the desert. A reporter for a Reno newspaper observed a CPRR train with flatbed cars carrying a "string of boarding and lodging houses" that were one to four stories high, the tallest nicknamed "the Hotel de China," with cooking facilities on the first floor and lodging on the upper floors. He saw Chinese peering out of the small upper windows as the passing houses swayed, mounted on a train car. Other smaller, better constructed and appointed buildings housed company officials.

The channel of the three-hundred-mile-long Humboldt River, running from about fifty miles east of Reno through most of northern Nevada, served as the main migration route through the state. The Central Pacific followed a route that snaked around mountains and through canyons. The challenging geography required Charles Crocker himself to come out and command the mass army. In advance of the railhead, he sent three thousand Chinese graders and four hundred horses to dig and blast through the twisting canyons. They graded "Fifteen-Mile Canyon" in six weeks, "Five-Mile Canyon" in three weeks, and eight-hundred-foot-deep "Twelve-Mile Canyon" with similar efficiency. As they advanced, the masses of Railroad Chinese received praise as being "the real pathfinders of empire." A journalist witnessed the smoke from the campfires of a thousand Chinese in their encampments along the Humboldt River valley. It was a dramatic scene but one that no photographer ever recorded. Along the way, the railroad spawned Lovelock, Winnemucca, Elko, Carlin, and other towns that eventually became home to hundreds of Chinese who worked on railroads well into the twentieth century.

A perceptive reporter for *Alta California* provided a lively account of the energetic work in the contour of Nevada, a dramatic contrast to the grueling effort to get through the granite in the Sierra:

Long lines of horses, mules and wagons are standing in the open
desert near the camp train. The stock is getting its breakfast of
hay and barley. Trains are shunting in from the west with supplies and materials for the day's work. Foremen are galloping
here and there on horseback giving or receiving orders. Swarms
of laborers, Chinese, Europeans and Americans, are hurrying to
their work . . . By the side of the grade smokes the camp fires of
the blue clad laborers who could be seen in groups waiting for
the signal to start work. These are the Chinese, and the job of
this particular contingent is to clear a level roadbed for the track.
They are the vanguard of the construction forces.

The reporter praises the Railroad Chinese as "systematic workers,"
calling them "competent and wonderfully effective because [they are]
tireless and unremitting in their industry."

The astonishing discipline and efficiency of the railroad workers
impressed another reporter who tried to describe what he had witnessed. The CPRR workers appeared to be a veritable factory of human muscle and energy in the desert: "It would be impossible to describe how rapidly, orderly and perfectly this is done without seeing
the operation itself," he wrote. "There are just as many employed as
can conveniently work, and no more." They worked with industrial efficiency, losing no time in continuously bringing supplies and men to
the line, where they toiled "with the velocity of steam." Rail after rail
was laid across the field in machinelike fashion, "the same operation
repeated ad infinitum." The company worked crews into the dark desert night, lighting the work area with sagebrush bonfires. Supply trains
came along regularly to provision and feed the workers. Time was of
the essence.

They were not pure machines, however, but also insisted on observing their customs, including celebrating their New Year, beginning about February 11, 1869, much to Crocker's frustration. A visitor to the line at this time offered a toast to Crocker over a meal that
unwittingly captured his peculiar dependence on, and identification
with, the Railroad Chinese. The visitor hailed the Pacific Railway and
declared that it was a "piece of crockery ware made out of China."
The witty play on Crocker's name delighted the other guests, who
broke out in laughter. Yet again, it was clear even to visitors to the

line how critical the Railroad Chinese were to this historic under-taking.

The CPRR wanted to cover the hundreds of miles that stretched eastward before the railhead in order to control as much territory as possible before having to meet the UP in central Utah. Pushed to the maximum of their abilities, the workers completed miles of track in a single day, compared to just one a month on average in 1867 in the Sierra. In October 1868 the CPRR reached Winnemucca, 325 miles from Sacramento, and four months later, in February 1869, it reached Elko, Nevada, 469 miles from the start. The line soon crossed into Utah, where tough grades, canyons, and ravines complicated the route. Five hundred workers labored for two months to cover another deep depression, again called the "Big Fill," 170 feet long and five hundred feet deep.

Photos taken by Alfred A. Hart during this time show the Railroad Chinese at work in the Nevada and Utah deserts and plains. No longer are there dense stands of tough evergreens, granite monoliths, and immense snowdrifts, but instead vistas of endless flatland and barren hills. Hart captures the human imprint on the desolate land by including long shots of the rail line extending far into the distance and isolated worker camps by the side of the tracks. One photograph by Hart, titled "China Camp, at End of Track" (above), shows an encampment of approximately forty canvas tents alongside the track, on which the camp train appears to sit. Smoke from what may have been dining cars or Strobridge's private residential car rises in the background. A body of water is seen at the edge of the frame. The focus, though, is on the worker encampment, which could have held seventy-five or more persons. The tents are of different sizes; one close to the camera is comparatively large and sturdy. The ties and weights holding down the canvas are even and tight. Surrounding it are several medium-sized structures that may have been used for storage and taking meals. Other tents are lightweight, with no sides. They may simply have offered protection from the strong sun. Still others appear to be A-frame tents for sleeping. They have staked-down sides and entry flaps but are insubstantial and are scattered haphazardly. No latrines or washing facilities are evident. Magnification shows perhaps twenty people milling about or sitting among the tents. It may have been Sunday, a day of no work, reserved for resting and attending to personal matters. Wet laundry hangs all around, draped over long poles, clotheslines, and tent tops. Pants, jackets, underwear, and long johns needed cleaning. The men were not embarrassed to air their modest clothing in public. They probably did not even know a camera was present, and if they did, they would not have cared much. They knew they would soon leave, never to return to this place, and their faces cannot be seen.

In another photograph, "Chinese Camp, Brown's Station" (above), Hart captures a similar collection of tents on either side of the track. Washbasins and other personal effects are scattered near the tents, and in the distance a large group of workers is active. In the foreground, two or three men take shelter under an awning—seeking respite, no doubt, from the merciless sun that hung over the baking desert.

Numerous Chinese workers appear in the distance in several of these images. In "End of Track on Humboldt Plains" (above), a location in eastern Nevada, Hart captures thirty or so workers, mainly Chinese, attending to already laid track. Perhaps they are doing repair work, as they don't seem especially engaged, or perhaps they have just been staged by the photographer, as suggested by the presence of a woman and a youngster in the lower left. Far in the distance, one can see a fuzzy cloud of activity where workers are pushing the end of the line forward. Clearly visible in the foreground are Chinese workers attired in different ways. Some continue to wear sunhats, others not. Most appear to be wearing high work boots. Notable is the remarkable uniformity of the visible completed road work, the results of Chinese labor. The bed is firm, the ties evenly spaced and well cut. The quality of the completed work of the CPRR line was publicly known at the time to be clearly superior to that of the UP, and the craftsmanship on display in Hart's photographs proves that the reputation was well earned.

• • •

In California, the Railroad Chinese far outnumbered white workers. As the route reached through Nevada and into Utah, however, the composition of the CPRR workforce changed as Native Americans and Mormons began to join. The most significant change came as the CPRR and UP converged and Chinese started to encounter Irish workers from the UP line. As they approached the meeting point, the railroad lines of the two companies ran parallel to each other in different locations, bringing the two groups into direct contact.

In the fall of 1868, Charles Crocker estimated that ten thousand Chinese, one thousand whites, and "any number" of Native Americans worked for the Central Pacific. Crocker and other company leaders had little direct contact with, let alone understanding of, the men who were actually building the railroad for them. Crocker confessed as much when a San Francisco reporter asked him about the work in Nevada. He said that in addition to Chinese and whites, he had hired men from Native tribes in the Humboldt channel to work for the company. He admitted that he did not know how many were employed because "no list of names was kept" and the men worked in "squads and not as individuals." Besides, Crocker ignorantly offered, "Indians and Chinese were so much alike personally that no human being could tell them apart." Perhaps because he viewed them as racially alike, he seems to have used them similarly. To avoid making the mistake of paying an individual twice, he said, the company devised a "scheme of employing, working and paying them by the wholesale." Overseers counted how many went to work, ate, and then returned to camp at night. The company then paid the overseer, who in turn divided up the wages among the men. Crocker proudly claimed that his method avoided "lengthy bookkeeping," saved time, and prevented "cheating." It was also a method that kept both Chinese and Native American workers nameless and anonymous to the company.

Chinese and Native peoples in the American West had a close and complicated relationship. Records show more than twenty incidents in which Native Americans attacked and killed Chinese miners in the California gold country in the 1850s. When the railroad entered central Nevada, local Shoshones reportedly took potshots at the Chinese, and Charles Crocker also circulated a story about efforts by Piutes to scare Railroad Chinese from working. He said that Native people had told the Chinese about enormous reptiles or human monsters that hid in the desert and were so large they could devour a human in a single bite. Frightened by the stories springing from the Nevada desert, a thousand Chinese supposedly deserted the line and had to be wooed back by the company. Crocker seemed to relish the story as it simultaneously highlighted Chinese ignorance and gullibility as well as Indian maliciousness.

In contrast, other pieces of evidence suggest that Chinese and Native peoples developed cooperative, even intimate relationships. Archaeological evidence from living sites of Chinese and Native people point to trade between the two groups. Interviews with Native Americans and Chinese through the years also include stories of close, friendly interaction along the railroad that occasionally included intermarriages that produced children. An unusual and compelling story is handed down through the Lee family of New York about how their railroad worker ancestor survived an Indian attack that left many Chinese dead. He was spared as the tribal chief, who had recently lost his own son, took an interest in the strapping young Chinese man and brought him to live with the tribe for two years before releasing him.

Stories of interactions between Railroad Chinese and Irish workers are much more fraught. Hundreds of thousands of Irish immigrated to the United States beginning in the 1840s, and reports of conflict between the two immigrant groups during railroad construction have circulated widely. Many Irish traveled to the Far West, and by the 1850s they had become a prominent part of California's population at the same time Chinese were arriving in the state. In 1860, the Irish were the second-largest foreign-born group behind Chinese, though the Irish population grew much more quickly, and they soon outnumbered Chinese. In 1867, San Francisco even elected its first Irish mayor, and the Irish continued to be active in politics, becoming a major element in the anti-Chinese labor movement that festered in the 1860s and exploded in the 1870s and 1880s. In railroad work, Irish formed a large proportion of the workforce for the Union Pacific, but hundreds also joined the CPRR as laborers, skilled workers, crew leaders, and supervisors. Mormons also came on the CPRR as it approached Salt Lake City, but there is little known about any interaction between them and Railroad Chinese.

Incidences of serious violence between the Irish and Chinese erupted as the lines of the rival CPRR and UP approached each other in Utah. In February 1869, a Utah newspaper reported an incident in which Irish workers used pick handles and explosives to attack the Chinese, seriously injuring several. The attackers ignored a company order to stop but found that the Chinese were a tough adversary. Chinese workers retaliated by setting loose their own blasts of dirt and rock against the Irish. A news report described Chinese as fighting with "unexpected vigor and accuracy."

Fighting between the Union Pacific's Irish and Chinese flared again two months later. Irish workers initiated fighting when they detonated explosions in the direction of the Chinese and seriously injured several. After Chinese responded with their own explosions directed at the Irish, the fighting stopped. Another report from early May 1869 recounts a similar incident, but with workers this time using nitroglycerine against each other. Several unfortunate mules were caught in the cross-fire and were decimated by the blasts. The two sides reportedly went to get firearms, but the fighting stopped before shooting could begin. Through it all, the defiant Chinese reportedly gained "due respect" from the Irish. It is a minor miracle that no loss of life on either side occurred during the mini-war.

In late May 1869, the national periodical *Harper's Weekly* devoted extensive space to covering the completion of the Pacific Railway and offered a different narrative of the relations between Chinese and Irish, one that emphasized interethnic connection. The periodical dramatized the completion of the railroad work in Utah with a detailed illustration showing many Chinese and "European" workers blasting hillsides and grading for the roadbed. They appear to be working in coordinated fashion, though also in conflict. In one corner of the illustration, a group of whites torment a Chinese by pulling on his queue. The caption of the image declares that it shows the "mingling of European and Asiatic laborers" in constructing the last mile of the Pacific Railway, and the accompanying article hails the efforts of the two immigrant groups. A "medley of Irishmen and Chinamen" completed the rail line, *Harper's* declared, and "typify its significant result, bringing Europe and Asia face to face, grasping hands across the American continent."

To push the work even further, the two companies pitted the workers against each other in competitions. In August 1868, Railroad Chinese had laid six miles and eight hundred feet of track in a single day. After UP workers also completed six miles of track in a day, Crocker claimed his teams could lay ten miles in a day. Thomas C. Durant, vice president of the UP, bet they could not do so. The ensuing construction challenge became legendary in railroad history, as ten miles of track in a day had never been accomplished before. Top leaders from both companies ventured out into the desert to watch the contest, which would enter history not only for the amount of ground it would cover but also for how much closer it brought the CPRR—and the Railroad Chinese—toward the end of the line.

On April 28, 1869, at seven in the morning, a train whistle marked the start of the CPRR army's work and the first supply train moved forward. The CPRR had prepared for the effort by loading five trains of sixteen flatcars each full of supplies. Each train carried enough material to cover two miles of track. Chinese had also distributed thousands of ties along the route in advance. Railroad Chinese unloaded kegs of bolts and spikes, fasteners, and iron rails from the sixteen flatcars in just eight minutes, and the supply train pulled away, letting another take its place.

Six-man teams then lifted small flatcars onto the track and loaded them with the rails and other materials that had been off-loaded. These horse-drawn cars were especially designed to slide the heavy iron rails off on rollers to be brought to the end of the completed line. There, Chinese unloaded the bolts, fasteners, and spikes, and two four-man teams of Irish workers lifted the 560-pound rails onto the ties. Chinese returned to straighten the track, drive the spikes into the ties, and bolt the fasteners. Four hundred Chinese followed and, using shovels and tampers, set the track firmly into the roadbed ballast. The small flatcars rolled back and forth along the rails to keep supplies moving. Sometimes they had to be lifted off the track to allow a fully loaded car to come forward. The line was a flurry of activity, with an uninterrupted flow of supplies, workers, foremen on horseback, and carriers of food, water, and tea under the blazing sun. The army laid a mile of track an hour, and at midday, with more than six miles of track laid, it was clear that they would win the challenge. At 1:30, the troops stopped to eat. The location was honored with the name "Victory."

A camp train pulled up to serve meals to five thousand workers. Did the Chinese eat boiled beef and potatoes, as was the usual fare for whites, or did they have their familiar food? We do not know, but the food was served punctually, and soon the workers resumed their advance. Among the lunch guests attending the unprecedented event was a U.S. Army officer, who shared his observations with Crocker. He said he had never seen such organization as he had witnessed that morning. "It was just like an army marching over the ground and leaving the track behind them," he praised. "[I]t was a good day's march for an army."

The ten-mile line was not just put down on flat ground but had to ascend the slope of Promontory Mountain. There were also curves that required tedious effort to bend the rails manually and attend to the particulars of the roadbed. The railroad army finally concluded its labors at 7:00 p.m., twelve hours after work began in the morning. The workers had handled 25,800 cross-ties, 3,520 iron rails, 28,160 spikes, 7,040 fishplates (a type of fastener), and 14,080 bolts and brought the CPRR three and a half miles to the east of Promontory Summit, the point where the lines of the two companies were to meet. As one journalist described it, several thousand Railroad Chinese and eight Irish rail handlers, "with military precision and organization," had laid ten miles and fifty-six feet of track in less than twelve hours, a stunning performance that had never been seen before. A San Francisco newspaper declared the feat "the greatest work in tracklaying ever accomplished or conceived by railroad men," and a railroad historian later described the Chinese effort as " the most stirring event in the building of the railroad." Celebratory accounts both then and since, however, included the names of the eight Irish iron movers but not one of the Chinese.

After the end of work, a supply train brought 1,200 men, almost all of them Railroad Chinese riding on flatcars, back to their camp at Victory, near the shores of the Great Salt Lake. Tomorrow would be another workday for the "Asiatic contingent of the Grand Army of Civilization," as they were called in the press. A week after the challenge, the CPRR sent almost all of the Railroad Chinese back westward to improve the completed line. Only a small force of workers stayed near Promontory to lay the last length of track. It is largely for that reason that few Chinese were present at the ceremony that would occur at

Promontory Summit, where Congress on April 9, 1869, determined the two lines would meet.

A few days after they had recovered from the ten-mile construction feat, some Chinese — Hung Wah, perhaps, and maybe a few others — decided to take a break. It may have been Sunday evening, a day off. They went to a bluff near Monument Rock, Utah. It was spring, and the vista must have been magnificent. They could see the rail line they had helped complete and, beyond it, the Great Salt Lake. It was a perfect place to enjoy the brown-glazed stoneware jug of Chinese rice wine they had brought along. It had come to them all the way from the Pearl River delta. Astonished at what they themselves had done in laying ten miles of track in a day, they might have reflected on their triumph over the odds, taken pride in their achievement, and celebrated. They also knew the CPRR would soon meet the Union Pacific line, and Hung Wah and the others may have reflected back on the years of toil and speculated about what they might do next with their lives in the months and years ahead. They might have become melancholy on the wine and thought about loved ones separated, far away in the villages, and their desire to return home. Or they might just have celebrated the coming end of railroad work and the chance to drift back to Truckee, Elko, or even San Francisco, where they could enjoy good food, attend an opera performance, or visit a "pleasure palace" that offered fresh opium and women. Bawdy joking and storytelling may have ensued. Done with the drink, they left the empty bottle and returned to camp. There was still work to do in the days ahead. Almost 150 years later, archaeologists studying the ground along the Transcontinental line stumbled across the jug intact, sitting on an outcrop. It had no written message inside, unlike those corked bottles that float for years in the ocean, waiting to wash ashore to tell a story. This bottle, though mute, had something to say. We just need to heed our imaginations and listen.

Though boosters predicted that thirty thousand people would attend the ceremonial linking of the Central Pacific and Union Pacific railways, many fewer actually showed up. Accounts do not agree on the number, but it falls between five hundred and fifteen hundred. Almost all were white males, a motley assortment of UP workers, gawkers, and soldiers brought to the site. Fewer than two dozen women and a couple of children attended. Twenty to thirty reporters were present to chronicle the historic day. No bunting or decorations brightened the scene. No band was present to play music during the ceremony. There was no stage or platform for the speakers, who could not be heard by the assembled crowd. All the speeches had been prepared in advance and were merely read.

At around 10:30 on the morning of May 10, "a clean-frocked squad" of eight Railroad Chinese brought the last rails of the CPRR forward to meet those of the Union Pacific, which had been laid by Irish workers. The UP photographer Russell captured this historic moment and aptly titled his image "Laying the Last Rail" (next page). Chinese workers put the rails in position and drilled holes in the ties so that the ceremonial spikes would not be damaged when "driven" in. The Chinese appeared rather indifferent to all the goings-on that day, seemingly taking everything "as a matter of course," according to one journalist. They simply did their work, "wielding the pick, shovel and sledge with consummate dexterity." Another journalist at the scene expressed his admiration of the efforts of the Railroad Chinese. "John Chinaman began the road," he wrote in the *San Francisco Daily Times*, "and it was fit that he should also end it." The Chinese then removed themselves from the scene, the two locomotives inched forward from west and east, and dignitaries took their places.

The event began a bit past noon and was over in about an hour. A short invocation, a forgettable, less than three-minute-long speech by Stanford, who occupied the center of the event, and brief remarks by other officials took up a few more moments. None of the speakers paid any attention to the workers, Chinese, Irish, or others, who had made the project possible. Company leaders clumsily enacted driving in ceremonial golden spikes with silver-headed mauls into a tie of polished laurel to connect the two lines. These precious materials were then carefully removed for safekeeping. "Done" is what the telegraphic announcement of the perfunctory deed was broadcasted across the country.

To emphasize their own importance, the top officials of the CPRR and UP declared that their combined laid track totaled 1,776 miles, the number of course of the date of the declaration of American independence.

After the brief event concluded, Chinese returned to replace the ceremonial materials with permanent ones. As noted by reporters at the site, it was Chinese workers who laid the rails and drove in the last spikes to complete the Transcontinental. The work was then *really* done. They and others in the crowd descended on abandoned props and carved them up for souvenirs. What relics Chinese might have kept from the day were lost to fires during the destruction of their communities in America, or perhaps just discarded over the years as the excitement of the day passed. No mementos of Promontory remain in the families of the Railroad Chinese. While the Golden Spike sits in the art museum at Stanford University, which Leland Stanford would go on to found, the polished laurel tie was destroyed in the great San Francisco earthquake and fire of 1906. Stanford hosted a brief party in his parlor car for dignitaries and then departed entirely from the scene in his sumptuous train car at 2:00. By 5:00, Promontory Summit was virtually deserted.

Strobridge held his own reception for reporters, military officers, and other visitors. After they had gathered, he stood and invited his "Chinese foreman and leader who had been with him so long," most likely Hung Wah, and other Railroad Chinese to the head of the table. His assembled guests listened with respect to his acknowledgment of their great contributions to the construction effort and warmly thanked them. The guests then rose, offered rousing cheers to the Chinese, and then they all sat together to dine. Though he did not name Hung Wah, a journalist who may have been present noted that one Railroad Chinese impressed him with his English-speaking ability and "extensive acquaintance with railroad matters." Newspapers noted the rare spectacle of Chinese workingmen and white male dignitaries sitting down to eat at the same table.

At the lively public celebration in Sacramento, E. B. Crocker, who had followed the actual construction of the CPRR line as closely as anyone with the exception of his brother Charles, hailed the completion of the Pacific Railway as "the greatest monument of human labor" and pointedly praised Chinese in his speech: "I wish to call to your minds that the early completion of this railroad we have built has been in large measure due to that poor, despised class of laborers called the Chinese, to the fidelity and industry they have shown." Sensitive to the indignities Chinese often suffered, Crocker wanted to make sure then that they received their due recognition. Several months later, Charles offered similar compliment to Chinese during his public speech welcoming Vice President Schuyler Colfax to Sacramento. Reportedly, Crocker "paid high tribute to the Chinese as a working class" and observed that California would greatly benefit from them, "an immigrant population willing to work."

As historically significant as the completion of the Pacific Railway was, the driving of the "Last Spike" at the formal celebration at Promontory Summit was anticlimactic. The mythic status the event gained over the years has obscured the reality of the actual moment, including the fact that it was held two days late. The celebratory event at Promontory Summit was to have occurred on May 8 but was delayed. During the preceding months, the leaders of the CPRR and UP had engaged in petty negotiation and bargaining to determine the site and had little respect, let alone affection, for each other. Many of the top leaders of both companies did not even bother to attend the event. Of the CPRR leaders, only Leland Stanford made it to the ceremony. Neither of the Crocker brothers nor Collis Huntington and Mark Hopkins traveled out to Promontory Summit.

San Francisco and Sacramento, however, with all their celebratory preparations booked and ready, went ahead anyway as planned on May 8 with huge, spectacular events that shut down both cities. San Francisco held an "immense procession" marked by "unbounded enthusi-asm," according to the local press. Celebrants filled the streets from early morning through the evening. The day began with the firing of cannons, and "Chinese bombs and crackers" continued to explode throughout the day. Grand celebrations also occurred in all the great midwestern and eastern cities. In Philadelphia, the Liberty Bell in In-dependence Hall rang out. The last time it had been heard was on the news of Robert E. Lee's surrender.

At Promontory Summit, however, nothing even remotely pleasant distinguished the event's physical location. It was isolated, dusty, bar-ren, flat, with no settlement in sight. Only rattlesnakes and buzzards felt at home in the sagebrush and alkaline dust and sand. Water had to be brought in from six miles distant. Where none had stood before, sev-enteen tents hastily appeared in the days just prior to the ceremony to house a bank, telegraph office, ticket station, eating establishments, and saloons. A couple of boxcars served as temporary offices for the railroad companies. After the event, a few more tents and some shoddy wooden buildings went up for more saloons, a gambling house, stores, brothels, and a Chinese laundry, but Promontory never became important and soon fell into oblivion when the railroad companies decided that their interests would be better served by moving their junction a few miles away to Ogden, an established town. Several hundred Railroad Chinese moved there to continue to work for the CPRR. A year after the driv-ing of the "Golden Spike," the population of Promontory Summit was just forty people, twenty-six of them Chinese on a maintenance crew. It became a place few people had any interest in visiting or even memory.

Several dramatic incidents and accidents in early May actually made for more exciting history. First, a special train bringing Leland Stan-ford out to Promontory slammed into a fifty-foot-long log felled by Chinese timber workers that had slid onto the track just past Truckee. One passenger was seriously injured. Stanford had to wait for replace-ments for the damaged engine and cars. A few days later, a mini-war broke out among the hundreds of Railroad Chinese who had worked on the ten-mile challenge and were encamped at Victory. It is unclear whether the cause of the conflict was money, politics, or ethnic and re-gional rivalries, but the unity and coordination they had exhibited just a few days earlier during the challenge were no longer. According to news reports, the fighting was serious, involving crowbars, picks, and guns. One Chinese was mortally wounded before Strobridge and several Chinese leaders subdued the combatants. Tensions among both Chinese workers and white company officials mounted as the events at Promontory approached.

Stanford and his elite party had to wait three tedious days for the UP party to arrive from the east. A collapsed bridge and torrential rains had delayed them, but their more sensational problem had been with hundreds of UP workers who had taken Thomas Durant, the company vice president, prisoner for nonpayment of back wages. He and the UP had treated their workers poorly and had engaged in financial mismanagement. The angry workers detached his "palace car" and surrounded it with armed guards. Durant had to wire for $800,000 and was warned not to seek help. If anyone came to try to release him, he was told, he would be run into the mountains and hanged or shot "with no mercy." Durant was finally released on May 8, when he paid the workers what was due them.

Shortly before the Promontory event, Daniel Cleveland, the writer who was fascinated with the Chinese in California, wrote about the impending completion of the Pacific Railway and its historic significance. He observed that the realization of the long-held dream of a rail line across America was the result of a "singular circumstance." Chinese, whom he characterized as "the most conservative people in the world" because of their faithful attachment to their old ways and customs, were then building eastward and would soon meet white American workers building westward. When they met, he declared, they would have completed "the most wonderful of the progressive achievements of this marvelous age," and "China and the United States will then strike hands, and feel more nearly drawn together in sympathy and interest than ever before." He concluded: "It is very appropriate that the people of the two mightiest nations of their respective continents should unite in the construction of this world's highway. May it draw and keep them close together, not only in commerce and interest, but in kindly sympathy and good offices." The Reverend John Todd echoed the sentiments. "China is our neighbor now," proclaimed the influential and distinguished minister, who delivered the benediction at the Promontory event. "The East and the West embrace; nay, we hardly know which is East or which is West." And, he emphasized, "The road could never have been built without the Chinamen."

In contrast to these expansive and sympathetic observations, a popular local judge at the San Francisco celebration presented a Euro-American chauvinist interpretation when he credited the construction accomplishment to "our people." In their veins, he said, flowed "the commingled blood of the four greatest nationalities of modern days," citing the French, Germans, English, and Irish. He made no mention of Chinese or anyone other than those four groups. His comments fit easily into the general tenor of nationalist celebratory remarks and prefigured the erasure of Chinese from railroad history as the excitement of Promontory Summit faded into the past.

Colorful descriptions of the staged activities, fawning tributes to the railroad barons, and declarations about the glowing commercial promise of the completed railroad fill the written accounts of those who were present at the Promontory Summit event. Photography supplements these texts and provides much less glamorous but fascinating perspectives on the day. The twenty-eight images taken by Alfred Hart, A. J. Russell, and Charles J. Savage on May 10 capture the forlornness of the gritty, dusty site and various scenes of listless people wilting in the sun, waiting for the event to begin. The soldiers in their heavy uniforms look bored and the onlookers curious but unanimated. Utah's vast plains and hills stretch to the far horizon in the background, dwarfing the human assembly.

The photographers captured a few images of the formal ceremony, but none are of much interest, and unsurprisingly few of these circulated widely afterward. Instead, A. J. Russell's image titled "East and West Shaking Hands," sometimes given as "Meeting of East and West," showing two locomotives drawn up head-to-head, has become iconic. (This image is shown in the book's introduction; see page 2.) The chief engineers for the Central Pacific and Union Pacific shake hands in the center of the photo. Train engineers toast each other with bottles while perched on the front of each engine. A hundred other men look toward the glass-plate camera. The photograph has come to represent the ambitious enterprise itself and the assumed excitement of the day.

Nowhere in the image, however, are the principals who participated in the formal ceremony. Nowhere is Leland Stanford, Thomas Durant and other UP officials, directors of either company, dignitaries and politicians, women, or the troops. The ceremony had concluded, and they all had withdrawn from the site. The hulking dark locomotives and the largely unidentified crowd remained. Russell arranged them for the impromptu shot. The background landscape is obscured. Perhaps that is why the image resonates: it seems to celebrate the machine and the everyday American, quintessential elements of the national identity outside of time and place.

But is the scene so devoid of personality? Look closely and you can actually see men in garments indicating they were immigrants from eastern Europe, wearing hats or boots that had come from far away. Most do not appear to be railroad workers at all. They are not wearing work clothes. Other reports mention the presence at Promontory of a diverse array of the people of the West: Native peoples, Mexicans, African Americans, Mormons, and Irish, along with Chinese. But where are the Chinese, the ones who were essential in realizing this moment for the CPRR?

Some interpret this omission as a deliberate slight, a purposeful exclusion from the historical moment. Though there is no evidence that the photographer arranged the crowd to omit Chinese, their absence has been taken as symbolic of the expurgation, or at least underappreciation, of the role the Chinese played in completing the Transcontinental. One UP official had called for taking a photograph that would show white and Chinese workers together completing the final work.

Look even closer, however, and a ghostly figure with his back to the camera, blurred because he was moving and not standing still like the rest of the crowd facing the camera, emerges in the mid-range center of the frame. From what can be seen of his tattered and patched clothes, hat, and stature, he is Chinese. He had probably been part of the crew that had laid the last rails. One fellow has his arm stretched out and holds a hat covering a face. Might the hidden fellow have been a Chinese standing next to the moving figure? Other Chinese may be mixed in with the crowd but are obscured. Another photographer, Charles Savage, captured that same scene a few minutes apart from Russell's and uses a similar composition. In Savage's work, a Chinese workman with a sledgehammer clearly appears at the left edge of the frame. He looks right at the camera, curious about the goings-on. He is not the ghostly individual in Russell's photograph, but he may have been another Chinese mixed in with the crowd.

None of the images taken by photographers at the Promontory event reveal very much of a Railroad Chinese presence. One photograph purporting to show Chinese at Promontory is by John B. Silvis. Remarkably, it does seem to show a crew of nine or ten Chinese working with a white foreman on a track running in front of a CPRR freight house and Silvis's train car. The image has the title "China section gang, Promontory" (above). The Chinese in the photo are weathered-looking, are holding iron tools, and wear leather boots and loose-fitting, patched clothing. One seems to be a youngster in his teens. These men fit the physical descriptions of Railroad Chinese, and the image provides remarkably clear views of faces—but the photo is not from the May 10 event. Silvis was not present then but took his image more than two years later at a location near Promontory.

Silvis's staged photograph responded to public curiosity about, and ignorance of, the Railroad Chinese. They were not invisible, but they were not well known either. As with Russell's iconic image, they are present in some form, but understanding and appreciating the reality of those individuals who toiled, mile by mile, to get to Promontory continued to elude an American public whose interest soon waned.

10

BEYOND PROMONTORY

The American eagle strides the heavens soaring
With half of the globe clutched in his claw.
Although the Chinese arrived later,
Couldn't you leave them a little space?

— HUANG ZUNXIAN, CHINESE CONSUL
GENERAL IN SAN FRANCISCO FROM
1882 TO 1885

THE COMPLETION OF THE PACIFIC RAILWAY INSPIRED A NEW way of thinking about the United States and its cartography. For decades before Promontory Summit, Americans largely thought of the nation in a North-South orientation. Its main characteristic was the division between slavery, centered in the South, and antislavery in the North, which shaped the country's politics, culture, economics, social structure, values, demographics, and ambitions. The victory of the North over the slave South eroded this division and established the foundation of a unified nation-state, though the legacy of slavery endured. After the end of the Civil War, the creation of a single, uninterrupted rail line that ran east to west across the continent encouraged a new directional way of thinking about the nation. Americans could see themselves continentally, as a widespread nation of almost contiguous states, once Colorado joined the union in 1876 (Utah remained a territory until 1896), which politically connected the two great oceans of the globe, and beyond the waters, two great divisions of the world: Europe and Asia. For many, the Transcontinental Railroad appeared to realize the providential destiny of the country as a great continent-empire that made a global imagination possible. Travel between New York and San Francisco, either overland or by sea, took months, and could even take one's life, before the completion of the Transcontinental. After May 10, 1869, one could make the trip in six days, at a fraction of the previous cost, comfortably and safely. California-grown strawberries could go east, as they did with Stanford for his banquet at Promontory, and visitors and settlers could venture out to the Far West. It also meant that Chinese could spread out from California, Oregon, and Nevada where they had concentrated and travel east, and they did. Chinese began to appear throughout the central regions of America, in Idaho, Wyoming, Colorado, Arizona, Texas, and beyond to the East and South. They used the railroad they had helped build to find their way all around Gold Mountain.

While national attention on the completed Pacific Railway focused principally on the commercial opportunities the rail line opened up for America in the Pacific and Asia, or on the national political significance of the iron lines that united the recently divided country, observers also took a keen interest in the demonstrated abilities of the Railroad Chinese who made the line possible. They, in fact, appeared to physically embody the interconnection between the Transcontinental's national and global significance. The migrant Chinese were the human link with Asia, but they—and their labor—were also poised to help the country attain even greater glory and prosperity. These alien Railroad Chinese, it appeared to many, could be critical for the further development of the American nation.

An article under the title "The Chinaman as a Railroad Builder," an encomium to the Railroad Chinese, appeared soon after the Promontory event in at least twenty publications in every region across the country, including the South, the Northeast, the mid-Atlantic, the central states, and the Far West. The *National Intelligencer,* the main paper for the nation's capital, and the New York–based *Scientific American* were among the most prominent periodicals that published it.

The Chinese laborer "occupied a prominent position" in completing the Pacific Railway, according to the article, because without him, the Central Pacific might never have gotten out of California. It was not just the availability of Chinese labor and its low cost that had been critical; the singular abilities of the Chinese worker were many and admirable. His attitude was exemplary, he had discipline and endurance, and his "mechanical skill is remarkable." The article was unrestrained even in comparing Railroad Chinese to whites. Chinese working for the CPRR "are more clever in aligning roads than many white men who have been educated to the business, and these Mongols will strike a truer line for a longer distance with the unassisted eye than most white men can with the aid of instruments. A good deal of nonsense had been talked about the Chinaman's want of stamina, and his alleged inferiority to the white laborer in point of strength and capacity for work. The Central Pacific, however, has pretty thoroughly settled that point: "[after many tests] it was found that John Chinaman had burrowed further into the rock than his antagonist, and was, moreover, less fatigued." Chinese had shown themselves to be "as fine railroad builders as can be found anywhere" and were now likely to move across the country to work on regional lines and other major construction projects. The article concluded with a salute to this talented workforce: "The Chinaman is a born railroad builder, and as such he is destined to be most useful to California, and, indeed, to the whole Pacific slope."

The *Daily Alta California,* the most prominent newspaper in the state, shared a similar opinion in its glowing report on the completion of the rail line. Reportedly, according to those who compared the work of the CPRR and UP, all declared that the Chinese "do a better, neater, and cleaner job, and do it faster and cheaper than the white laborers from the East." The paper concluded that there was really no comparison between the two, as Chinese "work with more method, precision, order, and regularity, and seems to take pride in his handiwork." The CPRR line was "infinitely superior in build and equipments."

After the completion of the Transcontinental there was an opening, a brief period of possibility and opportunity for Chinese in America that had not occurred before and would wither by the late 1870s. For several years, however, because of the positive national attention paid to the efforts of the Railroad Chinese, and coinciding with the national commitment to extend democracy to freed people through Reconstruction, a hopeful era for Chinese seemed to arise. Though violent Sinophobia continued to rage among white immigrant groups, many others in America expressed readiness to welcome huge numbers of

Chinese into the country and even grant them the privilege of citizenship. Chinese in America actually experienced what might be called a "post-Promontory promise" in America.

Legend has it that Railroad Chinese found themselves abandoned and discarded after the Promontory Summit event. They were allegedly set adrift in the deserts to find their way back to the Pacific coast. The belief, empathetic as it seeks to be, underestimates the standing the Railroad Chinese had achieved. They had become among the most experienced railroad builders in the country, and local and regional railroad builders valued what the Chinese could accomplish. The reputation of the Railroad Chinese preceded their actual presence around the country. Though many found themselves out of work or returned to China after Promontory, thousands of others located new work around the country. Ng Poon Chew, one of the early leaders among Chinese Americans, later observed that employment opportunities "were not wanting at all" after the completion of the Transcontinental. Even before the Promontory event, Railroad Chinese began to spread far beyond the Pacific Railway line.

As early as 1868, hundreds of Chinese joined railroad construction crews in the Eugene, Salem, and Portland, Oregon areas. Newspaper articles identified them as "railroad hands," indicating they were experienced, and favorably reported on their initial efforts. In the months after Promontory, even the UP hoped to recruit Railroad Chinese who had been employed on the CPRR to work on the improvement and maintenance of its line. Hundreds of Railroad Chinese became the main workforce on the line connecting Virginia City and Truckee. In June, five hundred Chinese described as "discharged hands from the Pacific Railroad" traveled by steamboat down the Mississippi to New Orleans, where they were expected to become agricultural workers. News reports in the summer and fall of 1869 tell of Chinese going to the Midwest for railroad work. Five hundred went to St. Joseph, Missouri; hundreds went to Paris, Texas; a thousand began work on the line built down California's Central Valley. Soon Chinese workers could be found in New Mexico, Montana, Tennessee, Louisiana, Minnesota, Massachusetts, New York, and New Jersey. Over the following years, they joined railroad construction projects in many other states throughout the country, where they proved most useful but also sometimes more expensive than first assumed. Some noted that the

CPRR had actually paid a "high price" for the labor of the Railroad Chinese.

Leading political and business figures publicly explored the idea of recruiting hundreds of thousands of Chinese to fill the many labor needs all around the country. The *New York Commercial Advertiser,* for example, reported that employers in Charleston, South Carolina, were preparing to bring fifty thousand Chinese for work in the rice and cotton fields. A Memphis, Tennessee, newspaper announced that 100,000 Chinese would come to the Mississippi Valley in a few years. And mass movement apparently had already begun: Chinese were starting to travel to the South and some observers expected them to replace African Americans, now freed from slavery, as the region's main labor force.

The novel idea of providing Chinese labor to southern plantations had emerged soon after the end of the Civil War and the end of slavery, but a new burst of interest spread over the South in the spring and summer of 1869. A major commercial convention in New Orleans pointedly resolved to recruit Chinese who had worked on the CPRR to come build railroads in the South. At Memphis in July, five hundred delegates from California and many southern states explored the idea of bringing Chinese directly from China. The labor contractor Cornelius Koopmanschap, who had made a name for himself providing Chinese to the CPRR, attended and claimed that he could help supply Chinese to "meet all the demands of the South." He was thinking on the order of tens of thousands. Another speaker, Tye Kim Orr, a resident of Chinese ancestry and schoolteacher who claimed to understand labor economics, boldly declared that China simply had "the best labor in the world" and the South should avail itself of it. Once large numbers of Chinese workers came to the southern coastal region, one newspaper predicted, it then could reemerge "as rich and productive as in the days of yore."

Over the next several years, news reports appeared throughout the country that favorably depicted the Chinese as workers and even just as humans. Seeing Chinese in person for the first time, some Union Pacific workers reportedly exclaimed, "Why, hang it, they are just like men, after all" and did not have tails like cows. Detailed descriptions of work contracts and the labor habits of Chinese addressed the widespread curiosity about them. One article by a Euro-American contractor, for example, told of the costs involved, ways to manage contracted Chinese, the critical importance of an English-speaking "headman" or number one, as he was described, through whom orders were given, food rations, medical care and medicines, bedding, tools, and even vacation time. The writer made it clear that the Chinese required three days off for their New Year holiday.

Individual Chinese also moved across the country. Former Railroad Chinese cooks started restaurants; doctors opened herbal stores; contractors became merchants and shopkeepers. Chinese workers joined at least sixty separate railroad projects across the country.

One of the largest projects was the Central Pacific line, which stretched down the San Joaquin Valley toward Los Angeles. More than a thousand Chinese worked on it, including a treacherous stretch through the Tehachapi Mountains that required boring seventeen tunnels. A thousand Chinese attacked the San Fernando Tunnel to break into the Los Angeles basin. At almost seven thousand feet in length, it became the longest tunnel west of the Appalachians. Thousands then worked on the Southern Pacific rail line, which linked Los Angeles to Arizona and Texas. The largest employer of Railroad Chinese was the Northern Pacific Railroad, which constructed rail lines in Washington, Idaho, and Montana in the 1870s and 1880s. Six thousand, and perhaps more, worked on the NPRR. Historical recovery of their experiences on these lines has just begun.

The Railroad Chinese, and their reputation, spread beyond the borders of the United States. For the next several decades, Chinese, including some who worked on the Transcontinental, helped build rail lines on every continent. They worked by the thousands in Hawaii, Cuba, Mexico, Peru, and even French colonial Africa. Even in far-off Britain, where the railroad construction boom began in the 1830s, the Pacific Railway and Railroad Chinese attracted close attention. Special correspondents produced reports for periodicals across the country considering the global implications of the Transcontinental and the contributions of the Chinese in completing it. One British newspaper called the Chinese migration to America a "revolution" and more historically important than the "intrigues and machinations of crowned heads or wily politicians." Chinese who worked on railroads in the United States returned to China and played prominent roles in its early railroad history. One man in particular, Chen Yixi (Chin Gee Hee), who lived much of his life in the Seattle area, became legendary for his efforts to build railroads in his home area in the Siyi.

In the 1880s, some ten to twelve thousand, many reportedly Railroad Chinese from the United States, labored to complete the challenging four-hundred-mile-long western portion of the Canadian trans-Pacific line through the Canadian Rocky Mountains. Work on the line was similar to that on the Pacific Railway, with extensive clearing of lands, grading for the track, laying ties and track, blasting rocks, and opening twenty-seven tunnels through granite mountains. Recruitment and management by labor contractors was similar to that on the CPRR. Workers came from the Siyi and formed teams like those in the United States. There was great loss of life and suffering. They sustained a high death rate, with estimated numbers ranging from six hundred to fifteen hundred, some 10 percent of the workforce, or one or two fatalities for each mile of track they laid. Further research might show that the Canadian experience, which is much better documented than the history of the CPRR, could serve as an analog to that of the United States in terms of work experience and fatalities.

The CPRR's recruitment of workers and the continuing demand for Chinese labor to meet American needs stimulated Chinese migration into the United States from 1869 to 1877. In those years, fifteen thousand Chinese entered the United States on average each year, with more than twenty thousand arriving in 1873. These are far lower than the grand numbers that were tossed around by the Big Four and post-Promontory entrepreneurs but appreciably greater than in previous years and indicate that Siyi people believed opportunities in America had not just continued to exist but expanded. The Chinese population in the United States increased by 50 percent in the decade from 1870 to 1880.

In New York City alone, in 1879 Chinese had established three hundred laundries, fifty groceries, twenty tobacco stores, ten drugstores, and six restaurants and other establishments; there were another fifty Chinese laundries and six cigar stores in Brooklyn, which was not yet part of New York City. In Jersey City, three factories employed Chinese labor exclusively. All told, there were more than 2,500 Chinese men living in the area, and many had established unions with local white women, mainly "Spanish" (that is, probably Latin American) and Irish, with three hundred marriages having already occurred. With the anti-

Chinese sentiment rising in the West, it was predicted that "considerable numbers" would soon settle in New York and other eastern cities.

With the spread of Chinese across the country and their employment in construction projects, fields, and factories far distant from the West Coast, a palpable shift in attitudes toward accepting Chinese as people and not just as laborers began to appear. The *Sacramento Daily Union* noted this "awakening interest" in the "Chinese question" on the East Coast, and though some detractors continued to characterize them as slave-like, other observers adamantly argued that Chinese were industrious, self-reliant, and "remarkable for their intelligence and good general qualities." In no way should they be considered servile coolies or slaves, their defenders argued. A New York newspaper declared that tarring this "most important labor movement of the age" with such labels was degrading; these people were not "coolies" but should be called by their "proper name": "Chinese." The years of toil put in by the Railroad Chinese—their dues, so to speak—undoubtedly helped prompt this unqualified declaration of regard for them.

The *Cincinnati Commercial,* the city's major newspaper, used an eye-catching headline that echoed this emerging respect for Chinese in the country. The lead article, covering its entire front page under the inspired headline "The American Chinamen," observed that the Chinese were making a place for themselves in the country. The heartland newspaper openly welcomed them as excellent new additions to the national family and observed that the "Chinese labor question" was now the most important issue before all "intelligent laboring people everywhere in the United States." The correspondent shared the results of his recent personal investigation of the Chinese population in California and offered high praise of them. The Chinese were a people of "industry, peaceableness, honesty, patience, conscientiousness, temperance, frugality and cleanliness," he offered, and from his discussions with CPRR officials, he learned of their inestimable contribution to the recently completed railroad project. Chinese construction work, he concluded, was completed "with perfect order and a discipline never heretofore attained on any public work in the country." They were far superior in industry, behavior, and ability than the Irish, the other immigrant group to which the Chinese were often compared. In fact, even in language acquisition, the writer claimed, the Chinese learned English faster than European foreigners. More Chinese than Irish could write their names in English, he declared. All in all, he was so thoroughly impressed with the Chinese, he insisted that their "manly straightforward being" would soon "win the confidence and support" of the people in the East. Indeed, the Chinese possessed all the "elements desirable in laborers and mechanics."

In August 1869, the well-regarded New York business periodical the *Merchants' Magazine and Commercial Review* eagerly anticipated the arrival of the industrious Chinese on the East Coast and in the South, not only for their potential contributions to the workforce, but also because they complemented the vast migration of immigrants from Europe. Millions had come to the United States from Europe, the newspaper observed, and now it was the turn of "millions" of Chinese to supplement the European immigrant population. As the provocative headline of the article announced, they were the "Coming Chinese," and they should be welcomed. When they first arrived, the author noted, the Chinese suffered persecution and abuse, but they persevered and have now "asserted their right to labor." Their great work on the Central Pacific Railroad had proved their worthiness. They were what an American should be: "frugal, industrious, teachable, patient and intelligent." They were described as literate in their own language and "anxious to acquire our language" and send their children to public schools. Soon, the newspaper anticipated, they would migrate throughout the southern states and become "familiar faces in New England factory towns," where, it was optimistically predicted, they would assimilate with the local populations and attain "homogeneity." Some white observers even believed that Chinese would before long replace Native peoples and African Americans, who were allegedly decreasing in number, as the leading racial minority in the country. Was it not symbolically noteworthy that "the American, the European, and John Chinaman" were represented at the event at Promontory, one journalist observed, but not "the negro and the Indian," asking, "Was not their absence significant?"

The appearance of new gendered terminology for the Chinese in popular discourse also indicates that their toil qualified them, at least in the informed opinion of important observers, as positive, *manly* additions to the nation. Articles began to praise them as worthy, virile

immigrants: they were called not just Chinamen, as they had been cus-
tomarily designated, but simply "men." In May 1870, the influential na-
tionally circulated periodical *Frank Leslie's Illustrated Newspaper* began
an unprecedented series of major articles under the telling, and frequently heard, title "The Coming Man." Famed Civil War correspondent and traveler to China Thomas W. Knox wrote the series, and illustrator Joseph Becker provided detailed visual impressions of many
dimensions of Chinese in America, including their travel and arrival,
interior locations in San Francisco's Chinatown, including temples and
theaters, scenes along the Pacific Railway and other work sites, and life
in their private spaces. The depictions are respectful and detailed. Such
comprehensive press attention to the Chinese in America had never
been seen before. The series ran weekly for months, with each install-
ment presenting a lengthy description of the life, personality, and ways
of the Chinese. Knox predicted, they "will come to our western shores,
not by dozens or hundreds, but by thousands and ultimately hundreds
of thousands." Moreover, they are a "recuperative race" and will "mul-
tiply rapidly," he wrote, as "they are not effete," echoing the new gendered image given them. By the close of the century, he asserted, their
numbers would dominate the American West, and in time the whole
"new world" would likely be "as Asiatic as it now is European." For
Knox, that future America full of Chinese was not frightening, and
though it was not imminent, the development would be just a matter of time. The vision of Chinese as the "coming man" so captured
American imaginations that other writers circulated both the phrase
and the sense that America was on the verge of a veritable social transformation.

Charles Crocker himself also employed gendered language to praise
Chinese. He maintained that the CPRR had treated them "like men,"
and they in turn treated the company "like men." The Chinese, he
publicly declared, "are men, good and true men." Extending the hand
of manly equality was Crocker's way of expressing sincere respect for
those who had made him very wealthy.

But perhaps the most telling evidence of the possibility of change in
the attitude of white Americans toward Chinese was the post-Promontory public discussion about extending to them the right to become
naturalized citizens. The post–Civil War political climate in the country prompted debate about naturalization privileges and race and the

Promontory event in 1869 had called attention to the growing presence and apparent importance of the alien Chinese in the country. So too did the successful conclusion of the Burlingame Treaty between China and the United States in 1868. Designed by Anson Burlingame, an American who had served as Lincoln's minister to China and then became China's minister to the United States, the agreement sought to establish a relationship of equality, mutual benefit, and reciprocity between the two countries. The treaty committed the parties to extending equal rights, protections, and privileges to the respective subjects of the two countries, including the ability to freely immigrate.

Many in the United States took these domestic and international developments to mean that the existing prohibition against Chinese naturalization should be dropped. The exemplary record of the Railroad Chinese also convinced many that Chinese would make decent and desirable Americans, and they openly said so. After studying California's Chinese, one writer from the Midwest confessed in September 1869, "I have been weaned of my prejudices against them," and boldly declared, "I am thoroughly impressed that they would make good citizens." A San Franciscan explicitly linked the issue to the centerpiece of national politics at the time, saying that extending citizenship to Chinese was consistent with, and required by, the objectives of Reconstruction. The Radical Republican principle that "all men are created equal" must be "impartially construed so as to take in the whole human race," he claimed, and because the Radical Republicans considered Chinese "the equal of the Europeans," the two races must "come here on terms of equality." Chinese should have access to citizenship, and for Radical Republicans in Congress to grant anything less would make them "hypocritical dogs." As early as August 1869, there were even reports about Chinese who had recently arrived in the Mississippi Delta voting in local elections in Louisiana.

In 1870, Congress passed a new Naturalization Act that expressly protected black former slaves who had been born outside the United States by extending naturalization privileges beyond whites to persons of African ancestry. The act, however, stopped short of eliminating all racial requirements. Leading congressmen had argued for doing just that, but others, especially from the South and West, vehemently opposed doing so, as it would mean Chinese would be admitted to citizenship, which was unacceptable to them. Nevertheless, the issue did not go away. Efforts to remove racial categories and extend naturalization to Chinese persisted through the 1870s, though without success. Chinese continued to be denied naturalized citizenship until 1943.

As Americans and Chinese wondered about improved prospects for a future in America, Chinese also looked back on their recent experiences to address that most important of life's responsibilities for them: attending to the departed. Even before the concluding events at Promontory Summit, Chinese began planning on recovering the remains of the many Chinese who had died during the construction effort. In 1868, a year before Promontory, Chinese leaders in San Francisco dedicated $10,000 to meet the expenses for disinterring the bones of a reported "three hundred Chinese persons" who were buried along the route of the Pacific Railway for repatriation to China for final burial, as custom dictated. This now raises one of the most sensitive and controversial issues in Railroad Chinese history: How many Chinese died during the building of the rail line?

Chinese who came to America risked death from accidents, disease, even murder. Death on board ship was a regular occurrence during the long voyage from China. The death or suffering of a "Chinaman" for most whites was not especially noteworthy. An example of this callousness is found in the travel journal of an American writer, Lucius Waterman. One day during his voyage across the Pacific, Waterman noted, a Chinese crewman "was attacked by a very peculiar disease, quite unknown among all civilized nations." Waterman added that he might enter details in his journal at a future time "if I feel like it." Either the same Chinese or another, Waterman also wrote, "put an end to his existence by jumping overboard after first attempting to kill himself." He "was suffering with a fever and was somewhat insane. No funeral honors in consequence. Passed the time as usual." The loss of a Chinese life was barely an event worth noting.

It is an understatement to say that California, and all of the American West, was a violent and dangerous place in the nineteenth century, but there was also no equal opportunity in suffering violence. Native peoples faced methodical, systematic murder. The remains of thou-

sands of Chinese, many of whom died violently, were regularly returned back to their home villages from America over the years. Spiritual belief required that the bodies of the dead be repatriated so the
deceased could be near their families for eternity. Shipping companies
accrued a handsome profit from the practice. Famed New York jurist
and future U.S. attorney general Edwards Pierrepont cynically noted in
an 1868 address that American shipping companies were then engaged
in a most advantageous exchange: they "take out dead Chinamen" to
China and "bring back live ones," he said. "Carcasses of defunct Chinamen" is how the *Sacramento Daily Union* crudely described the remains
returned to their homes.

The circumstances of daily life posed great risk for Chinese along
the Transcontinental. Where they lived and worked, and even how
they traveled, could kill them. Violent death could come suddenly,
anonymously, and take many in a second. On the Sacramento River
south of the starting point of the Central Pacific in October 1865, boil-
ers of a steamer suddenly exploded and destroyed almost all of its forward decks and what was called the "Chinese saloon." It was an undesirable place reserved for deck supplies and Chinese passengers, some
of whom may have been on their way to work on the railroad. The
blast killed fourteen whites and more than thirty Chinese "instanta-
neously" with hot steam, as was evident from the scalded skin on their
recovered bodies. The Chinese were twenty-nine men and one "China-
woman." Men identified as "scoundrels" were later arrested, carrying
packets and satchels of money and personal items taken from the bodies of the dead Chinese.

Not all deaths were by accident. From the first arrival of Chinese
migrants in the early 1850s, villains commonly selected them for robbery and vicious violence against their person, especially if they were
carrying gold panned from California streams. If by luck they discovered a rich source of the precious metal, their good fortune could turn
to misfortune and horrible slaughter at the hands of men who wanted
the wealth for themselves. In 1856 the *Shasta Republican* estimated that
"hundreds of Chinamen" had been "slaughtered in cold blood" over
the previous five years by "desperadoes." The newspaper angrily observed that although "the murder of Chinamen was of almost daily
occurrence," there had been only two or three convictions. Many in

California opposed executing a white man for murdering a Chinese, according to the paper.

Killing Chinese could also be a planned, collective action. In Grass Valley in the spring of 1868, near the CPRR line, a gang identified as Ku Klux Klan members robbed and lynched four Chinese. But the worst mass killing of Chinese was yet to come in the 1870s and 1880s, when massacres of dozens of Chinese occurred throughout the West.

One tale, handed down from generation to generation by Chinese Americans whose ancestors lived through these times, tells of an unfortunate Chinese miner in Mariposa County, south of the CPRR line, who was thrown in jail after he accidentally wounded a white miner in an altercation. Imprisonment did not satisfy twenty white men loaded with whiskey. They wanted blood. They stormed the jail and managed to slip a rope through the bars and around the prisoner. The gang gleefully pulled and pulled, squeezing the man's body against the bars until suddenly his agonized screams stopped. The rope flew out soaked with viscera. His body had been cut in two and his head battered to a pulp. The jail cell was a mass of gore. For years afterward, prisoners who inhabited the murder cell swore a Chinese ghost haunted the place. Try as they might, jailers could never completely cover over the bloodstains on the walls. They were still faintly visible more than seventy-five years later, the lingering presence of what became known as the Ghost of Hornitos.

There is little question that constructing the Central Pacific Railroad line claimed the greatest loss of life of Chinese in America. How many died is impossible to know, as the company kept no records of personnel killed on the job. Estimates from company officials many years later are in themselves unsettling in their vagueness. This has led to some preposterous legends, such as that the company murdered eight hundred unpaid Railroad Chinese by chaining them together and dumping them in the middle of Lake Tahoe to drown in the depths. The legend holds that their bodies remain preserved at the frigid bottom of the deep lake. There is no evidence for the horror story, but it has endured. Many Chinese workers certainly did die while constructing the CPRR; no fabrication is needed to establish that truth.

Louis M. Clement, one of the company's chief engineers, recalled, for example, that "during the winter months there was constant dan-

ger from avalanches, and many laborers lost their lives." James H. Strobridge, chief of construction, recalled "many instances" in the High Sierra in winter when "our camps were carried away by snowslides, and
men were buried and many of them were not found until the snow
melted the next summer." Tunnel engineer John Gilliss wrote that in
the ferocious winter of 1866–67, an avalanche at Tunnel No. 10 took the
lives of "some fifteen or twenty Chinamen." A. P. Partridge, a member
of a bridge-building crew, also remembered the terrible winters, and
he too said about the Chinese workers that "a good many were frozen to death" in 1867. The repeated use of the undefined term "many"
by these veteran railroad builders is disturbing. How many is *many*?
"Many" is far greater than "some," "a score," "dozens," or even "a hundred," all of which could have been offered as an estimate. But not one
of the officials provided any numbers. They could not, perhaps would
not, even venture a guess at the human toll.

No account of the experience of a Chinese worker during the construction of the Pacific Railroad line exists, but there is one from a
worker on the Canadian trans-Pacific line, which was built in the 1880s,
and his memoir emphasizes the horrors that he and his comrades suffered. Wong Hau-hon arrived in Canada in 1882 and joined hundreds
of other Chinese working on the Canadian Pacific Railway (CPR) in
the mountains of British Columbia. In 1926 when he was interviewed,
Wong shuddered when he was asked to recall death on the line. He
spoke of seeing corpses of many, many Chinese who had died from
disease along the route. Sometimes their bodies "were stuffed into
rock crevices or beneath the trees," awaiting the arrival of coffins. Others were hurriedly buried in crude boxes or just in blankets or grass
mats. "New graves dotted the landscape and the sight sent chills up
and down my spine," he said. Death from accidental explosions also
claimed many of his friends. A huge boulder thrown up by a blast fell
on one worker, Leung, and killed him. In another incident, a dynamite
misfire in a cave took the lives of ten or twenty Chinese; their bodies,
Wong recalled, "flew from the cave as if shot from a cannon. Blood and
flesh were mixed in a horrible mess." One of the CPR's main white labor contractors stated that approximately six hundred Chinese were
killed during construction of the line from accidents, poor food, and
severe weather conditions. His number was likely an underestimation.

Wong believed that three thousand Chinese had died, though his estimate was likely too high. The actual number, which will never be known, probably falls between these two extremes.

During the construction of the CPRR, local newspapers sometimes printed reports of accidents and deaths, but these were far from being comprehensive. Accounts from other sources such as individual memoirs tell of deaths that never found their way into the press. Partridge, the line supervisor, for example, recollected one of these deaths in his memoir. He recalled that one morning in the winter of 1867, when he and some friends were returning to Truckee by sleigh after a dance the night before at Donner Lake, they "saw something under a tree by the side of the road, its shape resembling the shape of a man. We stopped and found a frozen Chinaman." They threw the body into the sleigh and took it to town, where they "laid him out by the side of a shed and covered him with a rice mat, the most appropriate thing for the laying out of a Celestial." His chilling telling is unfeeling. He observed that "a good many" Chinese "were frozen to death" in the area but also gave no numbers.

Wong Geu, who was born in 1856 in China and arrived in America in 1878, provides another personal account. He settled in the Truckee area, where he worked as a track layer for the Southern Pacific. In the 1930s he told a researcher that he had once uncovered human bones at the snow sheds and tunnels near the summit. He concluded that they were the remains of Chinese railroad workers who had died from avalanches or tunneling accidents years before. He collected what he could find, arranged the bones, and reburied them in a solemn ceremony. He hoped the spirits of the departed workers had finally found some peace. This labor of honoring the dead was an obligation he felt duty bound to fulfill. After working for the railroad, he had gone on to work, of all things, as a comedian in San Francisco's Chinatown for many years, but he never forgot his somber effort to care for the remains of the compatriots he never knew.

Nineteenth-century newspapers did publish articles about specific incidents that resulted in the deaths of Railroad Chinese. Even in their brevity, the reports often convey a dreadful sense of the constant danger they faced. The casual language informing readers of these tragic and gruesome deaths, and the omission of any name or other indication of identity, also suggests that for many other Californians, the death of Chinese was barely newsworthy. They were just "China-men."

- In April 1866, an accidental explosion at Colfax on the line took the lives of six or seven workers, three or five being "Chinamen," all unnamed. The explosion was so powerful, the remains of some of the victims could not be found.

- Just before Christmas in 1866, a terrible snowslide buried "a gang of Chinamen," killing four or five of them. According to the *Dutch Flat Enquirer,* another "whole camp of Chinamen was covered up during the night and parties were digging them out when our informant left."

- A snowslide killed at least nineteen Chinese, with many more feared lost, according to a March 1867 news report.

- In May 1867, a Chinese worker excavating a line was killed when an embankment collapsed and buried him.

- In mid-June 1867, a huge explosion in a tunnel a mile from Cisco killed one white worker and at least "five Chinamen" who were "blown up, all of whom were horribly mangled." The news report described a horse and cart being blown a hundred feet in the air before they "came down in pieces."

- In December 1867, the *New York Evening Post* reported that twenty-two railroad workers on the Central Pacific died in an avalanche.

- In January 1868, at Truckee, snow crushed a cabin where Chinese were living. Five died, and five others were "seriously injured."

- In February 1868, "two Chinamen" were killed on the line near Emigrant Gap. A locomotive pushing a snowplow caused a snowslide that threw them under the train, which ran over one of them and "instantly" killed him.

- In 1868, two white railroad workers murdered two Chinese fellow workers in Toana, Nevada.

- In the spring of 1868, the melting snows revealed corpses of Chinese workers still upright, their tools in their hands. Snow had buried them the previous winter.

- A June 1868 item in the *Daily Alta California* reported that "a slide, in consequence of a blast, occurred near the summit tunnel, on the line of the Pacific Railroad, about noon day before yesterday, by which several Chinamen were killed." Another report, perhaps on the same incident, stated that "thirty Chinamen who were engaged in excavating a snow tunnel, near the Summit, were caved on and covered up by the snow."

- In October 1868, a huge accidental explosion killed three Chinese and two white laborers who were working along the Humboldt River in Utah.

- In December 1868, a locomotive smashed into a tree that Chinese were trying to remove from the tracks and "so killed one of the Chinamen." The report, under the headline "Accident to a Freight Train," focused on damage to the vehicle.

- Death could also come at the hands of a fellow Railroad Chinese. In early May 1869, at least one Chinese killed another in fighting near Promontory.

The uncertainty about deaths of Railroad Chinese fuels the single most emotional historical controversy in their history. For many today, the meager information about their deaths and desultory historical attention to their loss dishonor their sacrifice. Efforts have been made over the years to calculate, or at least estimate, the numerical toll alone. Numbers at the low end of the range, based principally on newspaper reports, suggest that fewer than 150 died. The Central Pacific, in its own interests, it has been argued, had no reason to see large numbers of workers die; the expense of recruiting and retaining them was a strong incentive to try to keep them out of harm's way, and thus the numbers must have been low. In response, others argue that the numbers were significantly higher, perhaps in the thousands, and cite ample evidence indicating that the leaders of the CPRR were desperate to lay as much track as fast as possible, as the very survival of the company depended on it, and they worried little about the working conditions of the Chinese. Their lives were expendable, financially as well as morally, and less important than making speedy progress. The almost complete absence of attention to worker fatalities in the correspondence among the CPRR's top leaders is itself evidence of the low regard they gave to the dangers facing the workers. The vast majority of space in the letters is devoted to discussing how to solve pressing issues of construction and finance. As Lewis Clement responded when asked how many Chinese worked on the line, "I never counted." And then, tellingly, he added, "I never took any particular interest in them, never cared about them so long as we got the work done." E. B. Crocker made the company's priorities clear in his own way in a private letter he sent to Collis Huntington in the harsh winter of 1867. Crocker informed Huntington that terrible accidents that took human lives were bound to happen during railroad construction, "in spite of all precautions," but the company must be prepared for them so that such accidents "will not stop the tracklaying beyond."

Relying solely on reportage provides an unreliable picture, as much evidence indicates that news of many Chinese deaths never made it into the newspapers at the time. In fact, a number of news items about deaths appear to have come from writers who happened to learn of the events simply by chance. No journalists were attached to the CPRR full-time. No article ever mentions that the company provided any information of its own on such incidents, and the CPRR never issued any public statement acknowledging the death of any railroad worker, Chinese or otherwise. Industrial relations then were a far cry from what they would become.

A compelling argument using evidence beyond newspaper accounts of accidents suggests that the death toll may well have climbed to over one thousand, though the case is far from conclusive. This estimate is based on reports about what appears to have been a mass repatriation of Chinese remains for shipment back to China for final burial after the Promontory event.

The story begins in mid-1869 with an article published by the *Cincinnati Commercial* that mentioned a sum of $10,000 that San Francisco Chinatown leaders had recently raised for the cost of retrieving and returning the remains of "300 Chinese persons" who were "buried on the line of the Central Pacific Railroad." Several months later, in early January 1870, the *Independent* in Elko, Nevada, which is located on the CPRR line, reported that Chinese had been unearthing the remains of their countrymen who had died nearby. In that area of Nevada, almost all the Chinese had worked for the CPRR. Another paper reported that as many as six freight cars carrying the remains of Chinese were sitting on tracks between small towns in eastern Nevada. The causes of death are not given. Also in late January, in what may have been part

228 • GHOSTS OF GOLD MOUNTAIN

of a coordinated effort, Chinese began disinterring the remains of "defunct brethren at the city cemetery" in Sacramento, "preparatory to shipping their bones to China." In March 1870, a Nevada newspaper reported on further efforts to uncover and prepare Chinese remains around Winnemucca, 125 miles to the west of Elko. These dead were "a goodly number of Johns," according to the news report, who had "delivered up the ghost along the line of the Central Pacific railroad" and were being prepared for repatriation. The remains were in containers "prepared and boxed in the most approved manner, and labeled with appropriate Chinese characters, given name, date of death, and company to which the deceased belonged." Two train cars had transported the remains to San Francisco. These separate news reports appear to indicate that Chinese were engaged in a coordinated remains repatriation operation of major proportions, its size far exceeding anything similar before or after.

In late June 1870, the *Sacramento Reporter*, under the headline "Bones in Transit," noted, "The accumulated bones of perhaps 1,200 Chinamen came in by the eastern train yesterday from along the line of the Central Pacific Railroad." The remains weighed "about 20,000 pounds." No detail was given on how the numbers were obtained. According to the newspaper, "nearly all of them are the remains of employees of the company who were engaged in building the road" and were on their way back for final burial in China. The *Daily Alta California*, the leading newspaper in the state, published out of San Francisco, reported the same information from Sacramento, including that the remains were of those "who died while in the construction of the Central Pacific Railroad and other service" and that they were "in *transitu* per railroad *en route* for China." Along with the information from 1869, these articles, and the information from a third newspaper that reported on the remains of about 150 other Railroad Chinese who died along the line and were interred locally, make a case that possibly as many as 1,200, or more, Chinese died during the construction of the CPRR from a variety of causes, including natural causes, industrial accidents and disasters, and diseases such as smallpox, which was known to have afflicted railroad labor camps.

Ambiguities and questions about the deaths remain, however: Where and how did the Chinese die? Why did the recovery of these remains occur so soon after the completion of the work on the CPRR?

Chinese custom allows for about ten years to pass before disinterment so that the flesh would decompose, leaving the bones, in which Chinese believed the spirit resided. Since their arrival in large numbers in California in the early 1850s, Chinese had regularly sent remains back to China in large shipments, the practice known as *jianyun* (bringing prosperity to descendants), which the English-language press frequently observed. Thousands had returned to their home villages over the years in such fashion, but no single repatriation had ever compared in size to the one of 1870.

The news articles did not provide details on how the remains were stored. Were they in coffins, which held the full remains of the recently deceased; "bone boxes," which held full or partial dry bone remains; or "spirit boxes" (*zhaohun xiang*), which held no physical remains? Spirit boxes were used when an individual was known to have died but the remains could not be recovered. The boxes were ritually consecrated near the death site to hold the spirit of the deceased in its own special container. These different sorts of vessels therefore varied considerably in weight and size, which means that the actual number of deaths could have been either lower or considerably higher than estimated in the news accounts.

Another way of looking at the deaths of Chinese who worked on the railroad is to consider the general death rate for Chinese in America. In late 1869, just six months after the events at Promontory, Chinese benevolent associations released their "census" of Chinese in America. Because the associations were intimately involved in welcoming arriving Chinese, collecting insurance monies and dues, monitoring debt, and guaranteeing the repatriation of remains, they kept detailed membership records, which probably give the most accurate tally of the population. Almost all Chinese in America belonged to one of the associations. According to their records. from the mid-1850s, when they were founded, to 1869, 7.5 percent of the Chinese who came to America died here, with the percentage varying considerably among the associations. For example, the Ningyung Benevolent Association, the largest, claimed 46,867 members over that period of time. Of these, 12,262 had returned to China, 27,118 remained in the United States, and 3,487 had died here. The second largest, the Yanghe Association, listed 28,207 members, of whom 21,820 were in the United States, 4,295 had returned to China, and 2,085 had died. The smallest association had a death rate of almost 20 percent. Various sources present figures that suggest that the risk of early death from disease, accident, or violence for Chinese in America, an almost all-young, all-male population, was high.

Other reports gave an even higher rate. The *Railroad Record*, a periodical on railroad matters, published population figures for the Chinese in January 1870. The journal claimed that 138,000 Chinese had arrived in California, and of these, 37,322 had returned to China; 16,426 had died; 41,000 still lived in California, including 31,700 "active laborers," 9,300 women and children, and the remainder old, ill, or in prison. The proportion of those who had died while in California was therefore 12 percent. Though the precise number of Railroad Chinese deaths will never be known, the toll was likely well into the hundreds, if not substantially higher.

The glimmer of possibilities for work for Railroad Chinese which appeared post-Promontory eroded steadily and then violently in the later 1870s and the 1880s. The reputation they had earned as exemplary workers, and the successes they were establishing as laborers, storekeepers, artisans, and merchants in the towns along the railroad and the regions it opened up for them, were now being used against them. A terrible economic recession in the 1870s stimulated the rise of racist populism. Agitators claimed that white workers could not compete against the hardworking and frugal Chinese, who were, in what seemed to be a contradictory prejudice, perceived as racially and culturally inferior in many fundamental ways. Racists held that white workers could not compete against Chinese, but also that they should not have to. The railroad that Chinese had helped build produced a terrible unintended consequence.

Just as Chinese used the railroad to spread across the country to places where they had never been before, white migrants from the East, many of them immigrants themselves, used the railroad to flood into the West, where they found Chinese already working and living. They saw Chinese as a threatening, undesirable race that deserved no place in a white man's country. Organized forces throughout the United States conducted what can be called "the great purge" to rid the nation of Chinese. They used political, often violent action, tragically, with great success. The massive numbers of "the coming man" that were once predicted never materialized. Instead, a veritable war against Chinese in America reduced their numbers decisively.

The opening shot of this war was fired in Los Angeles. In October 1871, a mob of five hundred attacked the Chinese quarter in Los Angles, then a small town. They ransacked and burned buildings occupied by Chinese and mutilated, shot, and lynched eighteen Chinese in the streets. Railroad Chinese who had traveled to southern California for railroad work there were likely among the victims. The massacre was the largest mass lynching in American history. Twenty-five rioters were indicted for murder, but none of them was ever convicted of the crime.

In June 1876, a heinous killing of a Chinese man occurred in Truckee in what is called the "Trout Creek Outrage." The mood of the town had turned viciously against Chinese, and hundreds of whites coordinated efforts to drive them out. Six or seven white men, members of a secret group called the Caucasian League, descended, fully armed, on two cabins inhabited by Chinese woodcutters along Trout Creek, not far from Truckee, at 1:00 a.m. on the eighteenth. They poured kerosene on the cabins and set them afire. As Chinese fled the burning buildings, the vigilantes shot them, killing one and wounding others, who fled into the woods. Though seven men were brought to trial, none were convicted of any crime and all were set free. A local newspaper called the shootings "one of the most cold-blooded and unprovoked murders ever recorded." During the next decade, white residents of Truckee used planned violence, arson, and mass intimidation to drive Chinese, many them former Railroad Chinese, out of the town. The 1900 census shows just two Chinese still living in Truckee. The so-called "Truckee method" of ridding the town of Chinese through real and threatened violence and boycotts against employers of Chinese gained national attention. The Chinese had to go, nationwide.

In October 1880, an armed mob of up to three thousand attacked the Denver Chinese community, which numbered a few hundred. The rioters, aiming to expel all Chinese from the city, burned residences, looted, and beat Chinese men and women, killing one. City officials rounded up more than two hundred Chinese and placed them in the county jail for their own "protection."

Formalizing these mob anti-Chinese sentiments, in 1882 Congress passed the first in a series of what are called the Chinese Exclusion Acts. Sinophobes agitated for this legislation to confirm the ineligibility of Chinese for citizenship and their exclusion from entering the United States. Opponents of these draconian measures cited the value of Chinese to America, including their work on building the nation's infrastructure. President Chester Alan Arthur vetoed an early version of the legislation and referenced Railroad Chinese as a reason for his decision, declaring that the Chinese "were largely instrumental in constructing the railways which connect the Atlantic with the Pacific." Congress overrode his veto and the objections of others, and in 1892 the restrictions were strengthened and continued under what was called the Geary Act, named for the sponsoring representative from California.

These federally sanctioned anti-Chinese actions did not satisfy extremists, however. Local mobs took matters into their own hands and used extralegal measures to rid the country of Chinese. In these perilous years, Huie Kin recalled, he and other Chinese feared they would be shot in the back if they left their homes.

In September 1885, an armed mob of 150 white workers attacked Chinese coal miners in Rock Springs, Wyoming, and killed at least twenty-eight. Chinese were, in the words of one article on the atrocity, "scalped, mutilated, branded, decapitated, dismembered, and hanged from gutter spouts." One was sexually mutilated. They were among more than three hundred working for the Union Pacific Railroad. Those not killed were driven out of town.

The worst incidence of violence against Chinese was the torture, mutilation, and murder of at least thirty-four Chinese miners in Hells Canyon, Oregon, in 1887. It is likely that some were former railroad workers. The "Evans Gang" ambushed the Chinese working along a remote section of the Snake River in eastern Oregon, and though the Chinese were armed and tried to defend themselves, the villains methodically picked them off and butchered their bodies. Some were scalped. The gang's lust for gold alone did not explain their savagery: racial hatred also burned in their hearts. None of the gang was ever convicted of the crime.

The number of expulsion efforts and killings of Chinese has been documented to be approximately 170 episodes, with seventy-five Chinese killed in just the years 1885–1887, the high point in anti-Chinese violence in the United States and its territories. Many Chinese fled the country, and by 1900, the Chinese population in the United States had dropped to 90,000 from its high point of 133,000 in 1882.

At issue in the controversy over the deaths of Chinese who perished during and after the construction of the Pacific Railroad is the deep anguish and anger many felt about the suffering Chinese endured in nineteenth-century America, which has yet to be fully acknowledged. The grief continues long after the moments of tragedy. Numbers can suggest dimensions; the deeper question is the meaning of historical experience to the living. For many, especially Chinese Americans, the history of the Railroad Chinese requires contending with a painful, aggrieved, and unsettled past. Many today who sympathize with the Railroad Chinese say that low-end estimates of violent deaths of Chinese during and after the building of the railroads demean them and the blood contribution Chinese have made to America.

Take, for example, a Railroad Chinese story provided by Sing Lum, born in Bakersfield in 1904. He became a moderately successful farmer, civic leader in local public education, and sprinter in senior track events. In 1984 the local school district honored him by naming a primary school after him. Late in life, Lum shared his memories with H. K. Wong, a San Francisco businessman and community historian. Lum recounted stories his grandfather and father had told him long ago, when he was a youngster, about the Chinese and the railroads. His grandfather, who may have worked in railroad construction, told him, "It was a hard, hard job to work on the railroad." And treatment from "the boss man," the "white man," was bad. "If they didn't like you, they'd just put a bullet through your head. Real tough times. Every day some killing going on," Lum was told. Many Chinese were buried right along the Southern Pacific railroad track, especially around Delano, in Kern County, which the line reached in 1873. Lum recalled marking old graves. "Many Chinese got killed," he said, "two or three hundred of them" during tunneling, and were buried in Caliente. In the 1920s their remains were sent back to China.

After the railroad work was done, Lum was told, "the railroad people didn't take the Chinese back to San Francisco. They let them walk back. See how cruel they were?" Then whites in Tulare County wouldn't let Chinese cross through the county. "They killed quite a few of them." Native Americans helped the stranded Chinese go west over the mountains to the coast and walk back north. They had nothing to eat. Many died. Lum then told Wong: "When we talk about how cruel these white people were to the Chinese, it just makes a fellow mad . . . [B]ack in the old days, the white man considered you as nothing, you're not even a human being."

Another tragic incident highlights historical amnesia and Chinese death. In the rugged Santa Cruz Mountains, through which one travels to get from Silicon Valley to the shore, few today know that many Chinese died building a railroad through this coastal range. There are no markers. There is almost nothing in the history books. Nevertheless, just before midnight on November 18, 1879, more than thirty Chinese railroad workers died horribly in an explosion while they were tunneling for a line that connected San Jose to Santa Cruz. Veterans of the Central Pacific work were likely among them. They were among one thousand Chinese then working on the line owned by James G. Fair, the silver baron of the Comstock Lode and an aspiring railroad boss. Earlier in the spring of that year, a tunnel explosion had terribly burned more than a dozen Chinese workers. After surviving in agony for weeks, five died at the Chinese hospital in San Francisco. The rest of the Chinese returned to work reluctantly, fearful of the bad omen.

The second calamity occurred 2,700 feet into the tunnel, when natural gas and seeping oil again exploded and took even more lives. Twenty-one Chinese and two whites were in the tunnel at the time. After twenty more Chinese, among them a man identified only as "Jim," who had alerted the telegraph operator about the disaster, rushed into the tunnel to aid the victims, a second, even more violent explosion shook the mountain. The tunnel acted like a giant cannon bore and blasted out fire, rock, equipment, and humans. A third explosion occurred a few minutes later. The two white men were burned, but they survived. Newspaper reports listed twenty-four Chinese killed inside the tunnel; seventeen others who were removed were "all horribly burned," with many dying in agonizing pain soon afterward. The "stench of burning flesh" belched from the portal. One horribly injured man identified as Ah Wo was found an hour later, dead in his cabin, with a silk scarf tied around his neck. His comrades said that that he had hanged himself, but evidence suggested that his friends had actually strangled him "to put him out of misery," as the news article put it. The mangled body of Jim, who had rushed into the burning tunnel to help his compatriots, was later found inside the tunnel. His friend Cook, the white telegraph operator, sadly identified his remains. Jim and Ah Wo are the only Chinese identified by name. Later reports placed the number of Chinese buried at the site at thirty-two. Two years later, a huge mudslide buried another camp of Railroad Chinese. A dozen of their bodies were eventually recovered, but the full number of those killed was never determined. They are forgotten souls.

Chinese took death rituals seriously, and the elaborate ceremonies at their funerals attracted a great deal of attention from white Americans. Chanting, wailing, burning symbolic items for use in the afterlife, and distribution of food often accompanied the occasion. A photograph of a Chinese funeral in Idaho circa 1880 offers a rare view of one of these moments (below). Chinese priests in gowns, banners from Chinese associations, and the grief on faces mark this sad occasion.

Some Railroad Chinese waited many years for death to come so that their remains, and spirits, could return to the villages where they were born. Ah Jim was born in 1826 in China and arrived in the United States in 1859 at a relatively old thirty-three years of age. He worked on railroads and eventually settled in Marysville, California, which had a sizable Chinese population and where he aged through many decades. In 1941 he was reportedly 115 years old, blind, and a public charge. He said he was anticipating his death because then his remains could finally be sent home to be with his ancestors, and descendants, in China.

It is not known whether Ah Jim's final wish was ever granted. We do not know whether his spirit is an abandoned, hungry ghost still haunting here or a content spirit at home. Over time, his life, like the lives of so many other Railroad Chinese, was simply forgotten. As with those who actually died during the construction of the Transcontinental, thoughtless glorification of its completion over the years overshadowed its tremendous human cost and made Ah Jim, one of the forgotten workers, yet another victim of the railroad.

CONCLUSION

As the excitement of the meeting at Promontory Summit faded into the past and Chinese were pushed to the margins of American life, the place of Railroad Chinese in the story of the Transcontinental consequently became hazy, even obscured. Occasionally, however, someone would remember them and recall their contributions. At the fiftieth anniversary of the completion ceremony on May 10, 1919, organizers located three workers who were said to have formed part of the crew that laid the last rail. Old and worn, Ging Cui, Wong Fook, and Lee Shao were brought out of retirement from Susanville, a small town of retired railroad workers in western Nevada. Reportedly, they had worked on railroads for more than fifty years, "none taking a leave of absence" until just three years earlier, when they finally stopped working and received pensions. Brought out to stand in a celebratory parade, they were dressed in period work clothes to recall a history that the anniversary celebration romanticized. But in the few photographs from the day, the three appear tired — a news report said they were in their nineties — and they hardly seem pleased with being put on display (below). The news reporter described them as "shy"; being honored was "a bit strange to them." "The strangers," as the local newspaper called them, "will be placed upon a float" with tools and other material from the construction era. Because their names are given several different ways in the news articles, we cannot even be sure of their actual identities. After the event, they fall into historical oblivion. We know nothing about what became of them, not even where they are buried.

Newspapers over the years occasionally mentioned other individual Railroad Chinese. In 1931, in brief articles, several California newspapers reported on the passing of Hung Wah. From the meager information contained in them, he apparently was the same Hung Wah of the railroad story, but it is not certain. If indeed he was, he had outlived his old friend William McDaniel; E. B. Crocker died in 1875, Charles Crocker in 1888, Leland Stanford in 1893, and James Strobridge in 1921.

The man identified as Hung Wah had died at 3:15 a.m. on April 14, 1931, at the age of ninety-six in the county hospital of Placerville, near Auburn, where he had been an "inmate" for twenty years. It seems he had become a ward of the county. He had been a well-known eccentric on the streets of the town, where he "hobbled about" collecting "scrap tin foil and other tit-bits of street refuse," which he carried back to hoard in his room. An attendant had to clear out the refuse regularly when the patient was out.

The articles described him as the "sole remaining pioneer Chinese of the gold rush days in California." Mention is also made of his work in lumber and mining, but none about the railroad. Local residents had given him demeaning nicknames that drew on long-standing slurs against Chinese, including "Hung Wah Rock," "Rock Canyon Charlie," "Charlie Bang Bang," and "King Tut." The news articles and hospital records provide no names of any relatives or friends. He died of heart disease, after living in California for eighty-one years. According to the burial permit, he was "single," and the names of his parents were "unknown." No funeral or memorial service was held, and he was quickly buried the day after his death in the county hospital cemetery. Three years later the cemetery itself was closed and abandoned. Today the grave markers are all gone, and one cannot even locate where he is buried. Hung Wah's was a pitiful end to a long and storied life. His lonely end, his life experiences largely later on forgotten, is emblematic of the void in the history of the Railroad Chinese.

If this is not Hung Wah of the Transcontinental, the story also ends sadly, but in a different way: Hung Wah of Auburn disappears from history entirely. There is no further mention of him in newspapers or public records, including of his death, in Auburn, except for the completion and apparently the final destruction of his entrepreneurial efforts. And for almost 150 years, his role in building the Transcontinental went unrecognized.

Here is the last that we know. After the completion of the Transcontinental, labor contractor Hung Wah made his way back to Auburn, where he continued his business activities. He leased acres of land, again contracted out labor, and ran a grocery store carrying Chinese goods. As one of the most prominent Chinese in town, however, he also encountered direct violence in 1880 as the racial mood in the state turned ugly. In the dead of night in July, a "thunderous" explosion, according to the local newspaper, shook the entire town, waking sleeping residents, breaking glass, and lifting structures from the ground. The sound was described as like that of an artillery explosion or an earthquake. Unknown villains had used black powder to blow up Hung Wah's wash house.

Located near the CPRR station, Hung Wah and his cousin's business had made a success washing laundry for nearby hotels, and the local newspaper surmised that "resentment" was the reason for the act. The explosion was so strong that "there was not a stick or timber of any kind left standing, and there was not a single board left whole." Hung Wah suffered a complete loss, and though he had at first thought about the expensive proposition of rebuilding, he abandoned the idea. Villains could always strike again. The reporter described him as "much depressed." No arrests were made, "nor are there likely to be any, we think, for public sentiment appears to be not greatly outraged by the affair." Maybe it was then that Hung Wah had had enough of Auburn and moved away for good, perhaps to Placerville, not far away, but far enough from Auburn and its festering anti-Chinese climate.

More uplifting are accounts of Railroad Chinese lives that come from Chinese Americans who have uncovered family histories. With some documentation and lore handed down through generations, the stories they have collected in recent years about their railroad ancestors, the first in their families to come to America, confirm that the foundations of the Chinese American community are inseparable from the Transcontinental. They also show that, while the ghosts of Gold Mountain remain silent in so many other contexts, they live on in the spirit and stories of their descendants who proudly cherish their ancestry and help keep history alive.

One such descendant is Gene O. Chan, a retired rocket propulsion designer. In 1855 his great-great-grandfather Jow Kee took two months to travel from southern China across the Pacific to land in San Francisco. He first went to work for mining companies, and his employers encouraged him to learn English. He Anglicized his name to Jim King, and in 1865, with his experience as a foreman and interpreter, he signed on with the CPRR. Chan, who uncovered his Railroad Chinese history over many years of effort, assumes that the railroad must have offered his ancestor wages and working conditions that were sufficiently attractive to lure him away from mining. Others in the mines must have followed suit as well, for Chan's ancestor is found on CPRR payroll records as "Jim King, Contracting Co.," similar to the way Hung Wah's labor contracting business was listed.

After working on the CPRR and gathering resources, Jim King settled in the Sacramento River delta, where he became a farmer and married a woman known as Hel Shee, with whom he had eight children. She is recalled as a "hard-working, wise and very frugal woman" who earned income from making fishing nets and sewing. They had success in farming and running gambling establishments. But as with other Railroad Chinese, tragedy struck. One day in 1898 or 1899, Jim King went missing. He was never seen again. Even today the family suspects foul play, as the region was awash with anti-Chinese violence then. But they can only speculate, for Jim King's body was never found.

Another family historian and American of Chinese descent, Russell N. Low, a physician, proudly tells the story of one of his ancestors, his great-grandfather Hung Lai Woh, who came to work on the CPRR in the mid-1860s. Though his name is similar to Hung Wah's, he was not the same person. Hung Lai Woh was accompanied by a brother who also worked on the line and lost an eye in a blasting accident. The two helped build the snow sheds that ran for miles to protect the line in the Sierra. A story circulates in the family about how one day Low's great-grandfather was walking atop a high wooden trestle when a train engine came right at him. He grabbed hold of a railroad tie and dangled in midair while the train rumbled past on the track above him. After the completion of the railroad, he made his way to San Francisco, where he learned to roll cigars, then a rising industry in the city. Hung Lai Woh later became a shopkeeper and ran his own cigar store in Chinatown. Like Jim King, he married a much younger Chinese woman, Tom Ying, in 1888. They had five children who eventually spread around the country. Low calculates that Hung Lai Woh and Tom Ying have more than one hundred descendants in the United States, including twelve great-great-great-grandchildren. Among them are engineers, military veterans, an opera singer, and a female fighter pilot.

Lim Lip Hong came from the Siyi to the United States when he was just twelve years old in the mid-1850s. After finding work washing clothes, building stone fences, and digging canals in the Sacramento River delta, he joined the effort to build the Pacific Railway; afterward he joined other lines in Utah, where he worked alongside Mormons. In Nevada he worked in mining and started a family, according to his descendants, with a Native woman, with whom he had several children, though he left them and went to San Francisco. What became of his Native American children is not known, unlike the history of his family resulting from his marriage to a young Chinese woman, Chan Shee, a seventeen-year-old beauty in San Francisco. They had seven children, seen below in the early 1900s with other relatives, and built a successful poultry and butcher business in the city's Potrero Hill district.

Lim Lip Hong had achieved success in business and in his personal life. His children were all born in the United States and thus American citizens. One of his great-great-grandsons is Michael Andrew Solorio, whose paternal grandparents were from Mexico and worked in agriculture after coming to the United States. It was at family gatherings on his mother's side when he was about twelve years old that he learned of Lim Lip Hong and the Transcontinental. Solorio's curiosity grew over the years, especially as he learned "how the railroad and Chinese migration played a significant role in the nation's history." He proudly points out that Chinese immigrants "helped shape today's United States," and therefore "feels very American and very engrained in this country." In 2017 he traveled to China to visit Lim Lip Hong's ancestral village. "I was so surprised to see how humble his background was," admits Solorio, who came to better appreciate the hard work of his family over the years that made his own life as a Stanford University undergraduate possible. The connection with history, he says eloquently, "inspires me to work hard and pursue my goals to leave my mark on this world, like my ancestors did."

Connie Young Yu, one of the leading and most dedicated historians in the Chinese American community, is an especially keen student of her own great-grandfather Lee Wong Sang. Born in Taishan, Lee left for the United States when he was just nineteen years of age. He joined the railroad, attracted by the high wages he could receive, and worked as a foreman and interpreter. Gold was what the Railroad Chinese valued, and great-grandfather Lee once bought a $20 gold piece with his wages and kept it on his person for good luck. One night, however, after he went to the latrine, he discovered that he had lost the valuable coin. He cried for a month. After his railroad work came to an end, he sent for his wife, whom he had wed before leaving China. Chin Shee, as she was known, did not have bound feet; she was smart and possessed a strong character. She arrived in the United States in the mid-1870s, and soon the couple began to have children, eventually four sons and a daughter. Lee became a successful merchant in San Francisco, but the memory of the railroad continued to play a prominent role in the family.

Stories about Chinese and the railroad filtered through the family over the years, but one especially moved Connie. She recalled her father telling her that as a youngster he listened to stories former railroad workers shared with her grandfather when they sat around having tea in the family store in the early decades of the twentieth century. They were old bachelors by then, never having been able to marry, as was the fate of many other nineteenth-century Chinese men in America. They described the hostile anti-Chinese climate they had to endure and their determined efforts to honor their compatriots who had died in building the CPRR. They told of the Chinese district associations sending people into the Sierra to look for the "remains of the Chinese who were killed on the railroad." They sometimes had maps indicating the location of remains, which when found often included identity and family information written on a piece of cloth placed inside a glass bottle. The representatives carefully packed up the remains in a box for repatriation to China. Connie's father spoke "very reverently" about this collecting of bones, which affected her deeply as a child. She says that she herself, two generations removed, grew up feeling a "kind of responsibility" to these men and their history. This helps explain her interest in these tales from the past. For her and many others, history is personal.

Seen collectively, Connie and other descendants' stories tell of life beyond individual experience. With the names and stories of real people, themes emerge. The descendants' stories usually describe Railroad Chinese who were acquisitive and entrepreneurial. They appear to have collected resources and knowledge during the construction of the CPRR which they used to establish themselves afterwards in communities large and small around the West. After attaining some financial stability, they decided to stay in America and not return to China as many others did. They were able to marry, usually to much younger women, sometimes even former prostitutes freed from their condition. They maintained close ties with China, returning on occasion, receiving relatives, or sending their own children back for a while for education or careers. Many gave generous financial or political support to China's efforts to oppose invasion and build itself into a modern nation. And, not surprisingly, all, almost without exception, had been contractors or headmen on the CPRR. They had had a feel for business and passed their drive, ambition, and good fortune on to their descendants. Sadly, few laborers, with little skill or resources for starting a family, left any progeny to tell their stories.

Railroad descendants' accounts are also offered with a varying mixture of pride, anguish, celebration, and resentment, as the complex story of the Transcontinental contains elements that sustain a wide range of sentiments. For many descendants, the tremendous contribution their ancestors made to completing the railroad firmly establishes Chinese within the fabric of the modern American nation. The railroad, it is seen, made the country's boom in the latter nineteenth century possible, and it was Chinese who made the railroad possible. The labor of the Railroad Chinese is thus the purchase of, and the irrefutable claim to, American place and identity. As the acclaimed writer Maxine Hong Kingston has written: "After the Civil War, China Men banded the nation North and South, East and West, with crisscrossing steel. They were the binding and building ancestors of this place."

Identification with the Railroad Chinese who suffered brutal working conditions and callous treatment by the CPRR is also reason for lamentation to this day. It is difficult to imagine the reality of the horrific lived experiences of family members long ago without a resulting sense of anguish and anger. What those Railroad Chinese had to endure! Their suffering is almost unimaginable.

Yet they more than survived; they also triumphed. Unbroken, they went on to build rich lives in America and in China and contribute to society. They were the progenitors of Chinese America and America itself in different ways. Admiration, even celebration, is due them.

And then there is resentment for the ignorance and prejudice that demeaned the Railroad Chinese and their descendants through the decades. Despite their sacrifice, the Railroad Chinese were tossed aside after the railroad work was done, their stories marginalized or omitted from the histories that followed, and efforts to recover their experience disrespected.

Railroad Chinese history never disappeared altogether, however, thanks to descendants who cherished their ethnic past and to dedicated writers, researchers, and scholars over many years who refused to abandon the memory of the Railroad Chinese. Because of these efforts, we know more about this history than ever before. Scholars and students in China today are taking up the pursuit of the history. Historical recovery will continue, and one day that elusive letter or diary from a railroad worker telling about his experiences 150 years ago may turn up. What a find that will be!

Though it is long overdue, in recent years the railroad workers are beginning to receive the recognition and honor they deserve, owing to years of dedicated efforts of community activists to have the history of the Railroad Chinese properly acknowledged. In May 2014 the U.S. Department of Labor formally inducted "Chinese Railroad Workers" into its Hall of Honor. In 2015 President Barack Obama and President Xi Jinping of China, during his state visit to the United States, explicitly called attention to the great contributions of the Chinese who worked on the railroad toward constructing early connections between the United States and China.

As we accumulate knowledge and honor the past, the ghosts of Gold Mountain must be feeling some comfort. They are no longer just "silent spikes" or "nameless builders" but are emerging as real historical actors. And recovering history, like the behavior of ghosts, is unpredictable and never really settled. The living continue to grapple with the past. So it is with the history of Railroad Chinese, as recovering their experiences and establishing the meaning of their lives will never end. One day a hungry ghost seeking resolution might lead a researcher to that elusive prize, the diary of a Railroad Chinese.

ACKNOWLEDGMENTS

Many friends and colleagues helped make this book possible. I have drawn especially from the work of more than a hundred scholars, archivists, and researchers in North America and Asia who contributed to the Chinese Railroad Workers in North America Project at Stanford University, which I have co-directed with Shelley Fisher Fishkin. Other project leaders include Associate Director Hilton Obenzinger, Director of Research Roland Hsu, Director of Archaeology Barbara L. Voss, and Digital Media Director Erik Steiner. Others who played leading roles in the project include Barre Fong, Teri Hessel, Kevin Hsu, Denise Khor, Gabriel Wolfenstein, and Connie Young Yu. Dongfang Shao and Evelyn Hu-Dehart helped establish the project. Many Stanford students conducted invaluable research in textual and digital materials. I thank all of the wonderful members of the project for their research, scholarship, and intellectual exchange.

For reading drafts or major portions of early versions of this book, I thank Sue Fawn Chung, Shelley Fisher Fishkin, Estelle Freedman, Roland Hsu, Sheila Melvin, Hilton Obenzinger, Phil Sexton, Victoria Sandin, Matt Sommer, Richard White, and Connie Young Yu. I thank them for sharing their knowledge, insight, and commentary.

I thank many dedicated librarians and archivists who provided invaluable help. Special thanks go to Stanford colleagues Benjamin Stone and Xiaohui Xue at Stanford Libraries, Monica Moore and Rachel Meisels in American Studies, John Groschwitz, Kelley Cortright, and Kristin Kutella-Boyd in the Center for East Asian Studies, and Sik Lee Dennig at East Asian Languages and Cultures; Steve Hindle and Li Wei Yang at the Huntington Library; and the archivists at the National Archives in San Francisco. I wish to thank many others who helped along the way. They include Julie Cain, Preston Carlson, Yong Chen, Zhongping Chen, Pat Chesnut, Mary Cory, Pin-chia Feng, Marilou Ficklin, Wallace Hagaman, Keren He, Annelise Heinz, Madeline Hsu, Hsinya Huang, Laura Jones, Richard Lapierre, Sue Lee, Beth Lew-Williams, Haiming Liu, Liu Jin, Chris Lowman, Sophie McNulty, Calvin Miaw, Joseph Ng, Laura Ng, Stephanie Niu, Roger Staab, Chris Suh, Selia Tan, Niuniu Teo, James Thieu, Bryce Tuttle, Nathan Weiser, Vivian Yan, Yuan Ding, Zhai Xiang, Zhang Guoxiong, and Hao Zou.

I thank the dedicated work of many local historical societies and libraries. Among these are the California State Railroad Museum Library and Archives, Chinese Historical Society of San Francisco, Colfax Railroad Museum, Donner Summit Historical Society, El Dorado County Historical Museum, Placer County Archives and Research Center, and the Searls Historical Library of Nevada County.

Don Lamm and Melissa Chinchillo provided invaluable help and guidance in representing me, and I am most grateful to them. At Houghton Mifflin Harcourt, I thank lead editor Alex Littlefield for his keen insights, vision, and assistance. I am grateful to Ivy Givens, Amanda Heller, and Jennifer Freilach for their attentive and careful efforts.

I want to give special thanks to pioneering Chinese American historians who opened the way forward in recovering the history of Chinese in America. William Hoy, H. K. Wong, Thomas Chinn, Him Mark Lai, and Philip Choy, now all passed, made enormous contributions in preserving, understanding, and interpreting history.

I could not have traversed the long road in completing this book without the assistance, patience, support, and love of Vicki, Chloe, and Maya. Thank you. The indomitable spirit of the Railroad Chinese runs through your veins.

NOTES

INTRODUCTION

page

1   *Hung Wah stepped:* Hung Wah was a real person. Newspaper accounts of this moment do not provide his name, but evidence points to him.

2   *Others at the time:* "Transcontinental Railroad Postscript," *San Francisco News Letter and California Advertiser,* May 15, 1869; "Pacific Railroad Inauguration," *Sacramento Daily Union,* January 9, 1863; and "UPRR Contractor Lewis D. Carmichael," http://discussion.cprr.net/2014/07/uprr contractor-lewis-d-carmichael.html (accessed August 18, 2018).

3   *"May God continue":* https://news.stanford.edu/news/2013/april/cantor google-partner-030313.html (accessed July 25, 2018).

4   *The Chinese railroad workers:* Strobridge was known among his contemporaries as demanding and sometimes physically abusive, certainly "bossy." But Cantonese speakers also commonly added an "ee" at the end of some English words to help with the pronunciation. "Bossy" could also just be nineteenth-century Chinese American English for "boss."

5   *"Chinese Laborers at Table":* "Pacific Railroad: Close of the Inauguration Ceremonies at Promontory Summit," *Chicago Tribune,* May 12, 1869; "Honors to John Chinaman," *San Francisco News Letter,* May 15, 1869; and "The Last Rail," *Daily Alta California,* May 12, 1869.

6 *"silent spikes"*: Huang Annian, ed., *The Silent Spikes: Chinese Laborers and the Construction of North American Railroads,* trans. Zhang Juguo (Beijing: China Intercontinental Press, 2006). The author gratefully acknowledges the dedicated efforts of Professor Huang Annian of Beijing in bringing the Chinese railroad workers' story to readers in China and for introducing the notion of "silent spikes." The term "nameless builders" comes from William F. Chew, *Nameless Builders of the Transcontinental Railroad* (Victoria, B.C.: Trafford, 2004). Chew was a retired engineer when he self-published his pioneering account.

 At the 1969 centennial: Dale Champion, "The Forgotten Men at Gold Spike Ceremony," *San Francisco Chronicle,* reprinted in *Chinese Historical Society of America Bulletin* 4, no. 5–6 (May–June 1969): 6, 7.

7 *"Railroad Chinese":* Emma Jinhua Teng, *Eurasian: Mixed Identities in the United States, China, and Hong Kong, 1842–1943* (Berkeley: University of California Press, 2013), 1–2.

 "The road could never": David L. Phillips, *Letters from California* (Springfield: Illinois State Journal, 1877),. 89–92; Rev. John Todd, *The Sunset Land; or, The Great Pacific Slope* (Boston: Lee and Shepard, 1870), 234.

8 *The Pacific Mail Steamship Company:* In 1876, the Pacific Mail Steamship Company, one of the most active shipping companies in the Pacific, which operated out of San Francisco, reported that it had carried 96,717 letters to China and Japan and received 159,717 from these two countries for the United States. Along with remittances sent home, business and church correspondence, and travelers' letters, this mail must have included many personal letters from Chinese and is evidence of literacy, or at least the busy activity of professional letter writers. See "Pacific Subsidies," news clipping, Stanford Family Scrapbooks, vol. 13, 41–44, Stanford Library Special Collections.

 This presents: The problem of recovering history when there is little or no documentation from the central subjects has been confronted through the use of creative interpretive methodologies and imaginative use of materials. For example, see the classic works Natalie Zemon Davis, *The Return of Martin Guerre;* Jonathan D. Spence, *The Question of Hu;* and Richard White, *The Middle Ground.*

9 *An international research project:* I give proper recognition to the Chinese Railroad Workers in North America Project at Stanford (CRWP) in the acknowledgments.

13 *Many years later:* Teng, *Eurasian,* 1–2.

1. GUANGDONG

15   In the second reign year: The second reign year of Haamfung (Xianfeng)
     of the Qing dynasty was 1852.
     Villagers constructed: In 2007, UNESCO designated the *diaolou* in Kaip-
     ing and Taishan, two of the Siyi, as a World Heritage site. These unusual
     structures once numbered several thousand. About 1,800 remain standing.
     An estimated one quarter: Madeline Y. Hsu, *Dreaming of Gold, Dreaming of
     Home: Transnationalism and Migration Between the United States and South
     China, 1882–1943* (Stanford: Stanford University Press, 2000), 31.

17   *The soil of the Siyi:* Sucheng Chan, *This Bittersweet Soil: The Chinese in Cali-
     fornia Agriculture, 1860–1910* (Berkeley: University of California Press, 1986),
     7–21.
     He fondly evoked: William Speer, *The Oldest and the Newest Empire: China and
     the United States* (Hartford: Scranton and Co., 1870), 472–73.

18   *The next settlement:* G. William Skinner, "The City in Late Imperial China,"
     in G. William Skinner, ed., *The City in Late Imperial China* (Stanford: Stan-
     ford University Press, 1977), 211–49.
     "The narrow streets": Speer, *Oldest and the Newest,* 473.
     Schooling was rudimentary: Augustus Ward Loomis, "What Our Chinamen
     Read," *Overland Monthly and Out West Magazine,* December 1868, 525–30;
     Stewart Culin, "China in America: A Study in the Social Life of the Chi-
     nese in the Eastern Cities of the United States," paper read before the
     American Association for the Advancement of Science, New York, 1887,
     https://catalog.hathitrust.org/Record/000336210 (accessed August 13,
     2018).

19   *The geography of:* Hsu, *Dreaming of Gold,* 18–27.

20   *The Siyi people:* Yan Phou Lee, *When I Was a Boy in China* (Boston: D.
     Lothrop, Lee & Shepard Co., 1887), 11–12.

21   *man named Huie Kin:* His full name was Huie Kin-kwong. He is also known
     as Xu Qin and Xu Qinguang. For his account, see Huie Kin, *Reminiscences*
     (Peiping: San Yu Press, 1932), 3–25. The Huie family history in America is a
     wonderful story that NPR has documented. See http://www.npr.org/
     templates/story/story.php?storyId=5699710 (accessed October 15, 2018).
     Much of the description Huie Kin gives of his home life, including the liv-
     ing arrangements of the family and children, and his departure from his
     village is similar to the stories provided by others, such as by Lee Chew
     in 1903. Lee came to the United States from the Siyi in the 1880s and for a
     time worked as a laundryman for railroad workers. Like Huie Kin, he was

just a teenager when he left for America, which he also claimed was his idea. He paid for his passage with money his father provided. Lee Chew, "The Biography of a Chinaman," *New York Independent*, February 19, 1903. Also, see the brief biography of Ng Poon Chew, who became an important Chinese American minister, publisher, and advocate in the early twentieth century. His village life, childhood, and travel experience are also very similar to the other accounts. Corinne K. Hoexter, *From Canton to California: The Epic of Chinese Immigration* (New York: Four Winds Press, 1976), 135–39.

23   *a new goddess:* Author's conversation with Selia Tan, December 15, 2017.
      Basic literacy for males: Huie, *Reminiscences*, 36; Lee, *Boy in China*, 50–62.
      The missionary William Speer: Speer, *Oldest and the Newest Empire*, 495.

24   *Located a little farther:* Hsu, *Dreaming of Gold*, 23.

25   *The bloodletting:* Yung Wing, *My Life in China and America* (New York: H. Holt, 1909), 54–55; David Faure, *Emperor and Ancestor: State and Lineage in South China* (Stanford: Stanford University Press, 2007), 277–83, 295; Hsu, *Dreaming of Gold*, 21–23.
      migrants from the Pearl River: Robert G. Lee, "Red Turbans in the Trinity Alps: Violence, Popular Religion, and Diasporic Memory in Nineteenth-Century Chinese America," *Journal of Transnational American Studies* 8, no. 1 (January 2017): 1–21.
      "Gold Mountain": The Chinese term can also be translated as "country of gold." Chinese overseas often referred to their homeland as the "Land of Tang," or Tangshan and themselves as *Tangren*, or "people of Tang."

26   *Chinese also settled:* Thomas Chinn, H. Mark Lai, and Philip P. Choy, *A History of the Chinese in California: A Syllabus* (San Francisco: Chinese Historical Society of America, 1969), 36–41.

27   *Though the Qing empire:* Gungwu Wang, *The Chinese Overseas: From Earthbound China to the Quest for Autonomy* (Cambridge: Harvard University Press, 2000), 43–65; Jack Leong, "The Hong Kong Connection for the Chinese Railroad Workers in North America," Chinese Railroad Workers in North America Project, digital publishing series, https://web.stanford.edu/group/chineserailroad/cgi-bin/wordpress/ (forthcoming).
      From the early 1850s: Elizabeth Sinn, *Pacific Crossing: California Gold, Chinese Migration, and the Making of Hong Kong* (Hong Kong: Hong Kong University Press, 2013), 43–60.

28   *Chinese labor recruiters:* Hsu, *Dreaming of Gold*, 29–33.
      The ship companies: "Mass Hiring of Workers in San Francisco," *California*

China Mail and Flying Dragon (Feilong), January 1, 1867. The paper was bilin-
gual. The article on hiring was in Chinese; translation by Tian Yuan.
A railroad company: Ibid.
The promise of well-paying: Law Yow, August 12, 1924, Survey of Race Relations, box 27, no. 191, Hoover Archives, Hoover Institution, Stanford.

29   *On February 15, 1875: Ezekiel B. Vreeland testimony and* appendix B, exhibit 1, in
Report of the Joint Special Committee to Investigate Chinese Immigration, United
States Senate, 44th Cong., 2nd sess. (Washington, D.C.: GPO, 1877), 173–80,
and 1147–58.
The 801 passengers: Ibid.
A second passenger list: Ibid., 1158–64.

30   *The migration experience:* Other personal accounts of out-migration and
village life in the Pearl River delta are consistent with much of Huie Kin's
account. See the collection of stories in Thomas W. Chinn, *Bridging the Pacific: San Francisco Chinatown and Its People* (San Francisco: Chinese Historical Society, 1989), 65–107; Teresa Sparks, *China Gold* (Fresno, Calif.: Acad-
emy Library Guild, 1954); Scott D. Seligman, *Three Tough Chinamen* (Hong
Kong: Earnshaw Books, 2012), 12–21; and Mae Ngai, *The Lucky Ones* (Boston: Houghton Mifflin Harcourt, 2010).
None of their fathers objected: The account of Huie Kin's emigration is
drawn from Huie, *Reminiscences,* 16–21.

33   *One journalist's report in 1870:* Thomas W. Knox, "The Coming Man," *Frank
Leslie's Illustrated Newspaper,* May 7, 1870. The travel journal of a young
writer, Lucius A. Waterman, completed during his return trip to the
United States onboard the Pacific Mail steamship *China* in early 1869, contains brief observations about the hundreds of Chinese on the ship. In
Hong Kong, it took on 400 Chinese women and 150 men. More Chinese
came onboard in Yokohama. He records that the ship heaved and rolled in
the winter seas, making the Chinese seasick. They observed the Chinese
New Year by gambling. Waterman reported on conflicts among the Chinese and an illness that drove a Chinese crewman mad. Entries for January
19, February 11, 19, 20, 1869, Lucius A. Waterman, "Journal," January 19–
March 23, 1869, Waterman, Lucius A., misc. vol. 467, https://research.
mysticseaport.org/item/lo34982/3/, Waterman Family Collection, G. W.
Blunt White Library, Mystic, Conn.

34   *Paradoxically, the Siyi:* Immanuel C. Y. Hsu, *The Rise of Modern China* (New
York: Oxford University Press, 1970), 248–50; and S. Wells Williams, *The
Middle Kingdom* (New York: C. Scribner's Sons, 1907), 555, 573–74.

Huie Kin's account is markedly: Huie, *Reminiscences,* 83. Also see Evelyn Hu-DeHart, "Chinese Labor Migrants to the Americas in the Nineteenth Century: An Inquiry into Who They Were and the World They Left Behind," in *The Chinese and the Iron Road: Building the Transcontinental Railroad,* ed. Gordon H. Chang and Shelley Fisher Fishkin (Stanford: Stanford University Press, 2019).

One careful tabulation: "Statistics of Cuba," *Railroad Record,* March 17, 1859, 37. Chinese knew the difference between conditions in Cuba and California. See Howland and Aspinwall to William O. Comstock, August 6, 1853, William Ogilvie Comstock Papers, folder August 1853, Massachusetts Historical Society, Boston.

These tragic numbers: M. Foster Farley, "The Chinese Coolie Trade: 1845–1875," *Journal of Asian and African Studies* (July–October 1968): 257–70.

35   *The Qing court:* Tian Yuan, "Summary of Imperial Memorials Regarding Trafficking of Guangdong Men to Overseas Employment in the Late Nineteenth Century," Chinese Railroad Workers in North America Project Archive, Stanford University.

In 1852 the Connecticut ship: Jules Davids, ed., *American Diplomatic and Public Papers: The United States and China,* ser. 1, vol. 17 (Wilmington, Del.: Scholarly Resources, 1973), xxxiii–xxxv, 312–16.

36   *Another American ship:* Ibid., xxxv, 349–51.

Other cases in the 1850s: Ibid., xxxvii, 349–51.

American officials in Hong Kong: Ibid., xxxvii, 407–68; and Farley, "The Chinese Coolie Trade." For more on the coolie trade and American involvement, see Sinn, *Pacific Crossing,* 50–55; and Watt Stewart, *Chinese Bondage in Peru, 1849–1874* (Durham: Duke University Press, 1951).

37   *From the deck:* D. L. Phillips, *Letters from California: Its Mountains, Valleys, Plains, Rivers, Climate and Productions* (Springfield: Illinois State Journal, 1877), 28–31. On the "coolie" controversy, see Mae Ngai, "Chinese Gold Miners and the 'Chinese Question' in Nineteenth-Century California and Victoria," *Journal of American History* 101, no. 4 (March 2015): 1082–1105.

Huie Kin recalled that: Huie Kin, *Reminiscences,* 24–25. After leaving the familiar terrain of San Francisco's Chinatown, Huie Kin worked at various odd jobs, including household work, for whites in the Oakland area for years before he joined the local Chinese Christian community and his life changed forever. He became a Protestant minister and later settled in New York City, where he would become a prominent member of the Chinese community. In 1933 he returned to China, where he died the next year.

2. GOLD MOUNTAIN

Arriving in this unfamiliar: J. S. Look, August 13, 1924, Survey of Race Relations, box 27, no. 182, Hoover Archives, Hoover Institution, Stanford University.

39   *Reporting on the arrival:* Albert S. Evans, "From the Orient Direct," *Atlantic Monthly,* November 1869, 542–48. The article is reproduced in Evans's 1873 volume *À la California.* Other descriptions of the arrival of Chinese appear in "Arrival of the 'Japan,'" *San Francisco Chronicle,* November 23, 1869; and Otis Gibson, *The Chinese in America* (Cincinnati: Hitchcock & Walden, 1877), 45.

41   *Immigration processing in San Francisco:* Decades later, after the passage of the Chinese Exclusion Acts, the experience would be very different. From 1910 to 1940, Chinese underwent harsh review and interrogation at the Angel Island immigration station in San Francisco Bay, which became notorious for mistreatment of arrivals.

42   *A bit later:* Evans suggests that the unfortunate women were from the boat-dwelling population in the Canton region, the *tanjia.* Evans, "From the Orient Direct."

43   *Evans wondered:* Ibid.

      Though much has been made: Thomas Chinn, Him Mark Lai, and Philip Choy, *A History of the Chinese in California: A Syllabus* (San Francisco: Chinese Historical Society of America, 1969), 18, 30–36.

      The initial reception: Mary Roberts Coolidge, *Chinese Immigration* (New York: Henry Holt, 1909), 21–23.

44   *In April 1854: Daily California Chronicle,* April 22, 1854.

      Charles Wolcott Brooks: Report of the Joint Special Committee to Investigate Chinese Immigration, 44th Cong., 2nd sess. (Washington, D.C.: GPO, 1877), 10–12, 402, 459, 513, and 518. Though there is still a lack of clarity over the exact number of Chinese in America in the nineteenth century, it appears that at the height, Chinese numbered no more than 119,000 at the end of the century. U.S. Census, "Comparison of Asian Populations During the Exclusion Years," http://www1.udel.edu/readhistory/resources/2005_2006/summer_06/hsu.pdf (accessed March 9, 2018); and see Chinn, Lai, and Choy, *A History of the Chinese.*

45   *Independent journalists, however:* "Chinamen as Free Immigrants," *Massachusetts Spy,* July 30, 1869, 2; "Indenture of Ahine, Chinaman," "Indenture of Awye, Chinaman," and "Indenture of Atu, Chinaman," Jacob P. Leese Papers, California Historical Society Archive of California; and see Jacob

P. Leese and Affon, "A California Businessman Contracts for Chinese Immigrant Labor," *HERB: Resources for Teachers,* https://herb.ashp.cuny.edu/items/show/789 (accessed March 21, 2018.) A fascinating example of an 1852 loan agreement between a local association and a migrant and his family seeking funds to travel overseas is displayed in the Jiangmen Wuyi Museum of Overseas Chinese, Jiangmen, Guangdong, cited in Joseph Ng, "Entrepreneurial Capitalism: The Making of Central Pacific Railroad, 1861–1899" (Ph.D. diss., Stanford University, 2018), 111–12.

The news report described: "Chinamen as Free Immigrants." One of the most knowledgeable persons about China in America at this time was S. Wells Williams, who had lived in China as a missionary and as a U.S. official for many years. He became a professor of Chinese language and literature at Yale in 1877. His book *Chinese Immigration* (New York: C. Scribner's Sons, 1879) provided ample evidence and personal testimony which established that Chinese were free emigrants and should therefore be treated like any other newcomers to the country.

46   *At the center of it:* Sue Fawn Chung, *In Pursuit of Gold: Chinese American Miners and Merchants in the American West* (Urbana: University of Illinois Press, 2011), 18–23. For the history of the *huiguan* and Six Companies, see Him Mark Lai, On *Becoming Chinese American: A History of Communities and Institutions* (Walnut Creek, Calif.: AltaMira Press, 2004), chap. 3.

Merchant Cantonese often had formed: Judy Yung, Gordon H. Chang, and Him Mark Lai, eds., *Chinese American Voices: From the Gold Rush to the Present* (Berkeley: University of California Press, 2006), 17–25; Yucheng Qin, *The Cultural Clash: Chinese Traditional Native-Place Sentiment and the Anti-Chinese Movement* (Lanham, Md.: University Press of America, 2016), 35–55; and Richard Cole and Gabriel Chin, "Emerging from the Margins of Historical Consciousness: Chinese Immigrants and the History of American Law," *Law and History Review* 17, no. 2 (Summer 1999): 325–64.

Still, Americans who: In the 1960s, Gunther Barth resurrected the anti-Chinese slanders of the nineteenth century in his influential history *Bitter Strength.* For a substantive and well-informed discussion of the historical controversies, see Yucheng Qin, "A Century-Old 'Puzzle': The Six Companies' Role in Chinese Labor Importation in the Nineteenth Century," *Journal of American–East Asian Relations* 12, no. 3–4 (Fall–Winter 2003): 225–54.

The organization repeatedly: Otis Gibson, *Chinese in America* (Cincinnati: Hitchcock & Walden, 1877), 259, 333–45.

47   *Leung Cook, a proprietor:* Leung Cook testimony, in Committee of the Sen-

ate of the State of California, *Chinese Immigration: The Social, Moral, and Political Effect of Chinese Immigration* (Sacramento: State Printing Office, 1876), 64–66. Also see the interview on the Six Companies with Long Dong, July 28, 1924, box 27, no. 171, Survey of Race Relations, Archives, Hoover Institution, Stanford.

48   *His photographs of Chinese:* Carleton E. Watkins, "Chinese Women, San Francisco," WA Photos 220, object 2001125, and "Chinese Actor, San Francisco," WA Photos 220, object 2001124, Beinecke Library, Yale University. For a collection of Watkins's work on Chinese, see http://www.carleton watkins.org/search.php?keyword=chinese&v=list&c=25&so=1&tmrg=n &smode=OR&ex (accessed July 10, 2018).

50   *As early as the 1850s:* Peter E. Palmquist, "In Splendid Detail: Photographs of Chinese Americans from the Daniel K. E. Ching Collection," in *Facing the Camera: Photographs from the Daniel K. E. Ching Collection* (San Francisco: Chinese Historical Society of America, 2001), 8–17. In the 1860s, the prominent San Francisco portrait studio of Bradley & Rulofson employed Fong Noy, Fong Ah-Sin, and Ah Chew. Fong Noy was a chemist. Watkins employed a number of Chinese, including one named Ah Fue, to help produce stereographs in 1873. Gordon H. Chang, Mark Dean Johnson, and Paul J. Karlstrom, eds., *Asian American Art: A History, 1850–1970* (Stanford: Stanford University Press, 2008), 2–3, 469–70.

Though his life: Compare Lai Yong's work with that of well-known fellow San Francisco photographers Eadweard Muybridge and Bradley & Rulofson. See WA Photos 357, object 2015037, 2015087, and 2015085, all at Beinecke Library, Yale University.

One striking image: WA Photos 357, object 2015070, 2015071, and 2015072, all at Beinecke Library, Yale University.

51   *Photography was not:* Lai Yong, Yang Kay, A Yup, Lai Foon, and Chung Leong, *The Chinese Question from a Chinese Standpoint,* trans. Rev. O. Gibson (San Francisco: Cubery & Co., 1874), 1–3, reprinted in Gibson, *Chinese in America,* 285–92.

52   *So too does the dispatch:* Evans, "From the Orient Direct." Evans was originally from the Hudson River valley but moved to Texas for a short while, where he served briefly as the mayor of San Antonio, before moving to San Francisco. Clarence Alan McGrew, *City of San Diego and San Diego County: The Birthplace of California (Chicago: American Historical Society, 1922), 106–7.*

Another keen observer: Daniel Cleveland, "The Chinese in California," unpublished manuscript, Daniel Cleveland Manuscripts, 1868–1929, mssHM

72175–72177, Huntington Library, San Marino, Calif.; Daniel Cleveland to Benson H. Lossing, May 27, 1868, Cleveland Letters to Lossing, BANC MSS C-B 858, Bancroft Library, University of California, Berkeley; and Cleveland to J. Ross Browne July 21, 1868, contained in Browne to Seward, July 24, 1868, "Diplomatic Correspondence," in *Papers Relating to Foreign Affairs Accompanying the Annual Message of the President to the 3d Sess., 40th Cong., pt. 1,* (Washington, D.C.: GPO, 1869), 530–44. The manuscript includes an entire chapter on the lives and work of Chinese railroad workers that will inform a later chapter in this book. The manuscript was completed sometime in early 1869, before the events at Promontory Summit.

3. CENTRAL PACIFIC

56   *"The change of the route":* Asa Whitney, *A Project for a Railroad to the Pacific* (New York: George W. Wood, 1849), 40.

Among those who: "Biographical Sketch," in *Memorial Addresses on the Life and Character of Leland Stanford,* United States Senate, 53rd Cong., 2nd sess. (Washington, D.C.: GPO, 1894), 11.

Other continental expansionists: Gordon H. Chang, "China and the Pursuit of America's Destiny: Nineteenth-Century Imaginings and Why Immigration Restriction Took So Long," *Journal of Asian American Studies* 15, no. 2 (June 2012): 145–69.

57   *Similarly, William Speer:* William Speer, *The Oldest and the Newest Empire: China and the United States* (Hartford, Conn.: S. S. Scranton and Co., 1870), 27–28; and for other views on the significance of Chinese in the West, see John David Borthwick, *Three Years in California* (Edinburgh: W. Blackwood, 1857); John Todd, *The Sunset Land; or, The Great Pacific Slope* (Boston: Lee and Shepard, 1870); Mary Cone, *Two Years in California* (Chicago: C. Griggs, 1876); Walter M. Fisher, *The Californians* (London: Macmillan, 1876); and Isabelle Saxon, *Five Years Within the Golden Gate* (Philadelphia: J. B. Lippincott & Co., 1868), 38–46.

In January 1855: Thomas Chinn, Him Mark Lai, and Philip Choy, *A History of the Chinese in California: A Syllabus* (San Francisco: Chinese Historical Society of America, 1969), 43.

Later in 1855: "The City," *Sacramento Daily Union,* November 8, 1855; and Speer, *Oldest and the Newest Empire,* 669.

Not just in prediction: Lucy M. Cohen, "The Chinese of the Panama Railroad: Preliminary Notes on the Migrants of 1854 Who 'Failed,'" *Ethnohistory* 18, no. 4 (Autumn 1971): 309–20; Lok C. D. Siu, *Memories of a Future*

Home: Diasporic Citizenship of Chinese in Panama (Stanford: Stanford University Press, 2005), 38, 39; *Railroad Record,* May 26, 1859, 162; Minutes of the Meetings of the Board of Directors, July 1, 1853–June 28, 1854, Records of the Panama Canal Panama Railroad Company, National Archives, Washington, D.C.

58   *Chinese began to work:* "News of the Morning," *Sacramento Daily Union,* June 15, 1858; "The Chinese in California," *New York Tribune,* May 1, 1869. Also see "China and the Indies — Our 'Manifest Destiny' in the East," *DeBow's Review* 15 (December 1853): 541–71; David Haward Bain, *Empire Express: Building the First Transcontinental Railroad* (New York: Viking, 1999), 207.

      On April 16, 1868: R. David Arkush and Leo O. Lee, eds., *Land Without Ghosts: Chinese Impressions of America from the Mid-Nineteenth Century to the Present* (Berkeley: University of California Press, 1989), 25–29.

59   *Political figures had at first:* Mary Roberts Coolidge, *Chinese Immigration* (New York: Henry Holt, 1909), 21–23.

      many white employers continued: Franklin A. Buck, *A Yankee Trader in the Gold Rush: The Letters of Franklin A. Buck* (Boston: Houghton Mifflin Co., 1930), 128–33.

      A wildly popular Massachusetts: J. Hutchinson and D. D. Emmett, "Ho! For California!" in *Songs of the American West,* comp. and ed. Richard E. Lingenfelter, Richard A. Dwyer, and David Cohen (Berkeley: University of California Press, 1968), 14–15.

60   *Anti-Chinese music:* Lyrics, "John Chinaman" (1855), and lyrics and score, "Get Out, Yellow-skins, Get Out!" in Lingenfelter, Dwyer, and Cohen, *Songs of the American West,* 299–309; and *American Murder Ballads,* comp. and ed. Olive Woolley Burt (New York: Oxford University Press, 1958), 155–58.

      Elite political support: Judy Yung, Gordon H. Chang, and Him Mark Lai, eds., *Chinese American Voices* (Berkeley: University of California Press, 2006), 9–12.

61   *One of the most eloquent:* Norman Asing, "To His Excellency Governor Bigler," *Daily Alta California,* May 5, 1852, reprinted in Yung, Chang, and Lai, *Chinese American Voices,* 9–12. In a curious twist, later in his career Bigler was appointed a federal commissioner to oversee the construction of the Pacific railroad.

      A decade later, Chinese: http://governors.library.ca.gov/addresses/08-Stanford.html (accessed August 18, 2018); and Gordon H. Chang, "The Chinese and the Stanfords: Nineteenth-Century America's Fraught Relationship with the China Men," in *Chinese and the Iron Road: Building the Transcontinental and Other Railroads in North America*, ed. Gordon H. Chang and Shelley Fisher Fishkin (Stanford: Stanford University Press, 2019). And see the excellent work by Julie Cain, "The Chinese and the Stanfords: Immigration Rhetoric in Nineteenth-Century California" (M.A. thesis, California State University, East Bay, June 2011).

62   *Jin Kee, for his part:* Ibid.
      In business, too: Ibid.

63   *The sectional conflict over slavery:* Bain, 57–148; and see Richard White, *Railroaded: The Transcontinentals and the Making of Modern America* (New York: Norton, 2011).

64   *The almost 1,800 miles:* "Magnitude," *Sacramento Daily Union*, October 14, 1865.

66   *forging the roadbed:* Edwin L. Sabin, *Building the Pacific Railway* (Philadelphia: J. B. Lippincott Co., 1919), 13.
      Stanford and the other leaders: Alfred E. Davis testimony, in *Testimony Taken by the Pacific Railway Commission*, vol. 6 (Washington, D.C.: GPO, 1887), 3620–26.

67   *Just a few hundred:* Lewis M. Clement and Leland Stanford testimony, ibid., 6:3224–26; Crocker testimony, in *Report of the Joint Special Committee to Investigate Chinese Immigration*, U.S. Senate, 44th Cong., 2nd sess. (Washington, D.C.: GPO, 1877), 666–69.
      In part because of: Alexander Saxton, *The Indispensable Enemy: Labor and the Anti-Chinese Movement in California* (Berkeley: University of California Press, 1971), 62; Oscar Lewis, *The Big Four: The Story of Huntington, Stanford, Hopkins, and Crocker, and of the Building of the Central Pacific* (New York: Alfred A. Knopf, 1938), 69–70. A calendar showing when the CPRR reached different locations and their distance from Sacramento is in George Kraus, *High Road to Promontory: Building the Central Pacific* (Palo Alto: American West, 1969), 308–10.
      The CPRR's labor predicament: "The Chinese in California," *Lippincott's Magazine*, July 1868, 36–41. Telegraph lines in California began to appear in the early 1850s, and Chinese came to use the technology with alacrity. See Albert Dressler, *California Chinese Chatter* (self-published, 1927).
      Chinese household servants: Calvin B. T. Lee, *Chinatown, U.S.A.* (New York: Doubleday, 1965), 17; Susie Lan Cassel, ed. *The Chinese in America: A History from Gold Mountain to the New Millennium* (Walnut Creek, Calif.: AltaMira, 2002), 314; author's conversation with a member of the Crocker family, 2016.

68 *When Charles Crocker:* Crocker testimony, in *Testimony Taken by the Pacific Railway Commission,* vol. 7 (Washington, D.C.: GPO, 1887), 3660; Bain, *Empire Express,* 208–9. Years later, Strobridge confessed that he had been very prejudiced against Chinese. "I did not believe we could make a success of it," Strobridge said, admitting that he had been wrong and had very much changed his mind. *Report of the Joint Special Committee to Investigate Chinese Immigration,* 44th Cong., 2nd sess. (Washington, D.C.: GPO, 1877), 723–28, 666–88.

   Strobridge knew the area: http://discussion.cprr.net/2009/07/name-of-wife-of-james-harvey-strobridge.html (accessed March 22, 2018); and Norman E. Tutorow, *The Governor: The Life and Legacy of Leland Stanford: A California Colossus* (Spokane: Arthur H. Clark Company, 2004), 244.

   According to a brief: "'Rock Canyon Charlie' Taken by Death at County Hospital," *Mountain Democrat,* April 17, 1931; and "Pioneer Chinese of Gold Rush Days Dies in Placerville," *Los Angeles Times,* April 15, 1931. Hung Wah's age at time of death is given as ninety-six. One news article gave his age on arrival as five, but this is likely inaccurate. It is improbable that he was five years old when he entered the United States, as that would have been in 1840, years before gold was discovered in 1848. The first Chinese to live in San Francisco appear to have arrived in the spring of 1848. They were servants of an American businessman who brought them with him from China. Catherine Coffin Phillips, *Portsmouth Plaza: The Cradle of San Francisco* (San Francisco: John Henry Nash, 1932), 104.

69 *the 1860 census identifies:* U.S. Census, Schedule 1, 19, Free Inhabitants in Township 105[?], in the County of Placer, State of California. I am much indebted to Bryanna M. Ryan, Curator of Archives, Placer County Archive & Research Center, for providing me with this and other information on Hung Wah. Email to author, September 14, 2017.

   In the 1850s: "Dutch Flat, California," https://en.wikipedia.org/wiki/Dutch_Flat,_California (accessed August 18, 2018); and Phil Sexton to author, email, August 1, 2018.

   Chinese had arrived: Jeff Crawford, "The Golden Mountains: Chinese in Placer County, 1848–1880," unpublished essay for Placer County Museums, "We Came for Gold" exhibition, April 15, 1998, 5; and *Autobiography of Charles Peters: The Good Luck Era; The Placer Mining Days of the '50s* (Sacramento: LaGrave Co., n.d.), 143–45.

70 *Chinese also patronized:* Crawford, "The Golden Mountain," 5–7.

   The region also experienced: District Court, Nevada County, *The People v.*

George W. Hall, September 22, 1853, photocopy in Hall, George, murder trial, Hagaman Chinese Collection, Searls Historical Library, Nevada City, Calif.

Violence against Chinese soared: Daniel Cleveland to J. Ross Browne, July 21, 1868, contained in Browne to Seward, July 24, 1868, "Diplomatic Correspondence," in *Papers Relating to Foreign Affairs Accompanying the Annual Message of the President to the 3d Sess., 40th Cong., pt.1* (Washington, D.C.: GPO, 1869), 530–44.

71   *In this volatile environment:* Placer County District Court, Case 1762, *William Roush v. J. E. Terry,* 1862, Placer County Archive & Research Center, Auburn, California. Teri Hessel provided a very helpful transcription of this difficult-to-read handwritten document.

Chinese males married: Marriage Certificate of Ah Chee and Sun Low, November 16, 1862, Carson City, Nevada, Carson City Recorder's Office, bk. 3, 296. Thanks to Judy Wickwire for providing this document.

72   *Hung Wah advertised: Placer Herald,* August 29, 1863, and October 15, 1864. *The January 1864 payroll:* CPRR Payroll no. 26 for January 1864 and no. 34 for February 1864, Central Pacific Railroad Collection, MS 79, California State Railroad Museum Library, Sacramento. Other payroll records are from California, Railroad Employment Records, 1862–1950, Ancestry.com.

73   *These workers greatly:* "City Intelligence," *Sacramento Union,* May 1, 1865; and Crocker testimony, in *Testimony Taken by the Pacific Railway Commission,* 7:3659–60.

4. FOOTHILLS

76   *Though a railroad conjures:* Wolfgang Schivelbusch, *The Railway Journey: The Industrialization of Time and Space in the 19th Century* (Berkeley: University of California Press, 1980); Edgar B. Schieldrop, *The Railway* (London: Hutchinson, 1939).

77   *No account of the experience:* Diary of Stephen Allen Curry, November 23, 1864, to June 16, 1865, Curry Family Collection, California Historical Society, San Francisco. Thanks to Roland Hsu for discovering this source.

80   *By mid-1865:* Sue Fawn Chung, *Chinese in the Woods: Logging and Lumbering in the American West* (Urbana: University of Illinois Press, 2015), 156.

A photograph taken: The best-known photographs of nineteenth-century Chinese are those of Arnold Genthe, who took them in San Francisco at the turn of the century. See John Kuo Wei Tchen, *Genthe's Photographs of San Francisco's Old Chinatown* (New York: Dover Publications, 1984).

Photographer Carlton Watkins: "Chinese-American Contribution to Transcontinental Railroad," http://cprr.org/Museum/Chinese.html (accessed August 17, 2018).

81 It was hardly: "City Intelligence," Sacramento Daily Union, May 1, 1865. Massive excavations: "City Intelligence," Sacramento Daily Union, September 4, 1865.

82 Records we do have: CPRR Payroll no. 128, for April 1865, Central Pacific Railroad Collection, MS 79, California State Railroad Museum Library, Sacramento. Thanks go to Preston Carlson, Sabrina Jiang, Lily Anna Nilipour, Niuniu Teo, and James Thieu for their research.

83 Below each: Ibid.

Ah Fong's Men	1317.56
Billy Yang's Men	1522.78
Ah Gou's Men	1396.45
Che Noa	458.05
Foo Sing	121.44
Hung Wah	3875.48
Sisson's Time	3335.41
Wang Wan	3278.34
Ah Wy	1756.10
Ah Kung	773.29
Ah Coons	3759.20
Cum Sing	2135.56
Hung Wah	221.20

84 The Chinese contractor: CPRR Payroll Record, April and May 1865, Central Pacific Railroad Collection, MS 79, California State Railroad Museum Library, Sacramento.
An early group photograph: Thanks go to Lim Lip Hong descendants for providing this photograph and the history of their great-grandfather.
Hung Wah's good fortune: CPRR Payroll Record, May 1865 and January–July 1866, California State Railroad Museum, Sacramento.

85 These Chinese workers: Catherine Coffin Phillips, Cornelius Cole, California Pioneer and United States Senator (San Francisco: J. H. Nash, 1929), 1929), 138.
In a July 1865 report: Leland Stanford, "To the Stockholders of the Central Pacific Railroad Company, July 13, 1865," Railroad Record, August 24, 1865, 323–24.

86 In October 1865: Leland Stanford, Statement Made to the President of the United

States, and Secretary of the Interior, on the Progress of the Work, October 10, 1865 (Sacramento: H. S. Crocker & Co., 1865), 990.

Company leaders also: Leland Stanford, E. H. Miller Jr., and Samuel S. Montague, "To the Board of Directors of the Central Pacific Railroad Company," January 5, 1867, reprinted in *Testimony Taken by the Pacific Railway Commission,* vol. 5 (Washington, D.C.: GPO, 1887), 3050, 3051; and Montague, annual report for 1865, cited in Erle Heath, "Trail to Rail," *Southern Pacific Bulletin,* May 19, 1927, chap. 15, 12.

87   *Many railroad histories:* Oscar Lewis, *The Big Four: The Story of Huntington, Stanford, Hopkins, and Crocker, and of the Building of the Central Pacific* (New York: Alfred A. Knopf, 1938), 75, photo caption facing page 80; and Maxine Hong Kingston, *China Men* (New York: Alfred A. Knopf, 1980), 130–32. Other well-known works that present the baskets account include Jack Chen, The *Chinese of America: From the Beginnings to the Present* (San Francisco: Harper & Row, 1982), 69; Wesley S. Griswold, *A Work of Giants: Building the First Transcontinental Railroad* (New York: McGraw-Hill, 1962), 123; Alexander Saxton, "The Army of Canton in the High Sierra," *Pacific Historical Review* 35 (1966): 141–52; John Hoyt Williams, *A Great and Shining Road* (New York: Times Books, 1988), 113–14; David Haward Bain, *Empire Express: Building the First Transcontinental Railroad* (New York: Viking, 1999), 238–39; David Montgomery, *The Fall of the House of Labor: The Workplace, the State, and American Labor Activism, 1865–1925* (Cambridge: Cambridge University Press, 1987), 67; and Stephen E. Ambrose, *Nothing Like It in The World: The Men Who Built the Transcontinental Railroad, 1863–1869* (New York: Simon & Schuster, 2000), 156–57. The most detailed account, including how the baskets were supposed to have been constructed and decorated, is in Corinne K. Hoexter, *From Canton to California: The Epic of Chinese Immigration* (New York: Four Winds Press, 1976), 74–76 and 79, but provides no sources. See the paintings by artists Jake Lee, ca. 1955, Chinese Historical Society collection, Chinese Historical Society, San Francisco; Tyrus Wong, illustration in William Harland Boyd, *The Chinese of Kern County: 1857–1960* (Bakersfield, Calif.: Kern County Historical Society, 2002) 24; unknown artist, illustration in Helen Hinkley Jones, *Rails from the West: A Biography of Theodore D. Judah* (San Marino, Calif.: Golden West Books, ca. 1950), 14–15; and Mian Situ, "Powder Monkeys," used on the dust jacket of this book.

As insistent as those: The most prominent critique of the baskets claim is Edson T. Strobridge, "The Central Pacific Railroad and the Legend of

Cape Horn: Laborers in Baskets, Fact or Fiction?" 2001, Central Pacific Railroad Photographic History Museum, http://cprr.org/Museum/Cape_Horn.html (accessed August 18, 2018).

88 *Another highly charged:* Sierra Nevada Geotourism, "Cape Horn and the Transcontinental Railroad," http://www.sierranevadageotourism.org/content/cape-horn-and-the-transcontinental-railroad/sie3CF4CAC-0C3AA88FF9 (accessed March 31, 2017); and Roger Staab to Roland Hsu, email, February 10, 2017, in author's possession.

An 1869 tour book: Wallace H. Atwell, *Great Trans-continental Railroad Guide* (Chicago: G. A. Crofutt & Co., 1869), 201–2. The section of the book is titled "Cape Horn." Sources with similar descriptions of Chinese lowered by ropes at Cape Horn include Henry Morford, *Morford's Scenery and Sensation Handbook of the Pacific Railroads and California* (New York: Chas. T. Dillingham, 1878), 164; William Minturn, *Travels West* (London: Samuel Tinsley, 1877), 227; *The Pacific Tourist: Adams & Bishop's Illustrated Trans-Continental Guide* (New York: Adams & Bishop, 1877 and 1884), 252; D. L. Phillips, *Letters from California* (Springfield: Illinois State Journal, 1877), 55; Robert L. Harris, "The Pacific Railroad Unopen," *Overland Monthly* 3 (1869), 248; and Caroline Amelia Clapp Chickering, letter to mother, November 9, 1876, published in *The Californian* 12, no. 1 cited in "Cape Horn—Ropes or Baskets," http://cprr.org/Museum/Chinese.html#baskets (accessed August 29, 2018).

Frederick A. Bee: Testimony, in *Report of the Joint Special Committee to Investigate Chinese Immigration,* 44th Cong., 2nd sess. (Washington, D.C.: GPO, 1877), 4.

One of the first mentions: The Central Pacific Railroad (New York: T. Nelson and Sons, 1870), 21.

89 *The most stirring description:* Isabella L. Bird, *A Lady's Life in the Rocky Mountains* (London: John Murray, 1894), 5.

90 *But the most compelling:* The *Pittsfield Eagle* report ran under the title "Wholesale Blasting" in the *Providence (R.I.) Evening Press,* December 14, 1868, as well as in the *New London (Conn.) Democrat,* January 2, 1869; *New England Farmer* (Boston), January 9, 1869; *Weekly Union* (Manchester, N.H.), January 19, 1869; *Portsmouth (N.H.) Journal of Literature and Politics,* February 6, 1869; *Bangor (Maine) Daily Whig and Courier,* February 11, 1869; and *Fayetteville (Tenn.) Observer,* May 27, 1869. Thanks go to Shelley Fisher Fishkin for locating these sources.

91 *Lastly, the topography:* Samuel S. Montague, Report of the Chief *Engineer*

upon Recent Surveys, Progress of Construction, and an Approximate Estimate of Receipts of the Central Pacific Railroad of California (N.p., October 8, 1864), 13. In a later report Montague writes that the construction around Cape Horn was less difficult than first anticipated and that two retaining walls were constructed. See his report dated December 25, 1865, http://cprr.org/ Museum/Cape_Horn.html (accessed October 19, 2018). Louis M. Clement briefly mentions Cape Horn in his 1865 journal, HM 66487, Huntington Library.

Several months later: Diary of Stephen Allen Curry, November 23, 1864–June 16, 1865, Curry Family Collection, California Historical Society, San Francisco. Thanks go to Roland Hsu for locating this collection.

There is also firm evidence: Bruce A. MacGregor, *Birth of the California Narrow Gauge: A Regional Study of the Technology of Thomas and Martin Carter* (Stanford: Stanford University Press, 2003), 533–49; and *Narrow Gauge Portrait: South Pacific Coast* (Felton, Calif.: Glenwood Publishers, 1975), 98. Thanks to Derek Whaley for providing these references.

92 *The mystery around:* The use of baskets may have occurred at a location other than Cape Horn. Farther east from Cape Horn is Crested Peak, a place where, according to a *New York Evening Post* report, published in a British paper, a "rugged precipice towers above you a thousand feet, with its shattered sides looking dreadfully as if they wanted to drop an immense fragment of rock on your head. The engineers were fain to tie themselves with ropes as they surveyed along here," and even the Chinese first objected to the work, with "but a thousand feet of precipice below them with a thousand more above them, and hanging on by the skin of their teeth." The use of baskets, however, is not specifically mentioned in the news report. Throughout the Sierra, ice on and between the rocks would have made stable footing impossible. "The Central Pacific Railroad," *Leeds Mercury,* December 28, 1867. A local California historian writes that baskets were used by workers "to chip away at the ledge east of Colfax and around Cape Horn" but provides no source. A. Thomas Homer, *Auburn and Placer County: Crossroads of a Golden Era* (Northridge, Calif.: Windsor Publications, 1988), 37. Railroad historian Phil Sexton also identifies Crested Peak as an area where baskets may have been used. Sexton to author, email, October 25, 2017.

Hart, who had come: The Stanford University library makes Hart's CPRR photos available online and provides a magnifying function for close study of images. This tool enables one to see Chinese who were obscure, indistinct, or undetectable in the original images.

93 *Hart's work impressed:* E. B. Crocker to Huntington, January 9, 1867, Huntington Letters.

Hart's work nevertheless: Alfred A. Hart photographs, 1862–1869, Special Collections, Green Library, Stanford University. Also see, Li Ju and Linda Ye, "A Photo Comparative Perspective of the Central Pacific Railroad," CRWP Digital Publishing Series (forthcoming).

97 *Captions for some photos:* "Wood Train and Chinamen in Bloomer Cut," in Lawrence & Houseworth Albums, Society of California Pioneers, http://www.californiapioneers.org/lh/search_image.php?id=1129&type=search&page=1&category=bloomer%20cut (accessed September 1, 2018).

hailed at the time: Article by Ralph Gibson, *Placer Historical Society Newsletter,* May–June 2011, https://www.trainorders.com/discussion/read.php?1,2632342 (accessed August 19, 2018).

Bloomer Cut, which was completed: According to a commemorative plaque at the site from the Native Sons of the Golden West, dated October 12, 1991, Chinese laborers were at least in part responsible for completing the cut, though some question the extent of their involvement. Ibid.

5. THE HIGH SIERRA

99 *During the construction months:* Maxine Hong Kingston writes movingly of this legend in *China Men* (New York: Alfred A. Knopf, 1980), 129–30. Thanks to Sik Lee Denning for discussions about the moon and the stars in Chinese tradition.

100 *In August 1865:* Albert D. Richardson, *Beyond the Mississippi: From the Great River to the Great Ocean* (Hartford, Conn.: American Publishing Co., 1869), 461–62; and "Richardson's Letters to the *Tribune,*" *Sacramento Daily Union,* December 18, 1865.

In terms of quality: George E. Gray, *Central Pacific Railroad Report* (Sacramento: H. S. Crocker, 1865), with letter from Stanford, 1, 8.

101 *familiar with black powder:* David Faure, *Emperor and Ancestor: State and Lineage in South China* (Stanford: Stanford University Press, 2007), 312–14.

Dramatic weather changes: Placer Herald, September 30, October 14 and 21, 1865; and Bain, *Empire Express,* 245–46 and 259–60.

102 *Snowfall began in September:* John R. Gilliss, "Tunnels of the Pacific Railroad," speech before the American Society of Civil Engineers, January 5,

1870, reproduced in *Transactions of the American Society of Civil Engineers* 1 (1872): 155–72.

Archaeology provides: Barbara L. Voss, "Archaeological Contributions to Research on Chinese Railroad Workers in North America," in *Chinese and the Iron Road: Building the Transcontinental and Other Railroads in North America,* ed. Gordon H. Chang and Shelley Fisher Fishkin (Stanford: Stanford University Press, 2019); Barbara L. Voss, "The Historical Experience of Labor: Archaeological Contributions to Interdisciplinary Research on Chinese Railroad Workers," and Paul G. Chace, "Celestial Sojourners in the High Sierras: The Ethno-Archaeology of Chinese Railroad Workers (1865–1868)," *Historical Archaeology* 49, no. 1 (2015): 4–23 and 27–33.

103 *Consistency in found objects:* Barbara L. Voss, "Living Between Misery and Triumph: The Material Practices of Chinese Railroad Workers in North America"; Voss, "Archaeological Contributions"; and Kelly J. Dixon with Gary Weisz, Christopher Merritt, Robert Weaver, and James Bard, "Landscapes of Change: Culture, Nature, and the Archaeological Heritage of Transcontinental Railroads in the North American West," all in Chang and Fishkin, *Chinese and the Iron Road;* and Kenneth P. Cannon et al., *The Archaeology of Chinese Railroad Workers in Utah: Results of Surveys in Box Elder and Emery Counties* (Logan, Utah: USU Archaeological Services, 2016).

104 *Large rectangular depressions:* Dixon et al., "Landscapes of Change."

Observers of the construction effort: Robert L. Harris, "The Pacific Railroad—Unopen," *Overland Monthly,* September 1, 1869, 244–52.

Author Daniel Cleveland: Daniel Cleveland, "The Chinese in California," unpublished manuscript, Daniel Cleveland Manuscripts, 1868–1929, mssHM 72175–72177, Huntington Library, San Marino.

106 *At Summit Camp:* R. Scott Baxter and Rebecca Allen, "The View from Summit Camp," *Historical Archaeology* 49, no. 1 (2015): 34–35.

Snow buried not only: Lewis M. Clement to Leland Stanford, July 21, 1887, and James H. Strobridge to Leland Stanford, July 23, 1887, reproduced in *Testimony Taken by the Pacific Railway Commission,* vol. 5 (Washington, D.C.: GPO, 1887), 2576–2578; Bain, *Empire Express,* 317–20; *Donner Summit Heirloom,* no. 96, August 2016, 1, 3. Some histories render John R. Gilliss's surname with only one "s."

108 *During late spring:* Sandy Lydon, *Chinese Gold: The Chinese in the Monterey Bay Region* (Capitola, Calif.: Capitola Book Co., 1985), 91; Watt Stewart, *Chinese Bondage in Peru: A History of the Chinese Coolie in Peru, 1849–1874* (Durham: Duke University Press, 1951), 230.

Potent odors permeated: Mary L. Maniery, Rebecca Allen, and Sarah Christine Heffner, *Finding Hidden Voices of the Chinese Railroad Workers: An Archaeological and Historical Journey* (Germantown, Md.: Society for Historical Archaeology, 2016), 22–57.

Food and diet: J. Ryan Kennedy, Sarah Heffner, Virginia Popper, Ryan P. Harrod, and John J. Crandall, "The Health and Well-Being of Chinese Railroad Workers," in Chang and Fishkin, *Chinese and the Iron Road.*

109 *Speaker of the House:* "City Items," *Alta California,* August 18, 1865.

110 *Inventory in a Chinese store:* Robert F. G. Spier, "Food Habits of Nineteenth-Century California Chinese," *California Historical Society Quarterly* 37, nos. 1 and 2 (March and June 1958): 79–84, 129–36; Sucheng Chan, *This Bittersweet Soil: The Chinese in California Agriculture, 1860–1910* (Berkeley: University of California Press, 1986), 82–86.

Railroad Chinese likely consumed: Dutch Flat Enquirer, February 24, 1866; Spier, "Food Habits."

In the mountain areas: Donner Summit Heirloom, no. 95 (July 2016): 1, 3–7.

111 *Southern Chinese have:* Charlotte K. Sunseri, "Alliance Strategies in the Racialized Railroad Economies of the American West"; J. Ryan Kennedy, "Zooarchaeology, Localization, and Chinese Railroad Workers in North America"; and R. Scott Baxter and Rebecca Allen, "The View from Summit Camp," all *Historical Archaeology* 49, no. 1 (2015): 85–99, 34–45, 122–33.

Journalists at the time: Spier, "Food Habits"; Kennedy et al., "Health and Well-Being."

Other evidence exists: Railroad Gazette, September 10, 1870, cited in Sue Fawn Chung, *Chinese in the Woods: Logging and Lumbering in the American West* (Urbana: University of Illinois Press, 2015) 157.

112 *California Chinese farmed:* Russell M. Magnaghi, "Virginia City's Chinese Community, 1860–1880," *Nevada Historical Society Quarterly* 24, no. 2 (Summer 1981): 130–58. Also see Yong Chen, *Chop Suey, USA: The Story of Chinese Food in America* (New York: Columbia University Press, 2014), 74–81; and Yong Chen, "Uncovering and Understanding the Experiences of Chinese Railroad Workers in Broader Socioeconomic Contexts," CRWP Digital Publishing series (forthcoming).

Hundreds of Chinese: Chan, *This Bittersweet Soil,* 79–108, 147–57; August Ward Loomis, "The Old East in the New West," *Overland Monthly,* October, 1868, 360–68; "How Our Chinamen Are Employed," *Overland Monthly,* March 1869, 231–40; Gordon Richards, "Life for Chinese in Truckee Not Easy in 1870," *Sierra Sun,* November 26, 2006; Voss, "Living Between Misery and

Triumph; and William Speer, *The Oldest and the Newest Empire: China and the United States* (Hartford, Conn.: S. S. Scranton and Co., 1870), 528.

Their meals invariably: "The California Chinese," *Weekly Arkansas Gazette*, November 27, 1866.

113 *When he was a youngster:* Pappy Clay, "Personal Life of a Chinese Coolie, 1868–1899," March 1, 1969, Kyle Wyatt Papers, Chinese Railroad Workers Project Archive, Stanford. Thanks to Kyle Wyatt for providing this.

On special occasions: "City Intelligence," *Sacramento Daily Union*, January 11, 1870; "Funeral Baked Meats," *Overland Monthly and Out West Magazine*, July 1869, 21–29; *Donner Summit Heirloom*, no. 100 (December 2016): 11–12; "Chinese Cookery," *Frank Leslie's Illustrated*, January 20, 1866, 283; and "Epitome of the Week," *Frank Leslie's Illustrated*, March 24, 1866, 547.

114 *Other Chinese labor contractors:* Chung, *Chinese in the Woods*, 39–40.

The Sisson, Wallace Company: Albert W. Sisson, William H. Wallace, and Clark W. Crocker were partners in Sisson, Wallace & Company, which became Sisson, Crocker & Company after Wallace's death. On its operations, see *Wallace et al. v. Sisson et al.*, June 9 1893, in Peter V. Ross, ed., *California Unreported Cases*, vol. 4 (San Francisco: Bender-Moss Company, 1913), 34–47.

The business records: Hao Zou, "Preliminary findings of research into the records of Ah Louis, Special Collections, Green Library, Stanford University." Thanks to Hao Zou for his work on the Ah Louis material. For similar arrangements between Chinese workers and merchants/contractors, see Sue Fawn Chung, *In Pursuit of Gold* (Urbana: University of Illinois Press, 2011), 16–18; and Lydon, *Chinese Gold*, 91, 94, 210–12, and 312.

115 *The Railroad Chinese were:* Voss, "Living Between Misery and Triumph"; and Chung, *Chinese in the Woods*, 81–86.

Railroad Chinese, however: *Overland Monthly*, September 1869, 244–49; and Voss, "Living Between Misery and Triumph."

A vast quantity of items: Maniery, Allen, and Heffner, *Finding Hidden Voices*, 40–41, 48–57; Marjorie Akin, James C. Bard, and Gary Weisz, "Asian Coins Recovered from Chinese Railroad Labor Camps," *Historical Archaeology* 49, no. 1 (2015): 110–21; and Lisa See, *On Gold Mountain* (New York: St. Martin's Press, 1995), 9–12

116 *Railroad Chinese even ate:* Maniery, Allen, and Heffner, *Finding Hidden Voices*, 35–39; Barbara Voss, "The Archaeology of Precarious Lives: Chinese Railroad Workers in Nineteenth-Century North America," *Current Anthropology* 59, no. 3 (June 2018): 287–313.

Material objects also tell: Kathryn Gin Lum, "Religion on the Road: How Chinese Migrants Adapted Popular Religion to an American Context," in Chang and Fishkin, *Chinese and the Iron Road;* and Arthur P. Wolf, "Gods, Ghosts, and Ancestors," in *Religion and Ritual in Chinese Society,* ed. Arthur P. Wolf (Stanford: Stanford University Press, 1974), 131–82.

117 *Figurines and images:* Stewart Culin, *The Religious Ceremonies of the Chinese in the Eastern Cities of the United States* (Philadelphia: Franklin Printing House, 1887), 3–5; Otis Gibson, *The Chinese in America* (Cincinnati: Hitchcock & Walden, 1877), 72–74. Thank you to Selia Tan for insight into Siyi spiritual practices.

Gui jie or zhongyuan jie: "The Feast of the Dead," *Daily Alta California,* April 4, 1870.

118 *In mid-August 1868:* Wolfram Eberhard, *Chinese Festivals* (New York: Henry Schuman, 1952), 129–33; and Thomas Arthur Deeble, "A History of Two Chinatowns in Grass Valley and Nevada City" (master's thesis, San Francisco State College, 1972), 128–35.

Entering town, Hung Wah: M. V. Foster, "Our Chinese Camp Meeting Described by an Eastern Visitor," letter to the *Piqua (Ohio) Helmet,* September 11, 1868, reprinted in the *Grass Valley Union Newspaper,* quoted in Wallace R. Hagaman, *Chinese Temples of Nevada City and Grass Valley, California, 1868–1938* (Nevada City, Calif.: Cowboy Press, 2001), 11–16.

119 *Old-time Chinese Americans:* I heard this story from elders when I was young.

6. THE SUMMIT

121 *On a sultry Fourth of July:* Sacramento Daily Union, July 4 and 6, 1866.

122 *Huzzahs to the republic:* "The Chinese in California," *Sacramento Daily Union,* July 9, 1866.

By the time: Leland Stanford, E. H. Miller Jr., and Samuel S. Montague, "To the Board of Directors of the Central Pacific Railroad Company," January 5, 1867, reprinted in *Testimony Taken by the Pacific Railway Commission,* vol. 5 (Washington, D.C.: GPO, 1887), 3050, 3051; and "The Building of the Iron Road," *Overland Monthly and Out West Magazine,* May 1869, 469–78.

123 *The dramatic contrast:* Gilliss, "Tunnels of the Pacific Railroad," 155–72.

In a formal report: Stanford, Miller, and Montague, "To the Board of Directors."

Ever watchful: Stanford, ibid.; and "The Use of Black Powder and Nitroglycerine on the Transcontinental Railroad," Linda Hall Library, https://rail

road.lindahall.org/essays/black-powder.html (accessed June 16, 2018).

124 *While Stanford wrote:* "The Building of the Iron Road," *Overland Monthly and Out West Magazine,* May 1869, 469–78.
The decision on how: Lewis M. Clement testimony, in *Testimony Taken by the Pacific Railway Commission,* vol. 6 (Washington, D.C.: GPO, 1887), 3231–33.

125 *Railroad Chinese had bored:* Gilliss, "Tunnels of the Pacific Railroad," 155–72.
Of the many daunting: Edwin L. Sabin, *Building the Pacific Railway* (Philadelphia: J. B. Lippincott Co., 1919), 120–21; and Gilliss, "Tunnels of the Pacific Railroad."

126 *The company had workers:* E. B. Crocker to Huntington, January 31, 1867, Huntington Letters, Collis P. Huntington Papers, 1856–1901, Microfilming Corporation of America, Sanford, N.C..

127 *Imagine the noise:* Sacramento Daily Union, April 22, 1867.
Work continued nonstop: E. B. Crocker to Huntington, January 7, 1867, Huntington Letters; Oscar Lewis, *The Big Four: The Story of Huntington, Stanford, Hopkins, and Crocker, and of the Building of the Central Pacific* (New York: Alfred A. Knopf, 1938), 81–84.
When the drifts: David Haward Bain, *Empire Express: Building the First Transcontinental Railroad* (New York: Penguin, 1999), 318.

128 *"Snow Plow. At Cisco":* The caption of another photo of this location taken at the same time establishes the month. It is likely that the year is 1867, following one of the worst winters on record.

133 *The work of the illustrator:* Joseph Becker, "An Artist's Interesting Recollections of Leslie's Weekly," *Leslie's Weekly,* December 14, 1905, 570; and Deirdre Murphy, "Joseph Becker's Central Pacific Trip, 1869," *Commonplace,* 7, no. 3 (April 2007): 1–10.

134 *One of Becker's:* Some writers have interpreted the image as showing Chinese anger toward the train. More likely this is a scene described by journalists like the one quoted in chapter eight.

135 *A small cache:* The drawings are in the Carl Becker Collection, Boston College.

136 *For a short while:* E. B. Crocker to Huntington, February 12, 1867, Huntington Papers; "Nitro-Glycerine Accident," *Sacramento Daily Union,* November 30, 1867; *Donner Summit Heirloom,* August 2012, 1, 4–6; and "The Use of Black Powder and Nitroglycerine on the Transcontinental Railroad."
Wanting to make progress: Gilliss, "Tunnels of the Pacific Railroad."

7. THE STRIKE

138 *In January 1867:* E. B. Crocker to Huntington, January 10, 1867, Huntington Letters, Collis P. Huntington Papers, 1856–1901, Microfilming Corporation of America, Sanford, N.C.

139 *Crocker further emphasized:* E. B. Crocker to Huntington, January 10 and 31, 1867, Huntington Papers. Crocker repeated his argument about the difficulty of keeping Chinese at work on the "hard rock" in a January 31, 1867, letter. As early as the fall of 1866, reports publicly circulated about the company's labor problems: "The Central Pacific Railroad Company finds it difficult to retain their Chinese laborers on the hard rock encountered at the South Yuba River. Several gangs have been entirely broken up by the laborers quitting work." *Montana Post,* September 8, 1866.
  Leland Stanford, CPRR secretary E. H. Miller: Leland Stanford, E. H. Miller Jr., and Samuel S. Montague, "To the Board of Directors of the Central Pacific Railroad Company," January 5, 1867, in *Testimony Taken by the Pacific Railway Commission,* vol. 5 (Washington, D.C.: GPO, 1887), 3050–51; and E. B. Crocker to Huntington, January 31, 1867. No extant copies of the flyer have been located.

140 *Work, income, and risk:* Shelley M. Bennett, *The Art of Wealth* (San Marino, Calif.: Huntington Library, 2013), 9.
  Field construction boss: Vallejo (Calif.) Evening Chronicle, January 11, 1869, cited in George Kraus, *High Road to Promontory* (Palo Alto: American West, 1969), 220–21.
  This ten- or eleven-car train: Alta California, November 9, 1868, cited ibid., 216–17.
  Strobridge, the company leader: Vallejo Evening Chronicle, January 11, 1869, in Kraus, *High Road,* 220–21, and photographs of Strobridge, his family, and the camp train, 180 and 224–25.

141 *Once, to satisfy their curiosity:* Charles Crocker testimony, November 14, 1876, *Report of the Joint Special Committee to Investigate Chinese Immigration,* 44th Cong., 2nd sess. (Washington, D.C.: GPO, 1877), 666–88; and E. B. Crocker to Huntington, January 7 and February 17, 1867, Huntington Letters.

142 *This pay disparity:* CPRR Payroll Record, November 1866, Central Pacific Railroad Collection, MS 79, California State Railroad Museum Library, Sacramento.

143 *Lewis M. Clement displayed:* Lewis M. Clement testimony, in *Testimony Taken by the Pacific Railway Commission,* vol. 6 (Washington, D.C.: GPO, 1887), 3217.

Arthur Brown, the engineer: Arthur Brown testimony, August 26, 1887; and Clement testimony, in *Testimony Taken by the Pacific Railway Commission,* 6:3603, 3219–320, and 3226; and *Alta California,* November 9, 1868, cited in Kraus, *High Road to Promontory,* 217.

Tunnel engineer Gilliss: Gilliss, "Tunnels of the Pacific Railroad" (1872): 155–72.

144 *Before the Senate committee:* Crocker testimony, *Report of the Joint Special Committee to Investigate Chinese Immigration,* U.S. Senate, 44th Cong., 2nd sess. (Washington, D.C.: GPO, 1877), 671–88.

Strobridge confirmed: James H. Strobridge testimony, ibid., 723–28.

145 *Strobridge's frank assessment:* Strobridge testimony, ibid., 723–28; and Crocker testimony, ibid., 671–88.

146 *A Chinese cook:* H. K. Wong, *Gum Sahn Yun: Gold Mountain Men* (San Francisco: Fong Brothers, 1987), 285.

147 *When the strike is mentioned:* See, for example, the foundational work of Philip S. Foner, *History of the Labor Movement in the United States,* vol. I (New York: International Publishers, 1947); and John R. Commons et al., *History of Labour in the United States* (New York: Macmillan, 1921). John Hoyt Williams briefly describes the strike in *A Great and Shining Road* (New York: Times Books, 1988), 181. David Haward Bain's account, *Empire Express: Building the First Transcontinental Railroad* (New York: Penguin, 1999), recognizes the strong position of the Chinese workers. Wesley S. Griswold, *A Work of Giants: Building the First Transcontinental Railroad* (New York: McGraw-Hill, 1962), draws almost entirely on Crocker's account of his role in the events. Progressive labor historian Alexander Saxton in his classic work *The Indispensable Enemy: Labor and the Anti-Chinese Movement in California* (Berkeley: University of California Press, 1971) does not even mention the strike, though he expresses great sympathy for the Chinese. The strike also does not appear in Edwin L. Sabin, *Building the Pacific Railway* (Philadelphia: J. B. Lippincott Co., 1919).

148 *Crocker, years later:* Charles Crocker's version is found principally in his Senate testimony; see *Report of the Joint Special Committee to Investigate Chinese Immigration,* 666–75.

In early February: E. B. Crocker to Huntington, February 12 and 17, 1867; and Mark Hopkins to Huntington, February 15, 1867, Huntington Letters.

149 *In early April:* "Going to the Front," *Sacramento Daily Union,* April 11, 1867. *A month later:* E. B. Crocker to Huntington, April 27, May 8, and May 16, 1867, Huntington Letters.

A week later: E. B. Crocker to Huntington, May 8 and 22, 1867, Huntington Letters.

150 *The press noted:* "Decrease in Chinese Population in California," *Daily Alta California,* July 31, 1867. Other reports noted an increase in Chinese joining the Central Pacific for work. "More Force on the Road," *Daily Alta California,* April 26, 1867. Leland Stanford to Mark Hopkins, May 18, 1867, Huntington Letters; and "The Chinese Labor Question," *Morning Oregonian,* March 6, 1867.

Within days of writing: E. B. Crocker to Huntington, May 27, 1867; Hopkins to Huntington, May 31, 1867; and E. B. Crocker to Huntington, July 2, 1867, Huntington Letters.

In early June: E. B. Crocker to Huntington, June 4, 1867; Mark Hopkins to Huntington, June 26, 1867, Huntington Letters.

151 *Then, on Wednesday: Meadow Lake Sun,* June 22, 1867.

On June 24: Meadow Lake Sun, June 29, 1867.

152 *Why the Railroad Chinese:* The date of the strike may also have fallen that year very close to *duanwujie,* the fifth day of the fifth month in the lunar calendar. Today it is known as the Dragon Boat Festival day. Also see Wolfram Eberhard, *Chinese Festivals* (New York: Henry Schuman, 1952), 69–96. John Moleda begins to explore alternative modes of understanding Railroad Chinese life, including the strike, in "Moral Discourse and Personhood in Overseas Chinese Contexts," *Historical Archaeology* 49, no. 1 (2015): 46–58.

The exact demands: "Facts Gathered from the Lips of Charles Crocker, Regarding His Identification with the Central Pacific Railroad, and Other Roads Growing Out of It," typescript, MSS, C–D 764, Bancroft Library, University of California, Berkeley, 30. It is not clear whether this account is of the June strike or another incident, however. Most writers cite "The Chinese Strike," *Sacramento Daily Union,* July 1 and 3, 1867, but the accounts may contain inaccuracies. E. B. Crocker privately wrote that Charles objected to the article, as it was "full of errors." E. B. Crocker to Huntington, July 10, 1867, Huntington Letters.

The strike apparently: J. O. Wilder in George Kraus, *High Road to Promontory* (Palo Alto: American West Publishing Co., 1969), 134.

153 *An agitated Strobridge:* E. B. Crocker to Huntington, May 8, 1867; Hopkins to Huntington, June 26, 1867, Huntington Letters; and "Strike of the Chinese for Eight Hours' Work and Twelve Hours' Pay on the Pacific Railroad," *Daily Alta California,* June 30, 1867. This article, "a special dispatch

from Cisco," stated that the Chinese had struck for $40 pay a month and an eight-hour day.

The Chinese strike continued: E. B. Crocker to Huntington, June 27, 1867, Huntington Letters; and *Sacramento Union,* July 6, 1867.

E. B. Crocker wrote to Huntington: E. B. Crocker to Huntington, June 28, 1867; and Hopkins to Huntington, June 28, 1867, Huntington Letters.

154 *A brash young visitor:* Greg Robinson, "'Les fils du ciel': European Travelers' Accounts of Chinese Railroad Workers," in *Chinese and the Iron Road: Building the Transcontinental and Other Railroads in North America,* ed. Gordon H. Chang and Shelley Fisher Fishkin (Stanford: Stanford University Press, 2019); and Comte Ludovic de Beauvoir, *Voyages autour du monde: Australie, Java, Siam, Canton, Pékin, Yeddo, San Francisco,* (Paris: H. Plon,1878), 856–58. Thanks to Greg Robinson for locating this account.

155 *Then, after a week:* E. B. Crocker to Huntington, July 2, 1867, Huntington Letters; *Sacramento Daily Union,* July 6, 1867.

156 *The company never learned:* "End of the Chinese Laborers Strike," *Daily Alta,* July 3, 1867; Mark Hopkins to Huntington, July 1, 1867, Huntington Letters.

157 *Though the company:* Charles Crocker testimony, September 20, 1887, *Testimony Taken by the Pacific Railway Commission,* vol. 7 (Washington, D.C.: GPO, 1887), 3659–60.

The self-discipline: Crocker testimony, in *Report of the Joint Special Committee to Investigate Chinese Immigration,* 669.

After the strike ended: E. B. Crocker to Huntington, July 6 and 10, 1867, Huntington Letters.

158 *Three weeks after the end:* E. B. Crocker to Huntington, July 23, 1867, Huntington Letters.

Railroad Chinese finally: "Letter from the Sierras," *Daily Alta California,* November 10, 1867; Ryan Dearinger, *The Filth of Progress* (Berkeley: University of California Press, 2016), 162–63.

159 *The labor crisis appeared:* E. B. Crocker to Huntington, September 12, 1867; Huntington to Crocker, October 3, 1867, Huntington Letters.

Chinese workers on later: "Western Slope Intelligence," *Daily Alta California,* August 8, 1869; Sandy Lydon, *Chinese Gold: The Chinese in the Monterey Bay Region* (Capitola, Calif.: Capitola Book Co., 2008), 94–95; "Pacific Slope Brevities," *San Francisco Chronicle,* October 17, 1869; *The New North-West,* November 25, 1870; and Shelley Fisher Fishkin, "The Chinese as Railroad Builders after Promontory," in Chang and Fishkin, Chinese and the Iron Road.

160 *Observers who came to see:* Robert L. Harris, "The Pacific Railroad—Unopen," *Overland Monthly,* September 1, 1869, 244–52.
At another location: Ibid.

161 *E. B. Crocker also visited:* E. B. Crocker to Huntington, August 10, 1867, Huntington Letters.
After the hard winter: Clement testimony, in *Testimony Taken by the Pacific Railway Commission,* 6:3205–7; Samuel S. Montague to Leland Stanford, July 1, 1869, ibid., 6:3481; Arthur Brown to Leland Stanford, July 25, 1887, ibid., 5:2581–82; Arthur Brown testimony, ibid., 6:3601–5.

162 *The previous summer:* Brown to Stanford, July 25, 1887; Montague to Stanford, July 1, 1869. One account claims that Chinese were mainly responsible for building the snow sheds near Truckee but provides no source. Carmena Freeman, "The Chinese in Nevada County a Century Ago," *Nevada County Historical Society Newsletter* 33, no. 1 (January 1979): 1–6.
Chinese were linked: Sue Fawn Chung, *Chinese in the Woods: Logging and Lumbering in the American West* (Urbana: University of Illinois Press, 2015), 59–65; "Across the Sierra Nevadas: The First Railway Passenger Train from Sacramento over the Mountains," *Alta California,* June 20, 1868.
The company realized: Clement testimony, August 29, 1887, in *Testimony Taken by the Pacific Railway Commission,* 6:3607.

163 *The most dramatic example:* Gilliss, "Tunnels of the Pacific Railroad"; GJG, "China Wall," CPRR Discussion Group, http://discussion.cprr.net/2008/03/china-wall.html; and "China Wall of the Sierra," https://www.hmdb.org/marker.asp?marker=23564 (both accessed June 12, 2018).
Such accolades came: Gilliss, "Tunnels of the Pacific Railroad."

164 *A New York reporter:* Alfred E. Davis testimony, in *Testimony Taken by the Pacific Railway Commission,* 6:3620; and "The Central Pacific Railroad," *New York Evening Post,* reprinted in *Leeds Mercury,* December 28, 1867.
Even snow at rest: Mark Hopkins to Huntington, June 16, 1868; and E. B. Crocker to Huntington, January 31, 1867, and April 20, 1868, Huntington Letters.
Despite these conditions: E. B. Crocker to Huntington, April 21, 1868, Huntington Letters.

8. TRUCKEE

165 *The Summit Tunnel finally:* "Across the Sierra Nevadas: The First Railway Passenger Train from Sacramento over the Mountains," *Alta California,* June 20, 1868; a shorter version appeared in *The Railroad Record,* July 16,

1868, 239–40; and see "The Chinese in California," *The Standard* (London), September 5, 1868.

168   *Chinese had made up:* Harry Laurens Wells, ed., *History of Nevada County* (1880; repr., Berkeley: Howell-North Books, 1970), 55, 61–66, 75, 103, 114, and 117–20.

Following the arrival: Sue Fawn Chung, *Chinese in the Woods: Logging and Lumbering in the American West* (Urbana: University of Illinois Press, 2015), 109–15; "Truckee Matters," *Sacramento Daily Union,* July 23, 1869; George Kraus, *High Road to Promontory* (Palo Alto: American West, 1969), 182–83; and Calvin Miaw, "Truckee, 1870," unpublished study, December 1, 2017, in author's possession.

169   *Truckee became the center:* Jean Pfaelzer, *Driven Out: The Forgotten War Against Chinese Americans* (New York: Random House, 2007), 167–70; Chung, *Chinese in the Woods,* 109–28; and see Michael Andrew Goldstein, "Truckee's Chinese Community: From Coexistence to Disintegration, 1870–1890" (M.A. thesis, University of California, Los Angeles, 1988).

In 1870, Chinese constituted: Goldstein, "Truckee's Chinese Community," 14.

170   *The census also listed:* Miaw, "Truckee, 1870"; Barbara Barte Osborn, "Old Chinese Herb Shop Getting a Face-Lift," *Sacramento Bee,* March 11, 2004, reprinted at http://www.chssc.org/History/OldChinatowns/chinatown truckee.html (accessed June 24, 2018).

The Chinese prostitutes likely: Marian S. Goldman, *Gold Diggers and Silver Miners: Prostitution and Social Life on the Comstock Lode* (Ann Arbor: University of Michigan Press, 1981), 69–72, 95–99.

Most Chinese males: Miaw, "Truckee, 1870." The *Morning Oregon,* October16, 1869, noted that Colfax personally witnessed the marriage of a Chinese couple performed by a justice of the peace in Truckee.

171   *Colfax Ah nevertheless appears:* Chung, *Chinese in the Woods,* 110–11; Daniel Cleveland, "The Chinese in California," unpublished manuscript, Domestic and Social Life, Daniel Cleveland Manuscripts, 1868–1929, mssHM 72175–72177, Huntington Library, San Marino, Calif.; Miaw, "Truckee, 1870"; and Goldstein, "Truckee's Chinese Community," 28, 40.

As they did elsewhere: Russell M. Magnaghi, "Virginia City's Chinese Community, 1860–1880," *Nevada Historical Society Quarterly* 24, no. 2 (Summer 198): 130–58.

The most common leisure activity: Arnop Bainbridge testimony, in *Report of the Joint Special Committee to Investigate Chinese Immigration,* U.S. Senate,

44th Cong., 2nd sess. (Washington, D.C.: GPO, 1877), 222, 224; Stewart Culin, "The Gambling Games of the Chinese in America," Series in Philology,
Literature and Archaeology 1, no. 4 (Philadelphia: University of Pennsylva-
nia, 1891); S. Wells Williams, *The Middle Kingdom* (New York: Charles Scribner's Sons, 1883), 825.

172   *Another extremely popular:* Magnaghi, "Virginia City's Chinese," 139.

173   *The drop-off in:* CPRR Payroll Record, June 1866, Central Pacific Railroad
Collection, MS 79, California State Railroad Museum Library, Sacramento;
Chung, *Chinese in the Woods,* 44, 46.
Turmoil in his personal life: Placer Herald, January 12, 19, 26, May 18, June 29,
and July 3, 1867.
The people of Auburn: https://www.findagrave.com/memorial/41711181
(accessed April 30, 2018); Carmel Barry-Schweyer, application for National
Register of Historic Places, Auburn, February 8, 2009, U.S. Department of
the Interior, http://ohp.parks.ca.gov/pages/1054/files/architectural%20
and%20historic%20resources%20of%20auburn%20mpd.pdf (accessed August 20, 2018).

174   *Within two weeks of the crime: Placer County Herald,* July 3, 1867.
A year later: Placer County Herald, July 18, 1868.

175   *Paying for sex:* Yong Chen, *Chinese San Francisco: A Trans-Pacific Community,
1850–1943* (Stanford: Stanford University Press, 2000), 76–79.
If Hung Wah happened: This is an imagined experience based on interpreting historical and cultural evidence.

176   *The desperation of Chinese:* "Large Invoice of Celestial Femininity," *Oregon
State Journal,* March 20, 1869.
Visiting brothels: Testimony of Otis Gibson, April 12, 1876, in Committee of
the Senate of the State of California, *Chinese Immigration: The Social, Moral,
and Political Effect of Chinese Immigration* (Sacramento: State Printing Office,
1876), 27–29.

177   *But in America:* Patrick Tinloy, "Nevada County's Chinese, Part I," *Nevada
County Historical Society Bulletin* 25, no. 1 (January 1971): 1–7; George Anthony Peffer, *"If They Don't Bring Their Women Here": Chinese Female Immigration Before Exclusion* (Urbana: University of Illinois Press, 1999), 91. Also
see testimony in Committee of the Senate of California, *Chinese Immigration,* 60, 109; and in *Report of the Joint Special Committee to Investigate Chinese
Immigration,* U.S. Senate, 44th Cong., 2nd sess. (Washington, D.C.: GPO,
1877), 14, 142.
Life for most of these women: Judy Yung, *Unbound Feet: A Social History of Chi-*

nese Women in San Francisco (Berkeley: University of California Press, 1995), 26–31.

178 *In the 1870s:* Magnaghi, "Virginia City's Chinese Community"; Benson Tong, *Unsubmissive Women: Chinese Prostitutes in Nineteenth-Century San Francisco* (Norman: University of Oklahoma Press, 1994), 94, 159–63; Yung, *Unbound Feet,* 41; Peffer, *"If They Don't Bring Their Women Here,"* 124n13; and Marian S. Goldman, "Sexual Commerce on the Comstock Lode," *Nevada Historical Society Quarterly* 21, no. 2 (Summer 1978): 99–129.

Though many Chinese men: Six Companies, "A Memorial to the State of California to Bar Prostitutes" (1868), in *Chinese American Voices: From the Gold Rush to the Present,* ed. Judy Yung, Gordon H. Chang, and Him Mark Lai (Berkeley: University of California Press, 2006), 23–24.

This public and private outcry: Augustus Ward Loomis, "Chinese Women in California," *Overland Monthly,* April 1, 1869, 344–51.

179 *A few years later:* "Letter by a Chinese Girl" (1876), in Yung, Chang, and Lai, *Chinese American Voices,* 15–16. Also see Otis Gibson, *The Chinese in America* (Cincinnati: Hitchcock & Walden, 1877), 127–56, 200–222; Judy Yung, *Unbound Voices: A Documentary History of Chinese Women in San Francisco* (Berkeley: University of California Press, 1999), 124–53; Yung, *Unbound Feet,* 35–36; Peggy Pascoe, *Relations of Rescue: The Search for Female Moral Authority in the American West, 1874–1939* (New York: Oxford University Press, 1990), 13–17, 153–65; and Ruthanne McCunn. *Thousand Pieces of Gold* (San Francisco: Designs, 1981).

Some Chinese prostitutes: Elizabeth Sinn, *Pacific Crossing: California Gold, Chinese Migration, and the Making of Hong Kong* (Hong Kong: Hong Kong University Press, 2013), 219–35; and Lucie Cheng Hirata, "Chinese Prostitutes in Nineteenth-Century America," *Signs* 5, no. 1 (1979): 3–29.

In the mid-nineteenth century: Yung, *Unbound Feet,* 33–34; Tong, *Unsubmissive Women,* 6–12; and Sinn, *Pacific Crossing,* 219–21.

180 *Outrage among whites:* Testimony in Committee of the Senate of California, *Chinese Immigration;* U.S. Senate, *Report of the Joint Special Committee to Investigate Chinese Immigration,* 655; and Sinn, *Pacific Crossing,* 219–20. On white views of Chinese sexuality, see Nayan Shah, *Contagious Divides: Epidemics and Race in San Francisco's Chinatown* (Berkley: University of California Press, 2001), 77–104.

Occasionally, white observers: Watt Stewart, *Chinese Bondage in Peru* (Durham: Duke University Press, 1951), 230; and Testimony, *Report of the Joint Special Committee to Investigate Chinese Immigration,* 239.

181 *In 1870, as hundreds:* "The Latest Chinese Importation: The Coming Man in Tennessee—His Experience on a Railroad," *New York Evening Post*, July 18, 1870.

182 *Wives of farmers:* Yung, *Unbound Feet*, 6–7.

Families hoped the tie: Marlon Hom, *Songs of Gold Mountain* (Berkeley: University of California Press, 1987, 44n61. The author's grandfather in America was married in this way. He faithfully financially supported his wife and adopted children in China throughout his entire life, though he never met them in person. In California he married a woman of Chinese ancestry born in America and had many children with her. They never went to China.

How could you bear: Zhang and Hsu, "The View from Home," in *Chinese and the Iron Road: Building the Transcontinental and Other Railroads in North America,* ed. Gordon H. Chang and Shelley Fisher Fishkin (Stanford: Stanford University Press, 2019).

183 *The quandary for unmarried:* Franklin A. Buck, *A Yankee Trader in the Gold Rush: The Letters of Franklin A. Buck* (Boston: Houghton Mifflin, 1930), 128. Buck makes interesting observations about Chinese he encounters in gold country in the 1850s. He describes them as very capable traders and merchants and praises their education and English language abilities.

In 1850, more than four thousand: Yung, *Unbound Feet*, 18, 24; Yung, *Unbound Voices*, 99; David Beesley, "From Chinese to Chinese American: Chinese Women and Families in a Sierra Nevada Town," *California History* 67, no. 3 (September 1988): 168–79; and Augustus Ward Loomis, "Chinese Women in California," *Overland Monthly*, April 1, 1869, 344–51.

Chinese gangsters victimized: Appendix to the Opening Statement and Brief of B. S. Brooks on the Chinese Question (San Francisco: Women's Co-operative Printing Union, 1877), 59–60.

The methods used to send: Yuan Ding with Roland Hsu, "Overseas Remittances of Chinese Railroad Workers in North America," and Liu Jin with Roland Hsu, "Chinese Railroad Workers' Remittance Networks: Insights Based on *Qiaoxiang* Documents," both in Chang and Fishkin, eds. *Chinese and the Iron Road;* Chen, *Chinese San Francisco,* 98–101.

184 *One popular art form:* Bell Yung and Eleanor S. Yung, eds., *Uncle Ng Comes to America: Chinese Narrative Songs of Immigration and Love* (New York: MCCM Creations, 2014).

185 Father, send money back: Zhang and Hsu, "The View from Home."
Don't marry your daughter: Ibid.

The lychee fruit: Tin-Yuke Char and C. H. Kwock, *The Hakka Chinese—Their Origin and Folk Songs* (Taipei: China Printing, 1969), 38.

186 We're guests stranded: Hom, *Songs of Gold Mountain*, 308–10, 257.

187 If you want to see: Zhang and Hsu, "The View from Home."
At the lunar January lantern show: Ibid.

9. THE GOLDEN SPIKE

189 *As the workforce surged forward:* Strobridge to Stanford, July 23, 1887, in *Testimony Taken by the Pacific Railway Commission,* vol. 5 (Washington, D.C.: GPO, 1887), 2580–81; Wesley S. Griswold, *A Work of Giants: Building the First Transcontinental Railroad* (New York: McGraw-Hill, 1962), 256.

In Utah there is: Mark Hopkins to Huntington, March 9, 1869, *Huntington Letters; and* Kenneth P. Cannon et al., *The Archaeology of Chinese Railroad Workers in Utah: Results of Surveys in Box Elder and Emery Counties,* Final Report to Utah Division of State History (Logan, Utah: USU Archaeological Services, 2016).

190 *Many workers lived out: Reno Crescent,* July 14, 1868.

The channel of the three-hundred: Edwin L. Sabin, *Building the Pacific Railway* (Philadelphia: J. B. Lippincott, 1919), 184.

As they advanced: "In Whirlwind Valley," *Overland Monthly and Out West Magazine,* February 1869, 11; and Sue Fawn Chung, "Beyond Railroad Work: Chinese Contributions to the Development of Winnemucca and Elko, Nevada," in *Chinese and the Iron Road: Building the Transcontinental and Other Railroads in North America,* ed. Gordon H. Chang and Shelley Fisher Fishkin (Stanford: Stanford University Press, 2019).

A perceptive reporter: Alta California, November 9, 1868, quoted in George Kraus, "Chinese Laborers and the Construction of the Central Pacific," *Utah Historical Quarterly* 37, no. 1 (Winter 1969): 41–57.

191 *The astonishing discipline: San Francisco Chronicle,* September 10, 1868, quoted in Kraus, "Chinese Laborers," 52.

They were not pure machines: Quote from George Kraus, *High Road to Promontory* (Palo Alto: American West, 1969), 210.

192 *Photos taken by Alfred:* Two authors put the number of residents at five hundred, though this seems high. Li Ju and Linda Ye, "A Photo Comparative Perspective of the Central Pacific Railroad," unpublished essay, Chinese Railroad Workers Project Archives, Stanford.

194 *Numerous Chinese workers:* In other photographs by Hart ("End of Track, Near Humboldt Lake," "Second Crossing of Humboldt River. 430 Miles

from Sacramento," and "Advance of Civilization on the Humboldt Desert"), Chinese workers appear indistinctly in the distance. These images also show the ample detritus littering the ground in the work camps which archaeologists would study 150 years later.

In "End of Track: Chinese may be included in some images that contain crowds of people at a distance. Sometimes one can see only a mass of bodies, all with hats, some of which could have been those typically worn by Chinese as seen in other photos. See "The Last Rail. The Invocation, Fixing the Wire, May 10, 1869," for example, taken by Hart at Promontory before the formal ceremony in May 1869. Indistinct groups of workers who may be Chinese also appear in the distance in images such as "Railroad Camp Near Victory. 10 1/4 Miles Laid in One Day" and "The First Greeting of the Iron Horse. Promontory Point, May 9th, 1869."

195 *In the fall of 1868:* San Francisco Chronicle, September 10, 1868; Kraus, "Chinese Laborers," 51–52.

Chinese and Native peoples: Benjamin Madley, *An American Genocide: The United States and the California Indian Catastrophe, 1846–1873* (New Haven: Yale University Press, 2016), 224, 225, 226, 481–522.

When the railroad entered: Kraus, "Chinese Laborers," 51; Hsinya Huang, "Tracking Memory: Encounters Between Chinese Railroad Workers and Native Americans," in Chang and Fishkin, *Chinese and the Iron Road;* Sue Fawn Chung, *In Pursuit of Gold: Chinese American Miners and Merchants in the American West* (Urbana: University of Illinois Press, 2014), 140, 149, 164; and Griswold, *Work of Giants,* 244–45.

196 *In contrast, other pieces:* Huang, "Tracking Memory"; and Sandra K. Lee and Douglas A. Lee, *The Lee Family of New York Chinatown Since 1888: An Historical Exhibition,* catalog (n.p., n.d.), 8.

Stories of interactions: Daniel J. Meissner, "California Clash: Irish and Chinese Labor in San Francisco, 1850–1870," in *The Irish of the San Francisco Bay Area: Essays on Good Fortune,* ed. Donald Jordan and Timothy J. O'Keefe (San Francisco: Irish Literary and Historical Society, 2005), 54–86; and Griswold, *Work of Giants,* 253.

Incidences of serious violence: Griswold, *Work of Giants,* 110–12, 303.

197 *Fighting between the Union Pacific's:* Grenville M. Dodge, *How We Built the Union Pacific Railway and Other Railway Papers and Addresses* (Washington, D.C.: GPO, 1910), 24, 68; Barry Patrick McCarron, "The Global Irish and Chinese: Migration, Exclusion, and Foreign Relations Among Empires, 1784–1904" (Ph.D. diss., Georgetown University, 2016), 116–17. Some histo-

rians take strong exception with Dodge and claim that little or no conflict existed between Chinese and Irish railroad workers. See http://cprr.org/ Game/Interactive_Railroad_Project/Fiction_or_Fact.html (accessed July 2, 2018).

In late May 1869: Harper's Weekly, May 29, 1869.

To push the work: Griswold, *Work of Giants,* 247–48, 306–7.

198 *Six-man teams then:* John Hoyt Williams, *A Great and Shining Road: The Epic Story of the Transcontinental Railroad* (Lincoln: University of Nebraska Press, 1988), 261–63; Sabin, *Building the Pacific Railway,* 200–202.

199 *A camp train pulled up:* Williams, *Great and Shining Road,* 261–63.

The ten-mile line was not just: Kraus, *High Road,* 252–53; "Ten Miles and 58 Feet of Track Laid Yesterday," *San Francisco Bulletin,* April 29, 1869, 2; *The Pacific Tourist: J. R. Bowman's Illustrated Transcontinental Guide of Travel, from the Atlantic to the Pacific Ocean,* ed. Frederick E. Shearer (New York: J. R. Bowman, 1882–83), 14; and Erle Heath, "A Railroad Record That Defies Defeat," *Southern Pacific Bulletin* 16, no. 5 (May 1928): 3–5. The descendants of a Railroad Chinese named Chin Lin Sou believe he was one of the supervisors over the army of Chinese workers. See, William Wei, *Asians in Colorado: A History of Persecution and Perseverance in the Centennial State* (Seattle: University of Washington Press, 2016), 76–77.

After the end of work: As early as May 4, the CPRR sent hundreds of Railroad Chinese away from Promontory Summit for work elsewhere. A few days later they were "almost all gone" from the Promontory area. "From the Railroad Front" and "The Railway Front," *Daily Alta California,* May 5 and 6, 1869; and Robert L. Spude and Todd Delyea, *Promontory Summit, May 10, 1869,* Cultural Resources Management, Intermountain Region, National Park Service, 2005, 14, 93.

200 *A few days after:* This story draws from the report of the actual discovery as described in Christopher W. Merritt, "The Continental Backwaters of Chinese Railroad Worker History and Archaeology: Perspectives from Montana and Utah," working paper presented to the Archaeology Network Workshop of the Chinese Railroad Workers in North America Project, October 2013, 5–6.

201 *The event began:* "The Last Rail," *Daily Alta California,* May 12, 1869; "John Chinaman at Lunch," *Chicago Tribune,* May 13, 1869; "The Pacific Railroad: Interesting Account of Its Completion," *New Hampshire Sentinel,* May 20, 1869; "A Significant Picture," *Galveston Tri-Weekly News,* June 4, 1869; "From the Railroad Front—The Ceremonies," *Sacramento Daily Union,* May 12,

1869; Spude and Delyea, *Promontory Summit*, 22–26; and David Haward Bain, *Empire Express: Building the First Transcontinental Railroad* (New York: Penguin, 1999), 658–67.

To emphasize: "The Pacific Railroad," *Sacramento Daily Union*, May 11, 1869.

202 *After the brief event:* "The Summit Deserted — A Scramble for Relics," *San Francisco Newsletter*, May 15, 1869; "The Last Tie," *Overland and Out West Magazine*, July 1869, 77–84.

Strobridge held his own: "Pacific Railroad: Close of the Inauguration Ceremonies at Promontory Summit," *Chicago Tribune*, May 12, 1869; "Honors to John Chinaman," *San Francisco Newsletter*, May 15, 1869; "The Last Rail," *Daily Alta California*, May 12, 1869; and "The Chinaman as a Railroad Builder," *Daily National Intelligencer*, May 27, 1869. And see "A Compliment to the Chinese," *Sacramento Daily Union*, May 3, 1869.

203 *At the lively public celebration: Sacramento Daily Union*, May 8, 1869; "Arrival of Vice President Colfax and Party," *Sacramento Daily Union*, August 13, 1869.

As historically significant: "Completion of the Pacific Railroad," *San Francisco Bulletin*, May 8, 1869.

San Francisco and Sacramento: "The Pacific Railroad," *San Francisco Daily Times*, May 10, 1869; "Railroad Celebrations East," *Daily Alta California*, May 12, 1869.

204 *At Promontory Summit, however:* Spude and Delyea, *Promontory Summit*, 20–21, 33–34, 49. See 1870 census of Promontory; Sue Fawn Chung to author, email, March 25, 2014.

Several dramatic incidents: "Second Despatch," *Daily Alta California*, May 8, 1869; Kraus, "Chinese Laborers," 56–57; Williams, *Great and Shining Road*, 263–65.

205 *Stanford and his elite party:* "Union Pacific Laborers Unpaid," *Sacramento Daily Union*, May 11, 1869; J. N. Bowman, "Driving the Last Spike at Promontory 1869," *Utah Historical Quarterly* 37, no. 1 (Winter 1969): 76–101; and Michael W. Johnson, "Rendezvous at Promontory: A New Look at the Golden Spike Ceremony," *Utah Historical Quarterly* 72, no. 1 (Winter 2004): 47–68.

Shortly before the Promontory: Daniel Cleveland, "The Chinese as Railroad Laborers," a chapter in "The Chinese in California," Daniel Cleveland Manuscripts, 1868–1929, MSS HM 72176, Huntington Library, San Marino, Calif.

"China is our neighbor now": Rev. John Todd, *The Sunset Land; or, The Great Pacific Slope* (Boston: Lee and Shepard, 1870), 291–92 and 234.

206 *In contrast to these expansive:* "The Railroad Celebration in San Francisco," *Sacramento Daily Union,* May 5, 1869; and "Completion of the Pacific Railroad," *San Francisco Bulletin,* May 8, 1869.

Colorful descriptions: Spude and Delyea, *Promontory Summit,* reproduces many of the images, most of them rarely seen, that were taken on May 10, 1869.

The photographers captured: Denise Khor, "Railroad Frames: Landscapes and the Chinese Railroad Worker in Photography, 1865–1869," in Chang and Fishkin, *Chinese and the Iron Road.*

207 *But is the scene:* Andrew J. Russell, H69.4592030, Oakland Museum of California. See the online version with "magnifying glass."

Some interpret this omission: Sidney Dillon, "Historic Moments: Driving the Last Spike of the Union Pacific," *Scribner's,* September 1892, 253–59; J. N. Bowman, "Pacific Railroad: The Last Spike Driven," *Railroad Record,* May 13, 1869, 147; Michael W. Johnson, "Rendezvous at Promontory: A New Look at the Golden Spike Ceremony," *Utah Historical Quarterly* 72, no. 1 (Winter 2004): 47–68; and *Cleveland Ohio Leader,* June 1893, Stanford Family Scrapbooks, vol. 4, p. 96, Special Collections, Green Library, Stanford University.

Look even closer: Bradley W. Richards, *The Savage View: Charles Savage, Pioneer Mormon Photographer* (Nevada City, Calif.: Carl Mautz Publishing, 1995), 48; and "A Significant Picture," *Galveston Tri-Weekly News,* June 4, 1869. Thank you to Victoria Sandin, who first alerted me to the ghostly figure.

208 *None of the images:* Spude and Delyea, *Promontory Summit,* 155.

IO. BEYOND PROMONTORY

210 *An article under the title:* Daily National Intelligencer, May 27, 1869; and *Scientific American,* July 31, 1869. The article appears to have come from *San Francisco Daily Times,* May 14, 1869.

The Chinese laborer: "The Railway Front," *Daily Alta California,* May 6, 1869.

212 *Legend has it that:* Ng Poon Chew, "Chinese Immigration," *Chinese Students' Monthly,* March 10, 1914, 398; and see "How Our Chinamen Are Employed," *Overland Monthly and Out West Magazine,* March 1869.

As early as 1868: Oregon State Journal, July 25, October 17, and November 7, 1868; *Morning Oregonian,* August 16, 1869; and *Railroad Record,* November 12, 1868. Also see Thomas C. Durant to D. W. Strong, October 10, 1868, in Testimony Taken by the Pacific Railway Commission, vol. 5 (Washington, D.C.: GPO, 1887), 2968–70; *Railroad Gazette,* October 8 and July 30, 1870, and March 25, 1871.

In the months after Promontory: Railroad Record, September 6 and 23, October 14, and December 12, 1869, and January 6, July 21, September 22, October 20, and November 24, 1870; *Daily Alta California,* May 8, August 7 and 8, 1869; *Sacramento Daily Union* April 30, 1870; *Times-Picayune,* July 14, 1870; *Nottinghamshire Guardian,* January 28, 1870; "Interesting to American Workmen," *Cincinnati Daily Inquirer,* September 22, 1870; and Gilbert H. Kneiss, "The Virginia and Truckee Railway," *Railway and Locomotive Historical Society Bulletin,* no. 45 (January 1938), Baker Library, Harvard Business School.

213 *Leading political and business:* "The Chinese," *Chicago Tribune,* June 14, 1869; "The Chinese," *Daily Alta California,* July 13, 1869; and "Letter from Alabama," *Daily Alta California,* August 7, 1869. The *Alta* reprinted articles from papers in New York and elsewhere. And see "The Celestials," *Marysville Daily Appeal,* October 6, 1869.

The novel idea: "Koopmanschap, and His Chinese Immigration Plans," *Daily Alta California,* August 1, 1869; "The Chinese in South Carolina," *San Francisco Daily Times,* August 26, 1869; and Moon-Ho Jung, *Coolies and Cane: Race, Labor, and Sugar in the Age of Emancipation* (Baltimore: Johns Hopkins University Press, 2006), 96–106, 113.

Over the next several years: "Second Despatch," *Daily Alta California,* May 8, 1869; and *Railroad Gazette,* September 10, 1870, 554.

214 *Individual Chinese also:* Shelley Fisher Fishkin, "The Chinese as Railroad Builders after Promontory," in *Chinese and the Iron Road: Building the Transcontinental and Other Railroads in North America,* ed. Gordon H. Chang and Shelley Fisher Fishkin (Stanford: Stanford University Press, 2019); and Shih-shan Henry Tsai, *The Chinese Experience in America* (Bloomington: Indiana University Press, 1986), 18–19.

One of the largest projects was: "Miscellaneous—Arrival of Chinamen at New Orleans," *Daily Alta California,* January 9, 1870; "Sambo's Successor: Arrival of Two Hundred and Fifty Chinamen at New Orleans—Queer Scenes and Incidents," *Daily Alta California,* January 30, 1870; Edward J. M. Rhoades, "The Chinese in Texas," *Southern Historical Quarterly* 81, no. 1 (1977): 5–10; Robert E. Wynne, "Reaction to the Chinese in the Pacific Northwest and British Columbia, 1850–1910 (Ph.D. diss., University of Washington, 1964), 84–85; Thomas Chinn, Him Mark Lai, and Philip Choy, *A History of the Chinese in California: A Syllabus* (San Francisco: Chinese Historical Society of America, 1969), 46–47; Alan Pollack, "1876 Southern Pacific Tunnels Through," https://scvhistory.com/scvhistory/pollack 0710tunnel.html (accessed October 15, 2018); Christopher W. Merritt, *The*

Coming Man from Canton: Chinese Experience in Montana, 1862–1943 (Lincoln: University of Nebraska Press, 2017), 73–85, 157–58; and Robert Weaver to author, email, July 5, 2017. For Utah, see Kenneth P. Cannon et al., *The Archaeology of Chinese Railroad Workers in Utah: Results of Surveys in Box Elder and Emery Counties,* Final Report to Utah Division of State History (Logan, Utah: USU Archaeological Services, 2016). For an overview, see Fishkin, "Chinese as Railroad Builders after Promontory."

The Railroad Chinese, and their: Raymond B. Craib, *Chinese Immigrants in Porfirian Mexico* (Albuquerque: University of New Mexico, 1996), 6; Jacques Meniaud, *Les pionniers du Soudan* (Paris: Société des Publications Modernes, 1931), 99, 100; Watt Stewart, *Chinese Bondage in Peru: A History of the Chinese Coolie in Peru, 1849–1874* (Durham: Duke University Press, 1951), 75, 89; Watt Stewart, *Henry Meiggs: Yankee Pizarro* (Durham: Duke University Press, 1946), 161–63; and Sophia V. Schweitzer and Bennet Hymer, *Big Island Journey* (Honolulu: Mutual Publishing, 2009), 74.

Even in far-off Britain: The Standard (London), May 18 and November 17, 1869–February 14, 1870; *Glasgow Herald,* 1866–1870; *Leeds Mercury,* November and December 1869; *Manchester Courier and Lancashire General Advertiser,* August 12, 1869; *Manchester Times,* December 18, 1869; Gordon H. Chang, "Chinese Railroad Workers and the U.S. Transcontinental Railroad in Global Perspective," in Chang and Fishkin, *Chinese and the Iron Road.* Thank you to Teri Hessel for her work in British periodicals.

Chinese who worked: Beth Lew-Williams, "The Remarkable Life of a Sometimes Railroad Workers: Chin Gee Hee, 1844–1929, in Chang and Fishkin, *Chinese and the Iron Road;* Willard G. Jue, "Chin Gee-Hee, Chinese Pioneer Entrepreneur in Seattle and Toishan," *Annals of the Chinese Historical Society of the Pacific Northwest* 1 (1983): 32–34; Ruthanne Lum McCunn, *Chinese American Portraits: Personal Histories, 1828–1988* (San Francisco: Chronicle Books, 1988), 55.

215 *In the 1880s:* Zhongping Chen, "The Construction of the Canadian Pacific Railway and the Transpacific Chinese Diaspora, 1880–1885," in Chang and Fishkin, *Chinese and the Iron Road;* Zhongping Chen to author, email, July 10, 2018; and Paul Yee, *Blood and Iron: Building the Railway* (Toronto: Scholastic Canada, 2010), 220–21.

The CPRR's recruitment: Thomas W. Chinn, H. Mark Lai, and Philip P. Choy, eds., *A History of the Chinese in California: A Syllabus* (San Francisco: Chinese Historical Society, 1969), 18–19; Herman B. Chiu and Andrew Taylor Kirk, "'Unlimited American Power': How Four California Newspapers Covered Chinese Labor and the Building of the Transcontinental Railroad, 1865–1869," *American Journalism* 31, no. 4 (2014): 507–24.

In New York City alone: "There is a steady growth in the Chinese population of New York and the contiguous cities." *Frank Leslie's Illustrated Newspaper,* October 4, 1879.

216 *With the spread of Chinese:* "The Chinese Question," *Sacramento Daily Union,* June 2, 1869; and "Letter from Alabama," *Daily Alta California,* August 7, 1869.

The Cincinnati Commercial: "The American Chinamen," *Cincinnati Commercial,* September 13, 1869.

217 *In August 1869:* "The Coming Chinese," *Merchants' Magazine and Commercial Review,* August 1, 1869, 123.

Some white observers: "A Significant Picture," *Galveston Tri-Weekly News,* June 4, 1869.

The appearance of new gendered: The series ran from May 7, 1870, through July 30, 1870.

218 *In May 1870, the influential:* "The Coming Man," *Frank Leslie's Illustrated,* July 30, 1870, 316; "The Latest Chinese Importation: The Coming Man in Tennessee—His Experience on a Railroad," *Evening Post,* July 18, 1870; and see a racist political cartoon that played on the popular notion, "The Coming Man," *San Francisco Wasp,* May 20, 1881. Philip P. Choy, Lorraine Dong, and Marlon K. Hom use the series title for the name of their book on Chinese and American popular culture, *The Coming Man: Nineteenth-Century Perceptions of the Chinese* (Hong Kong: Joint Publishing Company, 1994); also see Merritt, *The Coming Man from Canton.*

Charles Crocker himself: Testimony of Charles Crocker, in *Report of the Joint Special Committee to Investigate Chinese Immigration,* U.S. Senate, 44th Cong., 2nd sess. (Washington, D.C.: GPO, 1877), 666–75.

Extending the hand: "Chinese Labor," *New York Times,* July 18, 1869. On Leland Stanford's attitude toward Chinese, see Gordon H. Chang, "The Chinese and the Stanfords: Nineteenth-Century America's Fraught Relationship with the China Men," in Chang and Fishkin, *Chinese and the Iron Road.*

219 *Many in the United States:* "The American Chinamen"; Liping Zhu, *The Road to Chinese Exclusion: The Denver Riot, 1880 Election, and Rise of the West* (Lawrence: University of Kansas Press, 2013), 37–43.

A San Franciscan: "The Great Issue," *The Owyhee Avalanche,* July 3, 1869;

"Chinamen Voters in Louisiana, " *San Francisco Daily Times,* August 20, 1869.

In 1870, Congress: "Chinese Citizenship," *The Congregationalist,* October 23, 1878; and "Chinese in the United States," *San Francisco Daily Times,* August 21, 1869. Also see, Edlie L. Wong, *Racial Reconstruction: Black Inclusion, Chinese Exclusion, and the Fictions of Citizenship* (New York: New York University Press, 2015); and Elliott Young, *Alien Nation: Chinese Migration in the Americas from the Coolie Era Through World War II* (Chapel Hill: University of North Carolina Press, 2015).

220   *As Americans and Chinese:* "The American Chinamen," *Cincinnati Commercial,* September 13, 1869.

Chinese who came to: Lucius A. Waterman, Journal, January19–March 23, 1869, Waterman, Lucius A., misc. vol. 467, Museum of America and the Sea, Mystic, Conn.

It is an understatement: Three hundred repatriated remains are reported in "Summary of 1863," and about the same number for 1864 in "Summary of 1864," *Sacramento Union,* January 1, 1864, and January 2, 1865. The *City Intelligencer,* April 4, 1863, also reported that about three hundred coffins went to China in 1863.

221   *Famed New York jurist:* Remarks by Edwards Pierrepont, in *Banquet to His Excellency Anson Burlingame and His Associates of the Chinese Embassy by the Citizens of New York, June 23, 1868* (New York: Sun Book and Job Printing House, 1868), 47; *Sacramento Daily Union,* April 1, 1864.

The circumstances of daily life: "Latest News from the *Yosemite,*" *Sacramento Daily Union,* October 16, 1865.

Not all deaths were: News article quoted in *Appendix to the Opening Statement and Brief of B. S. Brooks, on the Chinese Question* (San Francisco: Women's Co-operative Printing Union, 1877), 4.

222   *Killing Chinese could:* "News of the Morning," *Sacramento Union,* April 16, 1868.

One tale: H. K. Wong, *Gum Sahn Yun: Gold Mountain Men* (San Francisco: Fong Brothers, 1987), 230–35.

There is little question: "Fact Checker: Is Lake Tahoe Filled with Hundreds of Preserved Bodies?" *Reno Gazette Journal,* August 22, 2011; and see as a possible source of a rumor that grew over the years "Truckee Matters," *Sacramento Daily Union,* July 23, 1869.

Louis M. Clement, one: Testimony of Clement, July 21, 1887, and testimony of Strobridge, July 23, 1887, in *Testimony Taken by the Pacific Railway Com-*

mission, vol. 5 (Washington, D.C.: GPO, 1887), 2577, 2580; John R. Gilliss, "Tunnels of the Pacific Railroad," paper read before the American Society of Civil Engineers, January 5, 1870, reprinted in *Transactions of the American Society of Civil Engineers* 1 (1872): 155–72.

223 *No account of the experience:* Wong Hau-hon, "Reminiscences of an Old Chinese Railroad Worker," reprinted in *Chinese American Voices: From the Gold Rush to the Present,* ed. Judy Yung, Gordon H. Chang, and Him Mark Lai (Berkeley: University of California Press, 2006), 39–42.

224 *During the construction:* "Reminiscences of A. P. Partridge," Lynn D. Farrar Collection, http://cprr.org/Museum/Farrar/pictures/2005–03–09–01–08.html (accessed July 15, 2018).

Wong Geu, who: H. K. Wong, *Gum Sahn Yun: Gold Mountain Men* (San Francisco: Fong Brothers Printing, 1987), 215.

225 *In April 1866:* "Explosion at Colfax—Six Men Killed," *Daily Alta California,* April 18, 1866; "Terrible Explosion, *Dutch Flat Enquirer,* April 21, 1866.

Just before Christmas: Sacramento Union, December 28, 1866. John R. Gilliss may have recalled the same slide but says that fifteen to twenty Chinese lives were lost. Gilliss, "Tunnels of the Pacific Railroad."

A snowslide: Sacramento Daily Union, March 5, 1867.

In May 1867: "Chinaman Killed," *Daily Alta California,* May 5, 1867.

In mid-June 1867: Meadow Lake Sun, June 22, 1867.

In December 1867: Account reprinted in "The Central Pacific," *Leeds Mercury,* December 28, 1867.

In January 1868: Brief, *Sacramento Daily Union,* January 21, 1868.

In February 1868: Brief, *Daily Alta California,* February 2, 1868.

In 1868, two white: Elko Independent, n.d., cited by Chris Graves, http://discussion.cprr.net/2005/10/how-many-chinese-were-dead-building-rr.html (accessed July 17, 2018).

In the spring of 1868: Edwin L. Sabin, *Building the Pacific* (Philadelphia: J. B. Lippincott, 1919), 121.

A June 1868 item: "Pacific Railroad Affairs," *Daily Alta California,* June 19, 1868; *Daily Alta California,* June 22, 1868.

226 *In October 1868: Daily Reveille* (Austin, Utah), October 21, 1868.

In December 1868: "Accident to a Freight Train," *Daily Alta California,* December 7, 1868.

Death could also: "The Final Connection to Be Made on Monday," *Daily Alta California,* May 8, 1869; and *San Francisco,* May 6, 1869.

227 *As Lewis Clement:* Lewis M. Clement testimony, in *Testimony Taken by the Pacific Railway Commission,* vol. 6 (Washington, D.C.: GPO, 1887), 3217.

E. B. Crocker made: E. B. Crocker to Huntington, January 31, 1867, Huntington Letters.

The story begins in mid-1869: "The American Chinamen," *Cincinnati Commercial,* September 13, 1869. The article is dated mid-August, which is when it was apparently written.

Several months later: Elko Independent, January 5, 1870; "California," *Daily Alta California,* January 28, 1870; *Humboldt Register,* March 12, 1870; also see J. P. Marden, "The History of Winnemucca," http://cprr.org/Museum/Winnemucca_Marden.pdf (accessed August 7, 2017).

228 *In late June 1870:* Sacramento Reporter, June 30, 1870; and "California," *Daily Alta California,* June 30, 1870. The accuracy of these two news articles has been questioned because of a third news report on the same day which provided an estimate of about fifty "defunct Chinamen, who died from disease or were killed by accident while working on the line of the Central Pacific Railroad." *Sacramento Daily Union,* June 30, 1870. This article reports that the remains were to be interred in "Conboie's private cemetery," located in Sacramento, which already held "the bones of about one hundred others similarly deceased." So was the number twelve hundred or fifty? A close reading of the articles shows there might be no contradiction. The two articles citing the larger number indicate that the remains were being sent back to China. Efforts made in the United States and in Hong Kong, however, have failed to locate any shipping records that could confirm the arrival of remains in 1870. The third article giving the smaller number says that the remains were being transported for local interment. "Conboie" refers to a Joseph Anthony Conboie, who served as Sacramento's undertaker for many years and Sacramento County coroner. In 1869 he purchased land that became known as the Sunset Hill Cemetery. He apparently operated his own funeral service, which Chinese used; see, for example, "City Intelligence," *Sacramento Daily Union,* February 18, 1870. His cemetery may have held the remains of Chinese who had made no prior arrangement for the return of their remains to China; or it may have been a "way station." Chinese regularly buried the dead and then disinterred them years later, after the flesh had decomposed. The number might therefore be approximately twelve hundred *plus* the fifty associated with Conboie. The exact number is impossible to establish. All the articles agree that the causes of death included accidents as well as disease. Interment of Chinese and others at

Conboie's cemetery began in September 1869, and by 1873 the total had reached five hundred persons, according to a news report that year. This same article reported that Conboie had entered into an agreement with Chinese associations to receive the "remains of those Chinese whose bodies might be brought here from the mountains and the interior for burial, prior to being shipped back to the Flowery Kingdom." *Sacramento Daily Union*, January 18, 1873, quoted in "Masonic Lawn Cemetery Predated by Earlier Established Cemetery," *Valley Community Newspapers*, February 13, 2014.

Ambiguities and questions: Elizabeth Sinn, *Pacific Crossing: California Gold, Chinese Migration, and the Making of Hong Kong* (Hong Kong: Hong Kong University Press, 2013), 265–75. The causes of death for a large number of Railroad Chinese is unknown. News reports, as noted earlier, mention only the known accidents. Company officials many years later recounted that avalanches and snowslides took many workers, but in these instances, it would have been very difficult to calculate numbers. Chinese, however, undoubtedly recorded these events, and teams would have tried later to recover the remains. This would have been a very difficult task, given the rubble, rock, water, and physical deterioration of the bodies. Did smallpox or other epidemics account for the deaths? There is documentation that in early 1869, an outbreak of smallpox took the lives of some white workers, perhaps a dozen. It terrified many, causing white tracklayers to leave work because of it; the company brought in Chinese to replace them, and they reportedly were eager to take on the labor. The outbreak apparently did not last long. C. Crocker to Huntington, January 20, 1869; E. B. Crocker to Huntington, January 23, 28, and March 16, 1869; and Mark Hopkins to Huntington, January 31, 1869, all in Huntington Letters. Microfilming Corporation of America, Sanford, N.C.; and *Oakland Daily News*, January 19, 1869.

229 *The news articles did not:* Sinn, *Pacific Crossing,* 275. The articles are unclear about the source of the numbers and how the calculations were made. For example, the claim of twenty thousand pounds of remains equating to 1,200 persons raises questions. It is unclear whether the weight of the remains involves entire bodies, partial remains, bones, or fragments. It is also unclear whether the weight includes coffins and shipping boxes. According to the forensic archaeologist John Crandall, only about 7 percent of a living individual's weight becomes "dry bone." Chinese males at the time weighed on average probably no more than 125 pounds. Cran-

dall to author, August 12, 2017. The same figure of 1,200 sets of Chinese remains returning to China is cited by the Reverend John Todd in *The Sunset Land; or, The Great Pacific Slope* (Boston: Lee and Shepard, 1870), 280; it was Todd who had delivered the invocation at the Promontory Summit ceremony. Though he does not provide the source of his information, he cites the number without qualification.

Another way of looking: Figures for this table are from Sue Fawn Chung, *In Pursuit of Gold: Chinese American Miners and Merchants in the American West* (Urbana: University of Illinois Press, 2014), 22–23, which gives the source as the *Oregonian*, December 6, 1869. If the total number of Chinese who worked on the CPRR was somewhere between twelve thousand and perhaps twenty thousand, taking turnover into account, a death toll of a thousand or more over five years is not unreasonable.

Name of association	Total members	Returned	Died	Remained
Ningyung	46,867	12,262	3,487	27,118
Yanghe	28,207	4,295	2,085	21,820
Siyi	19,111	8,015	1,005	10,061
Sanyi	15,023	3,202	987	10,834
Hehe	25,002	4,407	1,878	18,717
Renhe	4,374	1,112	983	2,281
	138,584			10,425
% died:				
7.5%				

230 *Other reports gave:* "Chinese Immigrants," *Railroad Record*, January 6, 1870, 466. The figures were repeated in "Chinese Immigrants in California," *Railroad Record*, February 10, 1870, 506. The periodical was a highly regarded source of information. Daniel Cleveland derived numbers similar to these and calculated that more than 13 percent of the Chinese who came to California by 1868 died in the state — about 6,000 out of 46,000. Unfortunately, Chinese associations that were involved in repatriation of remains adamantly refuse access to their archives. The Great Fire of 1906 also destroyed many records from this period.

231 *The opening shot:* Scott Zesch, *The Chinatown War: Chinese Los Angeles and the Massacre of 1871* (New York: Oxford University Press, 2012), 180.
In June 1876: Appendix to the Opening Statement, 68–71; Sue Fawn Chung, *Chi-*

nese in the Woods: Logging and Lumbering in the American West (Urbana: University of Illinois Press, 2015), 119; Wallace R. Hagaman and Steve F. Cottrell, *The Chinese Must Go!: The Anti-Chinese Boycott, Truckee, California, 1866* (Nevada City, Calif.: Cowboy Press, 2004), 9; and Jean Pfaelzer, *Driven Out: The Forgotten War Against Chinese Americans* (New York: Random House, 2007), 167–69.

In October 1880: "Anti-Chinese Riots in Denver, Colorado," *Frank Leslie's Illustrated Newspaper,* November 20, 1880; Liping Zhu, *The Road to Chinese Exclusion: The Denver Riot, 1880 Election, and Rise of the West* (Lawrence: University of Kansas Press, 2013), 166–92.

Formalizing these mob anti-Chinese: Gordon H. Chang, "China and the Pursuit of America's Destiny: Nineteenth-Century Imagining and Why Immigration Restriction Took So Long," *Journal of Asian American Studies* 15, no. 2 (June 2012): 145–69.

232 *In these perilous years:* Huie Kin, *Reminiscences* (Peiping: San Yu Press, 1932), 26–27.

In September 1885: "Rock Springs Massacre," Wikipedia.org (accessed July 31, 2017); and see Craig Storti, *Incident at Bitter Creek: The Story of the Rock Springs Chinese Massacre* (Ames: Iowa State University Press, 1991); and "Memorial of Chinese Laborers at Rock Springs, Wyoming (1885)," in Yung, Chang, and Lai, *Chinese American Voices,* 48–54.

The worst incidence of violence: R. Gregory Nokes, "'A Most Daring Outrage': Murders at Chinese Massacre Canyon, 1887," *Oregon Historical Quarterly* 107, no. 3 (Fall 2006); R. Gregory Nokes, *Massacred for Gold: The Chinese in Hells Canyon* (Corvallis: Oregon State University Press, 2009), 24–29, 42.

The number of expulsion: Beth Lew-Williams, *The Chinese Must Go: Violence, Exclusion, and the Making of the Alien in America* (Cambridge: Harvard University Press, 2018), 247–51.

233 *Many today who:* See discussion in CPRR Museum, http://discussion.cprr.net/2006/12/reparations-for-families-of-those-who.html and http://discussion.cprr.net/2007/01/dead-chinese.html (accessed August 11, 2017). Also see, Haiming Liu, "Chinese Railroad Laborers and Their Transcontinental Death Culture," CRRWP Digital publishing series (forthcoming).

Take, for example: Wong, *Gum Sahn Yun,* 96–100. Anti-Chinese sentiment was strong in the area in the 1880s and 1890s. William Harland Boyd, *The Chinese of Kern County* (Bakersfield, Calif.: Kern County Historical Society, 2002), 28, 29, 35, 151, and 184.

After the railroad work: Wong, *Gum Sahn Yun,* 99–100.

234 *The second calamity:* "Catastrophe on the South Pacific Coast Railroad—Explosion in the Tunnel," *Sacramento Daily Union,* February 14, 1879; "Another Tunnel Explosion—Terribly Fatal Effects," *Sacramento Daily Union,* November 19, 1879; "The Tunnel Explosion and a Farcical Inquest," November 21, 1879, *Sacramento Daily Union;* "Fatal Explosion," *Santa Cruz Weekly Sentinel,* November 22, 1879; "Death in a Tunnel—Terrible Catastrophe in the Narrow-Gauge Tunnel Through the Santa Cruz Mountains," *Los Angeles Herald,* November 20, 1879; "A Tunnel Horror: Nearly Thirty Men Killed by an Explosion in San Francisco," *Cleveland Plain Dealer,* November 19, 1879; *The Tunnel Disaster, Daily Alta California,* November 20, 1879; and Sandy Lydon, *Chinese Gold: The Chinese in the Monterey Bay Region* (Capitola, Calif.: Capitola Book Company, 2008), 92–101. A careful and moving study of this incident and others in the history of Railroad Chinese in the Santa Cruz area is presented in Bruce MacGregor, *The Birth of California Narrow Gauge: A Regional Study of the Technology of Thomas and Martin Carter* (Stanford: Stanford University Press, 2003), 533–36, 542–49, 553–57.

235 *Chinese took death rituals:* Sue Fawn Chung and Priscilla Wegars, eds. *Chinese American Death Rituals: Respecting the Ancestors* (Lanham, Md.: Alta Mira, 2005). In their home region, Chinese continue to care for remains returned from abroad in "Gold Mountain coffins" that are still unclaimed after more than a hundred years. This work is seen as a solemn responsibility for the living to bear. See Chinese Culture Center and Tung Wah Group of Hospitals, *Requiem* (San Francisco, Chinese Culture Center, 2018).
Some Railroad Chinese waited: "Ah Jim Waits to Join Honorable Ancestors," *Call Bulletin,* July 22, 1941, clipping in box 4, News Clippings Re: Biographies, Charles Leong Papers, Asian American Studies Archives, UC Berkeley.

CONCLUSION

237 *As the excitement:* "Driving of Gold Spike Celebrated at Ogden," *Salt Lake City Tribune,* May 11, 1919; *Ogden Standard,* May 8, 1919. The workers' names are given variously as Wong Fook, Lee Chao, Lee Shao, Lee Cho, Low Chai, Ging Cui, and Ah King. Thanks to Kevin Hsu for locating this information and articles. On the long association some Railroad Chinese had with railroad work, see "Old Central Pacific Men Still at Work," *Southern Pacific Bulletin,* October 1, 1914, 18.

238 *The man identified:* "'Rock Canyon Charlie' Taken by Death at County Hos-

pital," *Mountain Democrat,* April 17, 1931; "Pioneer Chinese of Gold Rush Days Dies in Placerville," *Santa Cruz Evening News,* April 14, 1931; and "Chinese Pioneer Dies," *Los Angeles Times,* April 15, 1931.

239 *He died of heart disease:* California Department of Public Health, Vital Statistics, "Hung Wah Rock: Permit for Removal and Burial," April 15, 1931, provided by Mary Cory, El Dorado County Historical Museum, Placerville, email to author; and https://www.edcgov.us/Government/Cemetery/Pages/county_hospital.aspx (accessed August 18, 2018). Federal records on departures and returns of Chinese from America show no evidence that Hung Wah ever left the country.
After the completion: Contract between Hung Wah and Peter Maher, June 24, 1879, Bryanna Ryan to author, email, July 13, 2018; Lillian Rechenmacher Oral History, March 28, 1991, Placer County Oral History Collection, Placer County Archive and Research Center, Auburn; and "Anti-Chinese," *Placer Weekly Argus,* July 24, 1880.

240 *One such descendant:* Gene O. Chan, with Connie Young Yu, "Jim King, Foreman of the Central Pacific: A Descendant's Story," in *Voices from the Railroad: Stories by Descendants of Chinese Railroad Workers,* ed. Sue Lee and Connie Young Yu (San Francisco: Chinese Historical Society of America, 2014), 9–13.

241 *Another family historian:* Russell N. Low, "Hung Lai Woh Was a Great Grandfather I never met," in Lee and Yu, *Voices from the Railroad,*. 15–19; and Russell N. Low, "The Story of Hung Lai Woh: Chinese Railroad Worker on the Transcontinental" (n.p., 2003).
Lim Lip Hong came: Andrea Yee, "Lim Lip Hong: An Indomitable Pioneer," in Lee and Yu, *Voices from the Railroad,* 21–26.

242 *Lim Lip Hong had achieved:* Michael Andrew Solorio to author, email, August 6, 2018.

243 *Connie Young Yu, one:* Connie Young Yu to author, email, September 22, 2017; Connie Young Yu, "Stanford Memories from a San Jose Chinatown Store," June 8, 2016, in author's possession; and Barre Fong, interview of Connie Young Yu, May 29, 2013, Chinese Railroad Workers Project Archives, Stanford.
Stories about Chinese: Connie Young Yu, "Three on the Payroll," and transcripts of oral histories with railroad descendants in the collection of the Chinese Railroad Workers Project, Stanford.

244 *Railroad descendants' accounts:* Many Chinese Americans worked diligently to keep their history from disappearing. Railroad Chinese history has been

of primary importance to generations of historians of the Chinese American community, including William Chew, Thomas Chinn, Philip Choy, William Hoy, Him Mark Lai, H. K. Wong, and Connie Young Yu, among others. Railroad Chinese have inspired a broad range of Chinese American writers including Frank Chin, David Henry Hwang, Maxine Hong Kingston, Alan Lau, Genny Lim, Lisa See, Shawn Wong, and Lawrence Yep. The Railroad Chinese are immortalized in the contemporary music of Jon Jang and Francis Wong. Pioneering Chinese American artists Jake Lee and Tyrus Wong and contemporary artists Alan Lau, Zhi Lin, Mian Situ (whose stunning work appears on the dust jacket on this book), and Hung Liu imagine work on the railroad and memorialize the experience. Actors Ruy Islandar, John Lone, Tzi Ma, Bryon Mann, Yuekun Wu, and Angela Zhou presented Railroad Chinese characters on stage and screen. Descendants of Chinese from the railroad era include authors Maxine Hong Kingston and Lisa See, and perhaps Mae Jamison, the first black female astronaut, among others. See Pin-chia Feng, "History Lessons: Remembering Chinese Railroad Workers in *Dragon's Gate* and *Donald Duk*," in *Chinese and the Iron Road: Building the Transcontinental and Other Railroads in North America*, ed. Gordon H. Chang and Shelley Fisher Fishkin (Stanford: Stanford University Press, 2019); and Julia H. Lee, "The Railroad as Message in Maxine Hong Kingston's *China Men* and Frank Chin's 'Riding the Rails with Chickencoop Slim,'" *Journal of Asian American Studies*, October 2015, 265–87.

"After the Civil War": Maxine Hong Kingston, *China Men* (New York: Vintage, 1989), 146.

245 *Though it is long overdue:* President Barack Obama, Proclamation, "Asian American and Pacific Islander Heritage Month, 2014," April 30, 2014. On U.S. textbooks and Chinese railroad workers, see William Gow, "The Chinese Railroad Workers in United States History Textbooks: A Historical Genealogy, 1949-1965," in Chang and Fishkin, *Chinese and the Iron Road*. On Chinese views of the railroad workers over the years, see Yuan Shu, "Representing Chinese Railroad Workers in North America: Chinese Historiography and Literature, 1949–2015," in Chang and Fishkin, *Chinese and the Iron Road*.

PHOTO CREDITS

Page 2: "East and West Shaking Hands at Laying Last Rail" by Andrew Russell. Courtesy of the Collection of the Oakland Museum of California.

Page 40: Philip P. Choy Papers. Courtesy of the Department of Special Collections, Stanford University Libraries.

Page 49: Carleton E. Watkins, Views of Southern California and Arizona. Western Americana Collection, Beinecke Rare Book and Manuscript Library, Yale University. WA Photos 220: 1004470 and 1004468.

Page 51: Carl Mautz Collection of Cartes-de-visite. Photographs Created by California Photographers. Western Americana Collection, Beinecke Rare Book and Manuscript Library, Yale University. WA Photos 357: 1062435, 1062437, and 1062439.

Page 81: "Filling in Secret Town Trestle, C.P.R.R." by Carleton Watkins. Courtesy of Phoebe A. Hearst Museum of Anthropology, University of California, Berkeley. (Catalog No. 13-1304ee)

Page 83: "Chinese Laborers Group Portrait" ca. 1976 from Security Pacific National Bank Collection. Reprinted by permission of Los Angeles Public Library.

Pages 90, 94, and 95: Alfred A. Hart Photographs, ca. 1862–1869 from the Department of Special Collections, Stanford University Libraries.

Page 96: Photograph from the collection of the Society of California Pioneers used with permission.

Page 105: *Frank Leslie's Illustrated Newspaper* (San Francisco, Saturday, June 04, 1870; pg. 189; Issue 766), published by Gale.

Page 105: *Frank Leslie's Illustrated Newspaper* (San Francisco, Saturday, June 11, 1870; pg. 205; Issue 767), published by Gale.

Pages 106–107: Photographs courtesy of The Bancroft Library, University of California, Berkeley.

Pages 128–133: Alfred A. Hart Photographs, ca. 1862–1869 from the Department of Special Collections, Stanford University Libraries.

Page 134: Robert B. Honeyman, Jr. Collection of Early Californian and Western American Pictorial Material, BANC PIC 1963.002:0808 — C. Courtesy of The Bancroft Library, University of California, Berkeley.

Page 135: "Chinese Railroad Workers and Landscape" and "Chinese Porters for Railroad" c. 1869–1870. Courtesy of the Becker Collection, Boston College, Boston, MA.

Page 155: Illustration by Comte Ludovic de Beauvoir, *voyages autour du monde.*

Pages 192–194: Alfred A. Hart Photographs, ca. 1862–1869 from the Department of Special Collections, Stanford University Libraries.

Page 202: "Laying the Last Rail" by Andrew Russell. Courtesy of the Collection of the Oakland Museum of California.

Page 208: "China section gang Promontory, c. 1869–1870" by J. B. Silvis. The Denver Public Library, Western History Collection, Call No. X-22221.

Page 235: Eugene Antz photo, ca. 1885. Courtesy of The Community Library Center for Regional History, Ketchum Community Library, Ketchum, Idaho.

Page 238: *Surviving Central Pacific Chinamen, Wong Fook, Lee Chao, Ging Cui,* 1919, gelatin silver print. Courtesy of Amon Carter Museum of American Art, Fort Worth, Texas.

Page 242: Photograph of Lim Lip Hong with his wife and seven children, c. 1905. Courtesy of Lim Lip Hong Family.

INDEX